OFFSHORE SPECIAL REGULATIONS

Governing Offshore Racing for Monohulls & Multihulls

Including US SAILING Prescriptions

US SAILING Edition 2012-2013

(ISBN 0-9821676-9-5)

Published by ISAF (UK) Ltd., Ariadne House, Town Quay, Southampton, S031 2AQUK

Revision December 2011

Issue Date; March 1, 2012
State Frequency; Published Bi-Annually
Authorized Organization's Name and Address
US SAILING
P.O. Box 1260
15 Maritime Drive
Portsmouth, RI 02871
Tel: 401-683-0800
Fax: 401-683-0840
Web: www.ussailing.org

Issue Number: Issue No. US Version 1 - 2012

Administration

The Offshore Special Regulations are administered by the ISAF Special Regulation Sub-Committee whose terms of reference are as follows: (www.sailing.org/regulations)

ISAF Regulation 6.8.8.3 – The Special Regulations Sub-Committee shall:

(a) be responsible for the maintenance, revision and changes to the ISAF Offshore Special Regulations governing offshore racing, under licence from ORC Ltd. Such changes shall be biennial with revised editions published in January of each year, except that matters of an urgent nature affecting safety may be dealt with by changes to the Regulations on a shorter time scale;

(b) monitor developments in offshore racing relative to the standards of safety and seaworthiness

Any queries please E-Mail: offshore@ussailing.com

Cover image courtesy of Jim Teeters.

A Word From US SAILING

Evolutionary, not revolutionary. That could well be the motto of the Offshore Special Regulations that you hold in your hands. Published every two years, this booklet is a compilation of current best safety practices, learned hands-on at sea in sailboats. It's an unfortunate fact that many of the regulations are as a result of studies conducted after a fleet of boats is subjected to storm conditions. But those studies provide insight into what works and what doesn't, what needs strengthening, and what training and skills will make a difference. The very fact that the regulations change over time is a reminder that we're still learning about safety at sea, and that we need to be open minded about new techniques and technology.

As in previous years, extracts of these regulations can be downloaded from the US Sailing web site at offshore.ussailing.org. Follow the link to Safety at Sea and ISAF Special Regulations. The extracts provide a compact view of the regulations for either monohull or multihull sailors in any of the seven categories of racing. You'll also find additional information on Safety at Sea Seminars and related training, crew overboard studies, pre-race vessel inspection, and other topics of interest to the offshore and inshore racer.

Want to do more? Consider organizing a Safety at Sea Seminar at your home club or in your local area. These one-or two-day seminars are an essential part of training prior to going to sea. More information can be found at offshore.ussailing.org.

We also welcome your feedback on the Offshore Special Regulations. Contact offshore@ ussailing.org, or volunteer to serve on the Safety at Sea Committee of US Sailing.

A special thanks to the US Editor of this booklet, SAS Volunteer Ron Trossbach, who receives the ISAF copy in an Excel Spreadsheet and adds the US Sailing Prescriptions to generate the separate Monohull and Multhull Extracts listed on the Contents Page, in time to meet the spring Safety at Sea Seminars explained above.

Cheers and Fair Winds,
Chuck Hawley
Chairman, Safety at Sea Committee

NOTE THAT Additional Extracts for each Category of sailboat racing in the US are also posted on the US SAILING Web Site at http://offshore.ussailing.org/SAS/ISAF_Special_Regulations.htm for all Race Organizers to use.

ISAF Offshore Special Regulations Governing Offshore Racing Monohulls & Multihulls
Including US SAILING Prescriptions

CONTENTS **PAGE No.**

Appendices

Appendix A parts I and II are minimum standards; B to H and N are advisory; J, K, L and M are minimum standards.

The Special Regulations Sub-committee was created in 1967 by the newly formed Offshore Rule Coordinating Committee, later the Offshore Racing Congress. As offshore racing extended into round-the- world and multihull activities, so too did the scope of Special Regulations, which now covers racing in seven categories. Interpretations, amendments, and also ISAF extract files for particular categories and boat types, are available on the ISAF web site (www.sailing.org/specialregs).

US SAILING extract files are available for individual categories and boat types (monohulls and multihulls) at http://offshore.ussailing.org/SAS/ISAF_Special_Regulations/Extracts.htm

In the US - Send all Questions and Recommendations to offshore@ussailing.org

US Edition 2012 - 2013

ISAF Special Regulations Governing Offshore Racing for Category 1 & 2 Monohulls
Including US SAILING Prescriptions

ISAF OFFSHORE SPECIAL REGULATIONS REQUIREMENTS FOR MONOHULL SAILBOATS

Including US SAILING Prescriptions
www.offshore.ussailing.org
Extract for Race Category 1 and 2 Monohulls
JANUARY 2012 - DECEMBER 2013

US Version 1 and 2 - 2012

Because this is an extract not all paragraph numbers will be present

Language & Abbreviations Used

Mo - Monohull
" ** " means the item applies to all types of yacht in all Categories except 5 or 6 for which see Appendix J or L.

A side bar indicates a significant change in 2012

US SAILING extract files are available for individual categories and boat types (monohulls and multihulls) at http://offshore.ussailing.org/SAS/ISAF_Special_Regulations/Extracts.htm

US SAILING prescriptions are printed in bold, italic letters

ISAF guidance notes and recommendations are printed in italics

The use of the masculine gender shall be taken to mean either gender

SECTION 1 - FUNDAMENTAL AND DEFINITIONS

		Category
1.01	**Purpose and Use**	
1.01.1	It is the purpose of these Special Regulations to establish uniform minimum equipment, accommodation and training standards for monohull and multihull yachts racing offshore. A Proa is excluded from these regulations.	**
1.01.2	These Special Regulations do not replace, but rather supplement, the requirements of governmental authority, the Racing Rules and the rules of Class Associations and Rating Systems. The attention of persons in charge is called to restrictions in the Rules on the location and movement of equipment.	**
1.01.3	These Special Regulations, adopted internationally, are strongly recommended for use by all organizers of offshore races. Race Committees may select the category deemed most suitable for the type of race to be sailed.	**

		Category
1.02	**Responsibility of Person in Charge**	
1.02.1	**The safety of a yacht and her crew is the sole and inescapable responsibility of the person in charge who must do his best to ensure that the yacht is fully found, thoroughly seaworthy and manned by an experienced crew who have undergone appropriate training and are physically fit to face bad weather. He must be satisfied as to the soundness of hull, spars, rigging, sails and all gear. He must ensure that all safety equipment is properly maintained and stowed and that the crew know where it is kept and how it is to be used. He shall also nominate a person to take over the responsibilities of the Person in Charge in the event of his incapacitation.**	**
1.02.2	Neither the establishment of these Special Regulations, their use by race organizers, nor the inspection of a yacht under these Special Regulations in any way limits or reduces the complete and unlimited responsibility of the person in charge.	**
1.02.3	**Decision to race -The responsibility for a yacht's decision to participate in a race or to continue racing is hers alone - RRS Fundamental Rule 4.**	**
1.03	**Definitions, Abbreviations, Word Usage**	
1.03.1	Definitions of Terms used in this document	**

TABLE 1

Age Date	Month/year of first launch
AIS	Automatic Identification Systems
CEN	Comité Européen de Normalisation
CPR	Cardio-Pulmonary Resuscitation
Coaming	includes the transverse after limit of the cockpit over which water would run in the event that when the yacht is floating level the cockpit is flooded or filled to overflowing.
DSC	Digital Selective Calling
EN	European Norm
EPFS	Electronic Position-Fixing System
EPIRB	Emergency Position-Indicating Radio Beacon
FA Station	The transverse station at which the upper corner of the transom meets the sheerline.
Foul-Weather Suit	A foul weather suit is clothing designed to keep the wearer dry and maybe either a jacket and trousers worn together, or a single garment comprising jacket and trousers.

GMDSS	Global Maritime Distress & Safety System
GNSS	Global Navigation Satellite System
GPIRB	EPIRB, with integral GPS position-fixing
ITU	International Telecommunications Union
GPS	Global Positioning System
Hatch	The term hatch includes the entire hatch assembly and also the lid or cover as part of that assembly (the part itself may be described as a hatch).
INMARSAT	This is Inmarsat Global Limited, the private company that provides GMDSS satellite distress and safety communications, plus general communications via voice, fax and data
IMO	International Maritime Organisation
IMSO	The International Mobile Satellite Organisation, the independent, intergovernmental organisation that oversees Inmarsat's performance of its Public Service Obligations for the GMDSS and reports on these to IMO
ISAF	International Sailing Federation.
ISO	International Standard or International Organization for Standardization.
Lifeline	rope or wire line rigged as guardrail / guardline around the deck
LOA	Length overall not including pulpits, bowsprits, boomkins etc.
LWL	(Length of) loaded waterline
Monohull	Yacht in which the hull depth in any section does not decrease towards the centre-line.
Moveable Ballast	Lead or other material including water which has no practical function in the boat other than to increase weight and/or to influence stability and/or trim and which may be moved transversely but not varied in weight while a boat is racing.
ORC	Offshore Racing Congress (formerly Offshore Racing Council)
OSR	Offshore Special Regulation(s)
Permanently Installed	Means the item is effectively built-in by eg bolting, welding, glassing etc. and may not be removed for or during racing.
PLB	Personal Locator Beacon
Proa	Asymmetric Catamaran
RRS	ISAF - Racing Rules of Sailing
SAR	Search and Rescue
SART	Search and Rescue Transponder
Series Date	Month & Year of first launch of the first yacht of the production series
SOLAS	Safety of Life at Sea Convention

Safety Line	A tether used to connect a safety harness to a strong point
Securely Fastened	Held strongly in place by a method (eg rope lashings, wing-nuts) which will safely retain the fastened object in severe conditions including a 180 degree capsize and allows for the item to be removed and replaced during racing
Static Ballast	Lead or other material including water which has no practical function in the boat other than to increase weight and/or to influence stability and/or trim and which may not be moved or varied in weight while a boat is racing.
Static Safety Line	A safety line (usually shorter than a safety line carried with a harness) kept clipped on at a work-station
Variable Ballast	Water carried for the sole purpose of influencing stability and/or trim and which may be varied in weight and/or moved while a boat is racing.

		Category
1.03.2	The words "shall" and "must" are mandatory, and "should" and "may" are permissive.	**
1.03.3	The word "yacht" shall be taken as fully interchangeable with the word "boat".	**

SECTION 2 - APPLICATION & GENERAL REQUIREMENTS

2.01	**Categories of Events** *In many types of race, ranging from trans-oceanic sailed under adverse conditions to short-course day races sailed in protected waters, six categories are established, to provide for differences in the minimum standards of safety and accommodation required for such varying circumstances:*	**
2.01.2	**Category 1** ***US SAILING prescribes that Category 1 races are of long distance, well offshore, in large unprotected bays, and in waters where large waves, strong currents, or conditions leading to rapid onset of hypothermia are possible, where yachts must be completely self-sufficient for extended periods of time, capable of withstanding heavy storms and prepared to meet serious emergencies without the expectation of outside assistance.***	MoMu1
2.01.3	**Category 2** ***US SAILING prescribes that Category 2 races are of extended duration along or not far removed from shorelines, where a high degree of self-sufficiency is required of the yachts but with the reasonable probability that outside assistance would be available for aid in the event of serious emergencies.***	MoMu2
2.02	**Inspection** A yacht may be inspected at any time. If she does not comply with these Special Regulations her entry may be rejected, or she will be liable to disqualification or such other penalty as may be prescribed by the national authority or the race organizers.	**

		Category
2.03	**General Requirements**	
2.03.1	All equipment required by Special Regulations shall:-	
a)	function properly	**
b)	be regularly checked, cleaned and serviced	**
c)	when not in use be stowed in conditions in which deterioration is minimised	**
d)	be readily accessible	**
e)	be of a type, size and capacity suitable and adequate for the intended use and size of the yacht.	**
2.03.2	Heavy items:	
a)	ballast, ballast tanks and associated equipment shall be permanently installed	**
b)	heavy movable items including e.g. batteries, stoves, gas bottles, tanks, toolboxes and anchors and chain shall be securely fastened	**
c)	heavy items for which fixing is not specified in Special Regulations shall be permanently installed or securely fastened, as appropriate	**
2.03.3	When to show navigation lights	**
a)	navigation lights (OSR 3.27) shall be shown as required by the International Regulations for Preventing Collision at Sea, (Part C and Technical Annex 1). All yachts shall exhibit sidelights and a sternlight at the required times.	**

SECTION 3 - STRUCTURAL FEATURES, STABILITY, FIXED EQUIPMENT

3.01	**Strength of Build, Ballast and Rig**	
	Yachts shall be strongly built, watertight and, particularly with regard to hulls, decks and cabin trunks capable of withstanding solid water and knockdowns. They must be properly rigged and ballasted, be fully seaworthy and must meet the standards set forth herein. Shrouds shall never be disconnected.	**
3.02	**Watertight Integrity of a Hull**	
3.02.1	A hull, including, deck, coach roof, windows, hatches and all other parts, shall form an integral, essentially watertight unit and any openings in it shall be capable of being immediately secured to maintain this integrity.	**
3.02.2	Centreboard and daggerboard trunks and the like shall not open into the interior of a hull except via a watertight inspection/maintenance hatch of which the opening shall be entirely above the waterline of the yacht floating level in normal trim.	**

		Category
3.02.3	A canting keel pivot shall be completely contained within a watertight enclosure which shall comply with OSR 3.02.2. Access points in the watertight enclosure for control and actuation systems or any other purpose shall comply with OSR 3.02.1.	**
3.02.4	Moveable ballast systems shall be fitted with a manual control and actuation secondary system which shall be capable of controlling the full sailing load of the keel in the event of failure of the primary system. Such failures would include electrical and hydraulic failure and mechanical failure of the components and the structure to which it mounts. The system must be capable of being operational quickly and shall be operable at any angle of heel. It would be desirable if this system was capable of securing the keel on the centreline.	**
3.03	**Hull Construction Standards (Scantlings)**	MoMu0,1,2
3.03.1		Mo0,1,2
a)	A yacht of less than 24m in hull length (measured in accordance with ISO 8666) with the earliest of Age or Series Date on or after 1 January 2010 shall have: • been designed,built and maintained in accordance with the requirements of ISO 12215 Category A * • on board a certificate of building plan review from a notified body recognized by ISAF. • on board a declaration signed and dated by the builder to confirm the yacht is built in accordance with the plans reviewed by the Notified Body.	Mo0,1,2
b)	A yacht of 24m in hull length and over (measured in accordance with ISO 8666) with the earliest of Age or Series Date on or after 1 January 2010 shall have: • been designed, built and maintained in accordance with the requirements of a Classification Society recognized by ISAF • on board a certificate of building plan review from a Classification Society recognized by ISAF • on board a declaration signed and dated by the builder to confirm the yacht is built in accordance with the plans reviewed by the Classification Society	Mo0,1,2
3.03.2		Mo0,1,2
a)	A yacht of less than 24m in hull length (measured in accordance with ISO 8666), with the earliest of Age or Series Date on or after 1 January 2010, if subject to any significant repair or modification to the hull, deck, coachroof, keel or appendages on or after the 1 January 2010, shall have • the repair or modification designed and built in accordance with ISO 12215 Category A* • on board a certificate of building plan review for the repair or modification from a notified body recognized by ISAF • on board a declaration signed and dated by the builder to confirm that the repair or modification is in accordance with the requirements of ISO 12215 Category A *	Mo0,1,2

		Category
b)	A yacht of 24m in hull length and over (measured in accordance with ISO 8666), with the earliest of Age or Series Date on or after 1 January 2010, if subject to any significant repair or modification to the hull, deck, coachroof, keel or appendages on or after the 1 January 2010, shall have • the repair or modification designed and built in accordance with the requirements of a Classification Society recognized by ISAF. • on board a certificate of building plan review for the repair or modification from a Classification Society recognized by ISAF • on board a declaration signed and dated by the builder to confirm that the repair or modification is in accordance with the plans reviewed by the Classification Society.	Mo0,1,2
3.03.3	In cases when a builder no longer exists a race organizer or class rules may accept a signed statement by a naval architect or other person familiar with the requirements of 3.031 and 3.03.2 above and in lieu of the builders declaration required by 3.031 and 3.03.2 above.	Mo0,1,2
3.03.4	A monohull with the earliest of Age or Series Date before the 1 January 2010 shall comply with 3.03.1, 3.03.2 and 3.03.3 above or with appendix M to these OSR. A multihull shall comply with appendix M to these OSR.	Mo0,1,2
	* or as from time to time specified by ISAF	
3.04	**Stability - Monohulls**	Mo0,1,2,3,4
3.04.2	A yacht shall be designed and built to resist capsize.	Mo0,1,2,3,4
3.04.3	*A race organizer should require compliance with a minimum stability or stability/buoyancy index. Attention is drawn to the stability index in the ORC Rules and Regulations*	Mo0,1,2,3,4
3.04.4	*Achievement of Design Category A under ISO 12217-2 may be accepted by a race organizer as a guide to general suitability for competition in a Special Regulations Category 1 race.*	Mo1
3.04.5	*Use of the ISO or any other index does not guarantee total safety or total freedom of risk from capsize or sinking*	Mo0,1,2,3,4
3.04.6	For boats with moveable or variable ballast the method in OSR 3.04.4 shall apply plus the relevant additional requirement of OSR Appendix K.	Mo0,1,2,3,4
3.04.7	Tanks for variable ballast shall be permanently installed and shall be provided with a system of isolating valves and pump(s) capable of manual operation at any angle of heel. A plan of the plumbing system shall be displayed aboard the boat.	Mo0,1,2,3,4
3.06	**Exits - Monohulls**	Mo0,1,2,3,4
3.06.1	Yachts of LOA of 8.5 m (28 ft) and over with age or series date after January 1995 and after shall have at least two exits. At least one exit shall be located forward of the foremost mast except where structural features prevent its installation.	Mo0,1,2,3,4

		Category
3.06.2	Yachts first launched on or after January 2014 have a hatch with the following minimum clear openings in compliance with ISO 9094: - Circular shape: diameter 450mm; - Any other shape: minimum dimension of 380mm and minimum area of 0.18m2. The dimension must be large enough to allow for a 380mm diameter circle to be inscribed. The measurement of the minimum clear opening is illustrated in Figure 1.	Mo0,1,2,3,4

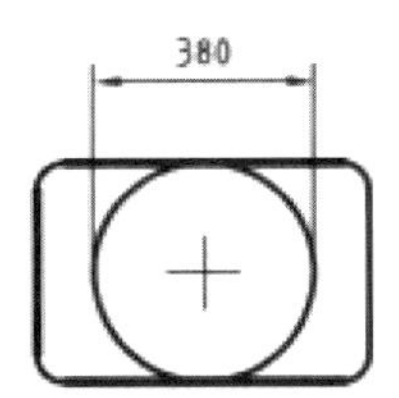

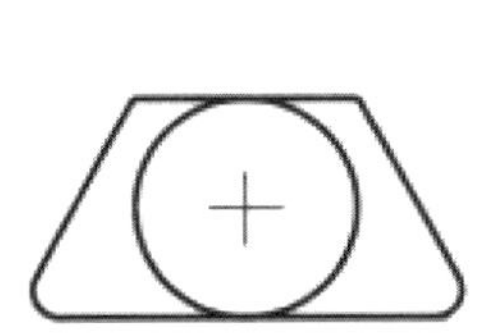
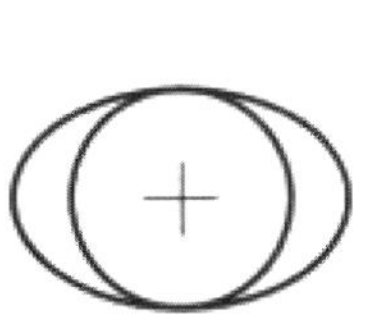
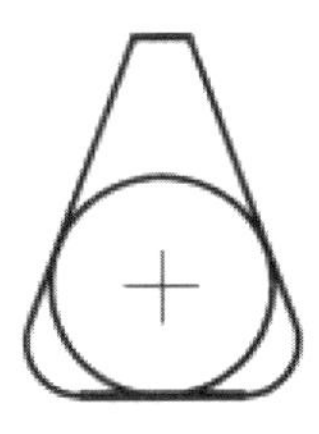

Figure 1 - Measurements of Minimum Clear Opening

3.06.3	*when first launched prior to January 2014, if possible have each escape hatch in compliance with the dimensions in OSR 3.07.2(a)(ii)*	Mo0,1,2,3,4
3.08	**Hatches & Companionways**	
3.08.1	No hatch forward of the maximum beam station, other than a hatch in the side of a coachroof, shall open in such a way that the lid or cover moves into the open position towards the interior of the hull (excepting ports having an area of less than 0.071m2 (110 sq in)).	**
3.08.2	A hatch fitted forward of the maximum beam station, located on the side of the coachroof, opening into the interior of the boat ,and of area greater than 0.071m2 shall comply with ISO12216 design category A and and be clearly labelled and used in accordance with the following instruction: "NOT TO BE OPENED AT SEA" Attention is drawn to SR 3.02.1	**
3.08.3	A hatch shall be:	
a)	so arranged as to be above the water when the hull is heeled 90 degrees. Hatches over lockers that open to the interior of the vessel shall be included in this requirement. A yacht may have a maximum of four (two on each side of centerline) hatches that do not conform to this requirement, provided that the opening of each is less than 0.071 sq m (110 sq in). Effective for boats of a series begun after January 1, 2009, a written statement signed by the designer or other person who performed the downflooding analysis shall be carried on board. For purposes of this rule the vessel's displacement condition for the analysis shall be the Light Craft Condition LCC (in conformity with 6.3 of the EN ISO 8666 standard and 3.5.1 of the EN ISO12217-2 standard).	Mo0,1,2,3,4
b)	permanently attached	**

		Category
c)	capable of being firmly shut immediately and remaining firmly shut in a 180 degree capsize (inversion)	**
3.08.4	A companionway hatch shall:	
a)	be fitted with a strong securing arrangement which shall be operable from the exterior and interior including when the yacht is inverted	**
b)	have any blocking devices:	**
i	capable of being retained in position with the hatch open or shut	**
ii	whether or not in position in the hatchway, secured to the yacht (e.g. by lanyard) for the duration of the race, to prevent their being lost overboard	**
iii	permit exit in the event of inversion	**
3.08.5	If the companionway extends below the local sheerline and the boat has a cockpit opening aft to the sea the boat shall comply with one of the following:	Mo0,1,2,3,4
a)	the companionway sill shall not extend below the local sheerline. or	Mo0,1,2,3,4
b)	be in full compliance with all aspects of ISO 11812 to design category A	Mo0,1,2,3,4
3.08.6	For boats with a cockpit closed aft to the sea where the companionway hatch extends below the local sheerline, the companionway shall be capable of being blocked off up to the level of the local sheerline, provided that the companionway hatch shall continue to give access to the interior with the blocking devices (e.g. washboards) in place	Mo0,1,2,3,4
3.09	**Cockpits - Attention is Drawn to ISO 11812**	
3.09.1	Cockpits shall be structurally strong, self-draining quickly by gravity at all angles of heel and permanently incorporated as an integral part of the hull.	**
3.09.2	Cockpits must be essentially watertight, that is, all openings to the hull must be capable of being strongly and rigidly secured	**
3.09.3	A bilge pump outlet pipe shall not be connected to a cockpit drain . See OSR 3.09.8 for cockpit drain minimum sizes	**
3.09.4	A cockpit sole shall be at least 2% LWL above LWL (or in IMS yachts first launched before 1/03, at least 2% L above LWL)	**
3.09.5	A bow, lateral, central or stern well shall be considered a cockpit for the purposes of OSR 3.09	**
3.09.6	In cockpits opening aft to the sea structural openings aft shall be not less in area than 50% maximum cockpit depth x maximum cockpit width.	**
3.09.7	**Cockpit Volume**	
i)	earliest of age or series date before April 1992: the total volume of all cockpits below lowest coamings shall not exceed 6% (LWL x maximum beam x freeboard abreast the cockpit).	MoMu0,1

		Category
ii)	earliest of age or series date April 1992 and after: as above for the appropriate category except that "lowest coamings" shall not include any aft of the FA station and no extension of a cockpit aft of the working deck shall be included in calculation of cockpit volume	**
Note	*IMS-rated boats may instead of the terms LWL, maximum beam, freeboard abreast the cockpit, use the IMS terms L, B and FA.*	**
3.09.8	**Cockpit Drains**	
	See OSR 3.09.1. Cockpit drain cross section area (after allowance for screens if fitted) shall be:-	
a)	in yachts with earliest of age or series date before 1/72 or in any yacht under 8.5m (28ft) LOA - at least that of 2 x 25mm diameter (one inch) unobstructed openings or equivalent	**
b)	in yachts with earliest of age or series date 1/72 and later - at least that of 4 x 20mm diameter (3/4 inch) unobstructed openings or equivalent	**
	US SAILING prescribes that cockpit drains shall be accessible for cleaning.	**
3.10	**Sea Cocks or Valves**	
	Sea cocks or valves shall be permanently installed on all through-hull openings below the waterline except integral deck scuppers, speed indicators, depth finders and the like, however a means of closing such openings shall be provided.	**
3.11	**Sheet Winches**	
	Sheet winches shall be mounted in such a way that an operator is not required to be substantially below deck.	**
3.12	**Mast Step**	
	The heel of a keel stepped mast shall be securely fastened to the mast step or adjoining structure.	**
3.14	**Pulpits, Stanchions, Lifelines**	
3.14.2	Lifelines required in Special Regulations shall be "taut".	**
a)	*As a guide, when a deflecting force of 50 N (5.1 kgf, 11.2 lbf) is applied to a lifeline midway between supports, the lifeline should not deflect more than 50 mm.*	**

		Category
3.14.3	The following shall be provided:	**
a)	a bow pulpit with vertical height and openings essentially conforming to Table 7. Bow pulpits may be open but the opening between the pulpit and any part of the boat shall never be greater than 360mm (14.2") (this requirement shall be checked by presenting a 360mm (14.2") circle inside the opening) 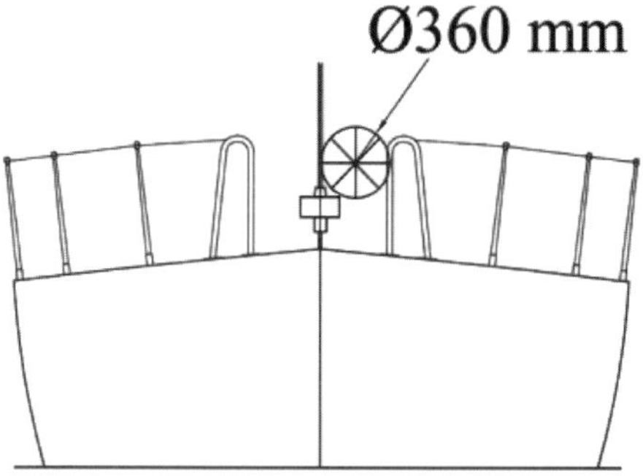 Ø360 mm **Figure 2 - Diagram Showing Pulpit Opening**	Mo 0,1,2,3,4
b)	a stern pulpit, or lifelines arranged as an adequate substitute, with vertical openings conforming to Table 7	Mo0,1,2,3,4
c)	lifelines (guardlines) supported on stanchions, which, with pulpits, shall form an effectively continuous barrier around a working deck for man-overboard prevention. Lifelines shall be permanently supported at intervals of not more than 2.20m (86.6") and shall not pass outboard of supporting stanchions	**
d)	upper rails of pulpits at no less height above the working deck than the upper lifelines as in Table 7.	**
e)	Openable upper rails in bow pulpits shall be secured shut whilst racing	**
f)	Pulpits and stanchions shall be permanently installed. When there are sockets or studs, these shall be through-bolted, bonded or welded. The pulpit(s) and/or stanchions fitted to these shall be mechanically retained without the help of the life-lines. Without sockets or studs, pulpits and/or stanchions shall be through-bolted, bonded or welded.	**
g)	The bases of pulpits and stanchions shall not be further inboard from the edge of the appropriate working deck than 5% of maximum beam or 150 mm (6 in), whichever is greater.	**

		Category
h)	Stanchion or pulpit or pushpit bases shall not be situated outboard of a working deck. For the purpose of this rule the base shall be taken to include a sleeve or socket into which the tube is fitted but shall exclude a baseplate which carries fixings into the deck or hull.	**
i)	Provided the complete lifeline enclosure is supported by stanchions and pulpit bases effectively within the working deck, lifeline terminals and support struts may be fixed to a hull aft of the working deck	**
j)	Lifelines need not be fixed to a bow pulpit if they terminate at, or pass through, adequately braced stanchions set inside and overlapping the bow pulpit, provided that the gap between the upper lifeline and the bow pulpit does not exceed 150 mm (6 in).	**
k)	Lifelines shall be continuous and fixed only at (or near) the bow and stern. However a bona fide gate shall be permitted in the lifelines on each side of a yacht. Except at its end fittings, the movement of a lifeline in a fore-and-aft direction shall not be constrained. Temporary sleeving in 3.14.6 (c) shall not modify tension in the lifeline.	**
l)	Stanchions shall be straight and vertical except that:-	**
i	within the first 50 mm (2 in) from the deck, stanchions shall not be displaced horizontally from the point at which they emerge from the deck or stanchion base by more than 10 mm (3/8 in),and	**
ii	stanchions may be angled to not more than 10 degrees from vertical at any point above 50 mm (2 in) from the deck.	**
m)	*It is strongly recommended that designs also comply to ISO 15085*	**

		Category
3.14.5	**Lifeline Height, Vertical Openings, Number of Lifelines**	

TABLE 7 **

LOA	earliest of age/ series date	minimum requirements	Category
under 8.5 m (28 ft)	before January 1992	taut single lifeline at a height of no less than 450 mm (18 in) above the working deck. No vertical opening shall exceed 560 mm (22 in).	**
under 8.5 m (28 ft)	January 1992 and after	as for under 8.5 m(28 ft) in table 7 above, except that when an intermediate lifeline is fitted no vertical opening shall exceed 380 mm (15 in).	**
8.5 m (28 ft) and over	before January 1993	taut double lifeline with upper lifeline at a height of no less than 600 mm (24 in) above the working deck. No vertical opening shall exceed 560 mm (22 in)	**
8.5 m (28 ft) and over	January 1993 and after	as 8.5 m (28 ft) and over in Table 7 above, except that no vertical opening shall exceed 380 mm (15 in).	**
all	all	on yachts with intermediate lifelines the intermediate line shall be not less than 230 mm (9 in) above the working deck ***and shall be of the same construction and general arrangements as required for the upper.***	**

3.14.6	**Lifeline Minimum Diameters, Required Materials, Specifications**	
a)	Lifelines shall be of : - stranded stainless steel wire or - Single-braided High Modulus Polyethylene (HMPE) (Dyneema®/ Spectra® or equivalent) rope	** ** **
	US SAILING note. An article describing the best techniques for using Dyneema line, particularly in the life line application, is posted at http://offshore.ussailing.org/SAS.htm	
b)	The minimum diameter of all lifelines is specified in table 8 below.	**

		Category
c)	Stainless steel lifelines shall be uncoated and used without close-fitting sleeving, however, temporary sleeving may be fitted provided it is regularly removed for inspection.	**
d)	*When stainless wire is used, Grade 316 is recommended.*	**
e)	When HMPE (Dyneema®/Spectra®) is used, it shall be spliced in accordance with the manufacturer's recommended procedures.	**
f)	A taut lanyard of synthetic rope may be used to secure lifelines provided the gap it closes does not exceed 100 mm (4 in). This lanyard shall be replaced annually at a minimum.	**
g)	All wire, fittings, anchorage points, fixtures and lanyards shall comprise a lifeline enclosure system which has at all points at least the breaking strength of the required lifeline wire.	**

TABLE 8 **

LOA	minimum wire or rope diameter
under 8.5m (28ft)	3 mm (1/8 in)
8.5m - 13m	4 mm (5/32 in)
over 13m (43ft)	5 mm (3/16 in)

3.14.7	Pulpits, Stanchions, Lifelines - Limitations on Materials	

TABLE 9 **

Earliest of Age or Series Date	detail
before January 1987	carbon fibre is not recommended in stanchions pulpits and lifelines.
January 1987 and after	stanchions, pulpits and lifelines shall not be made of carbon fibre.

3.17	Toe Rail or Foot - Stop	Mo0.1,2,3
3.17.1	A toe rail of minimum height 25 mm (1 in) shall be permanently installed around the foredeck from abreast the mast, except in way of fittings and not further inboard from the edge of the working deck than one third of the local half-beam.	Mo0.1,2,3
3.17.2	The following variations shall apply:-	Mo0.1,2,3

		Category

TABLE 10 Mo0.1,2,3

LOA	Earliest of Age or Series Date	minimum requirements	Mo0.1,2,3
any	before January 1981	a toe rail minimum height of 20 mm (3/4 in) is acceptable.	
any	before January 1994	an additional lifeline of minimum height 25 mm (1 in) and maximum height 50 mm (2 in) is acceptable in lieu of a toe rail (but shall not count as an intermediate lifeline).	
any	January 1994 and after	the toe rail shall be fitted as close as practicable to the vertical axis of stanchion bases but not further in-board than 1/3 the local half-beam.	

3.18	**Toilet**	
3.18.1	A toilet, permanently installed	MoMu.1,2
3.19	**Bunks**	
3.19.2	Bunks, permanently installed	**
3.20	**Cooking Facilities**	
3.20.1	A cooking stove, permanently installed or securely fastened with safe accessible fuel shutoff control and capable of being safely operated in a seaway.	MoMu. 0,1,2,3
3.21	**Drinking Water Tanks & Drinking Water**	MoMu. 0,1,2,3
3.21.1	**Drinking Water Tanks**	MoMu. 0,1,2,3
a)	A yacht shall have a permanently installed delivery pump and water tank(s):	MoMu. 0,1,2,3
ii	dividing the water supply into at least two compartments	MoMu1
3.21.3	**Emergency Drinking Water**	MoMu. 0,1,2,3
a)	At least 9 litres (2 UK gallons, 2.4 US gallons) of drinking water for emergency use shall be provided in a dedicated and sealed container or container(s)	MoMu. 1,2,3
3.22	**Hand Holds**	
	Adequate hand holds shall be fitted below deck so that crew members may move about safely at sea.	**

		Category
	A hand hold should be capable of withstanding without rupture a side force of 1500N - attention is drawn to ISO 15085.	
3.23	**Bilge Pumps and Buckets**	
3.23.1	No bilge pump may discharge into a cockpit unless that cockpit opens aft to the sea.	**
3.23.2	Bilge pumps shall not be connected to cockpit drains. (OSR 3.09)	**
3.23.3	Bilge pumps and strum boxes shall be readily accessible for maintenance and for clearing out debris	**
3.23.4	Unless permanently installed, each bilge pump handle shall be provided with a lanyard or catch or similar device to prevent accidental loss	**
3.23.5	The following shall be provided:	
a)	two permanently installed manual bilge pumps, one operable from above, the other from below deck. Each pump shall be operable with all cockpit seats, hatches and companionways shut and shall have permanently installed discharge pipe(s) of sufficient capacity to accommodate simultaneously both pumps	Mo0,1,2
f)	two buckets of stout construction each with at least 9 litres (2 UK gallons, 2.4 US gallons) capacity. Each bucket to have a lanyard.	**
3.24	**Compass**	
3.24.1	The following shall be provided:-	
a)	a marine magnetic compass, independent of any power supply, permanently installed and correctly adjusted with deviation card, and	**
b)	a magnetic compass independent of any power supply, capable of being used as a steering compass which may be hand-held	MoMu 0,1,2,3
3.25	**Halyards.**	
	No mast shall have less than two halyards, each capable of hoisting a sail.	**
Boom Support	***US SAILING prescribes that some means must exist to prevent the boom from dropping if support from the mainsail and/or halyard fails. Topping lifts or supporting vangs are acceptable for this purpose.***	**
3.27	**Navigation Lights (see OSR 2.03.3)**	
3.27.1	Navigation lights shall be mounted so that they will not be masked by sails or the heeling of the yacht.	**
3.27.2	Navigation lights shall not be mounted below deck level and should be at no less height than immediately under the upper lifeline.	**
3.27.3	Navigation light intensity	

		Category

TABLE 11

LOA	Guide to required minimum power rating for an electric bulb in a navigation light
under 12 m (39.4 ft)	10 W
12 m (39.4 ft) and above	25 W

	US SAILING prescribes that in the US compliance with the recommendations of COLREGS shall suffice in satisfying these regulations. COLREGS requirements are as follows;	**

TABLE 14

LOA	*Light*	*Luminous*	*Minimum Range of Visibility*
under 39.4 ft	*Side*	*0.9 candelas*	*1 mile*
	Stern	*4.3 candelas*	*2 miles*
39.4 ft and above	*Side*	*4.3 candelas*	*2 miles*
and less than 164 ft	*Stern*	*4.3 candelas*	*2 miles*

3.27.4	Reserve navigation lights shall be carried having the same minimum specifications as the navigation lights above, with a separable power source, and wiring or supply system essentially separate from that used for the normal navigation lights	MoMu 0,1,2,3
3.27.5	spare bulbs for navigation lights shall be carried, or for lights not dependent on bulbs, appropriate spares.	**
3.28	**Engines, Generators, Fuel**	
3.28.1	**Propulsion Engines**	**
a)	Engines and associated systems shall be installed in accordance with their manufacturers' guidelines and shall be of a type, strength, capacity, and installation suitable for the size and intended use of the yacht.	**
b)	An inboard propulsion engine when fitted shall: be provided with a permanently installed exhaust, coolant, and fuel supply systems and fuel tank(s); be securely covered; and have adequate protection from the effects of heavy weather.	**

		Category
c)	A propulsion engine required by Special Regulations shall provide a minimum speed in knots of (1.8 x square root of LWL in metres) or (square root of LWL in feet)	MoMu 0,1,2,3
e)	An inboard propulsion engine shall be provided for yachts	Mo0,1,2 Mu0
3.28.2	**Generator**	
	A separate generator for electricity is optional. However, when a separate generator is carried it shall be permanently installed, securely covered, and shall have permanently installed exhaust, cooling and fuel supply systems and fuel tank(s), and have adequate protection from the effects of heavy weather.	**
3.28.3	**Fuel Systems**	
a)	Each fuel tank provided with a shutoff valve. Except for permanently installed linings or liners, a flexible tank is not permitted as a fuel tank.	MoMu 0,1,2,3
b)	The propulsion engine shall have a minimum amount of fuel which may be specified in the Notice of Race but if not, shall be sufficient to be able to meet charging requirements for the duration of the race and to motor at the above minimum speed for at least 8 hours	MoMu 0,1,2,3
3.28.4	**Battery Systems**	
a)	When an electric starter is the only method for starting the engine, the yacht shall have a separate battery, the primary purpose of which is to start the engine	MoMu 0,1,2,3
b)	All rechargeable batteries on board shall be of the sealed type from which liquid electrolyte cannot escape. Other types of battery installed on board at 1/12 may continue in use for the remainder of their service lives.	MoMu 0,1,2,3
3.29	**Communications Equipment, EPFS (Electronic Position-Fixing System), Radar, AIS**	**
	Provision of GMDSS and DSC is unlikely to be mandatory for small craft during the term of the present Special Regulations However it is recommended that persons in charge include these facilities when installing new equipment.	MoMu 0,1,2,3
3.29.1	The following shall be provided:	**
a)	A marine radio transceiver (or if stated in the Notice of Race, an installed satcom terminal), and	MoMu 0,1,2,3
i	an emergency antenna when the regular antenna depends upon the mast.	MoMu 0,1,2,3
b)	When the marine radio transceiver is VHF:	MoMu 0,1,2,3
i	it shall have a rated output power of 25W	MoMu 0,1,2,3

		Category
ii	it shall have a masthead antenna, and co-axial feeder cable with not more than 40% power loss	MoMu 0,1,2,3
iii	*the following types and lengths of co-axial feeder cable will meet the requirements of OSR 3.29.1 (b)(ii): (a) up to 15m (50ft) - type RG8X ("mini 8"); (b) 15-28m (50-90ft) - type RG8U; (c) 28-43m (90-140ft) - type 9913F (uses conventional connectors, available from US supplier Belden); (d) 43-70m) 140-230ft - type LMR600 (uses special connectors, available from US supplier Times Microwave)*	MoMu 0,1,2,3
iv	*it should include channel 72 (an international ship-ship channel which, by common use, has become widely accepted as primary choice for ocean racing yachts anywhere in the world)*	MoMu 0,1,2,3
e)	A hand-held marine VHF transceiver, watertight or with a waterproof cover. When not in use to be stowed in a grab bag or emergency container (see OSR 4.21)	MoMu 1,2,3,4
f)	Independent of a main radio transceiver, a radio receiver capable of receiving weather bulletins	**
i)	An EPFS (Electronic Position-Fixing System) (e.g. GPS)	MoMu 0,1,2,3
n)	An AIS Transponder	MoMu1,2
3.29.2	*Yachts are reminded that no reflector, active or passive, is a guarantee of detection or tracking by a vessel using radar.*	**
a)	*The attention of persons in charge is drawn to legislation in force or imminent affecting the territorial seas of some countries in which the carriage of an AIS set is or will be mandatory for certain vessels including relatively small craft.*	**

SECTION 4 - PORTABLE EQUIPMENT & SUPPLIES for the yacht (for water & fuel see OSR 3.21 and OSR 3.28)

4.01	**Sail Letters & Numbers**	
4.01.1	Yachts which are not in an ISAF International Class or Recognized Class shall comply with RRS 77 and Appendix G as closely as possible, except that sail numbers allotted by a State authority are acceptable .	**
4.01.2	Sail numbers and letters of the size carried on the mainsail must be displayed by alternative means when none of the numbered sails is set.	**
4.02	**Hull marking (colour blaze)**	**Mo0,1 Mu0,1,2,3,4**
4.02.1	To assist in SAR location:-	
b)	*Each yacht is recommended to show at least 1 m^2 of fluorescent pink or orange or yellow colour as far as possible in a single area on the coachroof and/or deck where it can best be seen*	MoMu1

		Category
4.02.3	*Each yacht is recommended to show on each underwater appendage an area of highly-visible colour*	MoMu0,1
4.03	**Soft Wood Plugs**	
	Soft wood plugs, tapered and of the appropriate size, shall be attached or stowed adjacent to the appropriate fitting for every through-hull opening.	**
4.04	**Jackstays, Clipping Points and Static Safety Lines**	
4.04.1	The following shall be provided:	
a)	Jackstays:-	MoMu 0,1,2,3
	shall be provided-	
i	attached to through-bolted or welded deck plates or other suitable and strong anchorage fitted on deck, port and starboard of the yacht's centre line to provide secure attachments for safety harness:-	MoMu 0,1,2,3
ii	comprising stainless steel 1 x 19 wire of minimum diameter 5 mm (3/16 in), high modulus polyethylene (such as Dyneema/Spectra) rope or webbing of equivalent strength;	MoMu 0,1,2,3
	US SAILING prescribes that wire jackstays (jacklines) may be of configurations other than 1 X 19.	
iii	which, when made from stainless steel wire shall be uncoated and used without any sleeving;	MoMu 0,1,2,3
iv	*20kN (2,040 kgf or 4,500 lbf) min breaking strain webbing is recommended;*	MoMu 0,1,2,3
4.04.2	**Clipping Points:-**	
	shall be provided-	
a)	attached to through-bolted or welded deck plates or other suitable and strong anchorage points adjacent to stations such as the helm, sheet winches and masts, where crew members work for long periods:-	MoMu 0,1,2,3
b)	which, together with jackstays and static safety lines shall enable a crew member-	MoMu 0,1,2,3
i	to clip on before coming on deck and unclip after going below;	MoMu 0,1,2,3
ii	whilst continuously clipped on, to move readily between the working areas on deck and the cockpit(s) with the minimum of clipping and unclipping operations.	MoMu 0,1,2,3
c)	The provision of clipping points shall enable two-thirds of the crew to be simultaneously clipped on without depending on jackstays	MoMu 0,1,2,3
e)	*Warning - U-bolts as clipping points - see OSR 5.02.1(a)*	

		Category
4.05	**Fire Extinguishers**	
	Shall be provided as follows:	
4.05.1	Fire extinguishers, at least two, readily accessible in suitable and different parts of the yacht	**
4.05.2	Fire Extinguishers, at least two, of minimum 2kgs each of dry powder or equivalent	MoMu 0,1,2,3
4.05.4	A fire blanket adjacent to every cooking device with an open flame	**
4.06	**Anchor(s)**	
4.06.1	An anchor or anchors shall be carried according to the table below:	**
a)	The following anchors shall be provided	
i	For yachts of 8.5 m LOA (28 ft) and over there shall be 2 anchors together with a suitable combination of chain and rope, all ready for immediate use	MoMu 1,2,3
ii	For yachts under 8.5 m LOA (28 ft) there shall be 1 anchor together with a suitable combination of chain and rope, all ready for immediate use	MoMu 1,2,3
4.07	**Flashlight(s) and Searchlight(s)**	
4.07.1	The following shall be provided:-	
a)	A watertight, high-powered searchlight, suitable for searching for a person overboard at night and for collision avoidance with spare batteries and bulbs, and	**
b)	a watertight flashlight with spare batteries and bulb	**
4.08	**First Aid Manual and First Aid Kit**	**
4.08.1	A suitable First Aid Manual shall be provided	**
	In the absence of a National Authority's requirement, the latest edition of one of the following is recommended:	
a)	*International Medical Guide for Ships, World Health Organisation, Geneva*	MoMu0,1
c)	*Le Guide de la medecine a distance, by Docteur J Y Chauve, published by Distance Assistance BP33 F-La Baule, cedex, France.*	**
d)	*PAN-PAN medico bordo' in Italian edited by Umberto Verna, www.panpan.it*	MoMu 2,3,4
e)	*Skipper's Medical Emergency Handbook by Dr Spike Briggs and Dr Campbell Mackenzie www.msos.org.uk*	**
	US SAILING endorses the above and additionally recommends the following manuals: Advanced First Aid by Peter Eastman, M.D., Cornell Maritime Press and A Comprehensive Guide to Marine Medicine by Eric A. Weiss, M.D. and Michael E. Jacobs, M.D., Adventure Medical Kit.	
4.08.2	A First Aid Kit shall be provided	**

		Category
4.08.3	*The contents and storage of the First Aid Kit should reflect the guidelines of the Manual carried, the likely conditions and duration of the passage, and the number of people aboard the yacht.*	**
4.09	**Foghorn**	
	A foghorn shall be provided	**
4.10	**Radar Reflector**	
4.10.1	A passive Radar Reflector (that is, a Radar Reflector without any power) shall be provided	**
a)	If a radar reflector is:	**
i	octahedral with triangular plates making up each pocket it must have a minimum diagonal measurement of 456 mm (18in).	**
ii	octahederal with circular sector plates making up each pocket it must have a minimum diameter of 304mm (12in).	**
iii	not octahedral it must have a documented RCS (radar cross-section) of not less than 10 m2 at 0° elevation and be capable of performance around 360° in azimuth.	**
	US SAILING prescribes that in the US, radar reflectors shall have a minimum documented "equivalent echoing area" of 6 sq. m. Octahedral reflectors shall have a minimum diameter of 12 inches.	**
	The minimum effective height above water is 4.0 m (13 ft).	**
b)	*The passive and active devices referred to in these notes and in 4.10.1 and 4.10.2 above are primarily intended for use in the X (9GHz) band*	**
4.10.2	*The most effective radar response from a yacht may be provided by an RTE (Radar Target Enhancer) which may be on board in addition to the required passive reflector. An RTE should conform to ISO 8729-2:2009. An RTE is strongly recommended.*	MoMu 1,2,3,4
b)	*The display of a passive reflector or the operation of an RTE is for the person in charge to decide according to prevailing conditions.*	**
4.10.3	*When available, a passive radar reflector in compliance with ISO8729-1:2010 will offer improved performance over earlier models and has a size typified by a cylinder of not more than weight 5kg, height 750mm and diameter 300mm.*	**
4.10.4	*S (3GHz) band radar is often used by ships in bad weather to complement X (9GHz) band radar. On S (3GHz) band a passive reflector offers about 1/10 the response obtained on the X (9GHz) band. Unless specifically designed to operate in the S(3GHz) band, an RTE will provide no response at all.*	**
4.11	**Navigation Equipment**	
4.11.1	Charts	

		Category
	Navigational charts (not solely electronic), light list and chart plotting equipment shall be provided	**
4.11.2	*Reserve Navigation System*	
	Navigators are recommended to carry a sextant with suitable tables and a timepiece or an adequate reserve navigation system so that total reliance is not placed on dead-reckoning and a single form of EPFS (Electronic Position-Fixing System) (see Volpe Report at www.navcen.uscg.gov/archive/2001/Oct/FinalReport-v4.6.pdf)	MoMu 0,1
4.12	**Safety Equipment Location Chart**	
	A safety equipment location chart in durable waterproof material shall be displayed in the main accommodation where it can best be seen, clearly marked with the location of principal items of safety equipment.	**
4.13	**Echo Sounder or Lead Line**	
4.13.1	An echo sounder or lead line shall be provided	MoMu 1,2,3,4
4.14	**Speedometer or Distance Measuring Instrument (log)**	
	A speedometer or distance measuring instrument (log) shall be provided	MoMu 0,1,2,3
4.15	**Emergency Steering**	
4.15.1	Emergency steering shall be provided as follows:	
a)	except when the principal method of steering is by means of an unbreakable metal tiller, an emergency tiller capable of being fitted to the rudder stock;	MoMu 0,1,2,3
b)	crews must be aware of alternative methods of steering the yacht in any sea condition in the event of rudder loss. At least one method must have been proven to work on board the yacht. An inspector may require that this method be demonstrated.	MoMu 0,1,2,3
4.16	**Tools and Spare Parts**	
	Tools and spare parts, including effective means to quickly disconnect or sever the standing rigging from the hull shall be provided.	**
4.17	**Yacht's name**	
	Yacht's name shall be on miscellaneous buoyant equipment, such as lifejackets, cushions, lifebuoys, lifeslings, grab bags etc.	**
4.18	**Marine grade retro-reflective material**	
	Marine grade retro-reflective material shall be fitted to lifebuoys, lifeslings, liferafts and lifejackets. See OSRs 5.04, 5.08.	**
4.19	**EPIRBs**	
4.19.1	A 406 MHz EPIRB shall be provided	MoMu1,2

		Category
b)	*It is recommended that a 406 MHz EPIRB should include an internal GPS, and also a 121.5MHz transmitter for local homing.*	MoMu 0,1,2
c)	Every 406 MHz EPIRB shall be properly registered with the appropriate authority.	MoMu 0,1,2
d)	Every ship's 406 MHz EPIRB shall be water and manually activated.	MoMu 0,1,2
e)	*EPIRBs should be tested in accordance with manufacturer's instructions when first commissioned and then at least annually.*	MoMu 0,1,2
f)	*A list of registration numbers of 406 EPIRBs should be notified to event organizers and kept available for immediate use.*	MoMu 0,1,2
g)	*Consideration should be given to the provision of a locator device (eg an "Argos" beacon) operating on non - SAR frequencies, to aid salvage if a yacht is abandoned.*	MoMu 0,1,2
h)	*Beacons with only 121.5MHz are no longer recommended for distress alerting. Satellite processing of 121.5 MHz is being phased out. 121.5MHz will continue to be used for local homing by on-board D/F systems and for local homing by SAR units. Type "E" EPIRBs are no longer supported and should be replaced immediately.*	MoMu 0,1,2
	US SAILING requires the use of 406 EPIRBs (with or without GPS input), as USCG advises that rescue efforts will be launched immediately upon receipt of a distress signal from these units. USCG also advises that some PLB and INMARSAT "E" transmissions are not monitored by U.S. Rescue Coordination Centers and that slight delays are likely to occur while the commercial ground stations forward an alert to the USCG.	MoMu 0,1,2
4.20	**Liferafts**	MoMu 0,1,2
4.20.1	**Liferaft Construction and Packed Equipment**	
4.20.2	Liferaft(s) shall be provided capable of carrying the whole crew when each liferaft shall comply with either:-	MoMu1,2
a)	Liferafts shall comply with SOLAS LSA code 1997 Chapter IV or later version except that they are acceptable with a capacity of 4 persons and may be packed in a valise. A SOLAS liferaft shall contain at least a SOLAS "A" pack or	MoMu1,2
b)	***for liferafts manufactured prior to January 2003 (1/06 in the U.S.) OSR Appendix A part I (ORC), or***	MoMu1,2
c)	OSR Appendix A part II (ISAF) when, unless otherwise specified by a race organizer, the floor shall include thermal insulation, or	MoMu1,2
d)	ISO 9650 Part I Type I Group A (ISO) when each liferaft shall contain at least a Pack 2 (<24h) and	MoMu1,2

		Category
i	shall have a semi-rigid boarding ramp, and	MoMu1,2
ii	shall be so arranged that any high-pressure hose shall not impede the boarding process, and	MoMu1,2
iii	shall have a topping-up means provided for any inflatable boarding ramp, and	MoMu1,2
iv	when the liferaft is designed with a single ballast pocket this shall be accepted provided the liferaft otherwise complies with ISO 9650 and meets a suitable test of ballast pocket strength devised by the manufacturer and	MoMu1,2
v	compliance with OSR 4.20.2 (d) i-iv shall be indicated on the liferaft certificate.	MoMu1,2
	US SAILING recommends that liferafts be equipped with insulated floors for events that take place in waters of less than 68 deg F (20deg C).	MoMu1,2
	US SAILING prescribes that liferafts shall be equipped with canopies.	MoMu1,2
4.20.3	**Liferaft Packing and Stowage**	MoMu 0,1,2
	A Liferaft shall be either:-	MoMu 0,1,2
a)	packed in a transportable rigid container or canister and stowed on the working deck or in the cockpit, or:-	MoMu 0,1,2
b)	packed in a transportable rigid container or canister or in a valise and stowed in a purpose-built rigid compartment containing liferaft(s) only and opening into or adjacent to the cockpit or working deck, or through a transom, provided that:-	MoMu 0,1,2
i	each compartment is watertight or self-draining (self-draining compartments will be counted as part of the cockpit volume except when entirely above working deck level or when draining independently overboard from a transom stowage - see OSR 3.09) and-	MoMu 0,1,2
ii	the cover of each compartment is capable of being easily opened under water pressure, and-	MoMu 0,1,2
iii	the compartment is designed and built to allow a liferaft to be removed and launched quickly and easily, or-	MoMu 0,1,2
iv	in a yacht with age or series date before June 2001, a liferaft may be packed in a valise not exceeding 40kg securely stowed below deck adjacent to a companionway.	MoMu 0,1,2
c)	The end of each liferaft painter should be permanently made fast to a strong point on board the yacht.	MoMu 0,1,2

		Category
4.20.4	**Liferaft Launching**	MoMu 0,1,2
a)	Each raft shall be capable of being got to the lifelines or launched within 15 seconds.	MoMu 0,1,2
b)	*Each liferaft of more than 40kg weight should be stowed in such a way that the liferaft can be dragged or slid into the sea without significant lifting*	MoMu 0,1,2
4.20.5	**Liferaft Servicing and Inspection**	MoMu 0,1,2
	IMPORTANT NOTICE Recent evidence has shown that packaged liferafts are vulnerable to serious damage when dropped (eg from a boat onto a marina pontoon) or when subjected to the weight of a crew member or heavy object (eg an anchor). Damage can be caused internally by the weight of the heavy steel CO2 bottle abrading or splitting neighbouring layers of buoyancy tube material. ISAF has instituted an investigation into this effect and as an interim measure requires that every valise-packed liferaft shall have an annual certificate of servicing. A liferaft should be taken for servicing if there is any sign of damage or deterioration (including on the underside of the pack). Persons in charge should insist on great care in handling liferafts and apply the rules NO STEP and DO NOT DROP UNLESS LAUNCHING INTO THE SEA.	MoMu 0,1,2
a)	Certificates or copies, of servicing and/or inspection shall be kept on board the yacht. Every SOLAS liferaft and every valise-packed liferaft shall have a valid annual certificate of new or serviced status from the manufacturer or his approved service station.	MoMu 0,1,2
b)	A liferaft built to OSR Appendix A part I ("ORC") packed in a rigid container or canister shall either be serviced annually or may, when the manufacturer so specifies, be inspected annually (not necessarily unpacked) provided the yacht has on board written confirmation from the manufacturer's approved service station stating that the inspection was satisfactory.	MoMu 0,1,2
c)	A liferaft built to OSR Appendix A part II ("ISAF") packed in a rigid container or canister shall either be serviced annually or may, when the manufacturer so specifies, have its first service no longer than 3 years after commissioning and its second service no longer than 2 years after the first. Subsequent services shall be at intervals of not more than 12 months.	MoMu 1,2
d)	A liferaft built to ISO 9650 Part 1 Type Group A, packed in a rigid container or canister shall be serviced in accordance with the manufacturer's instructions but NOT less frequently than every three years	MoMu 1,2

		Category
e)	A liferaft built to ISO 9650 Part 1 Type Group A packed in a valise shall be inspected annually by an approved manufacturer's agent and serviced in accordance with the manufacturer's instructions but NOT less frequently than every three years.	MoMu 1,2
f)	Liferaft servicing certificates shall state the specification that the liferaft was built to. See OSR 4.20.2	MoMu 1,2
4.21.2	***Grab Bags to Accompany Liferafts***	
a)	*A yacht is recommended to have for each liferaft, a grab bag with the following minimum contents. A grab bag should have inherent flotation, at least 0.1 m^2 area of fluorescent orange colour on the outside, should be marked with the name of the yacht, and should have a lanyard and clip.*	MoMu 0,1,2
b)	*Note: it is not intended to duplicate in a grab bag items required by other OSRs to be on board the yacht - these recommendations cover only the stowage of those items*	MoMu 0,1,2
4.21.3	***Grab Bag Recommended Contents***	
a)	*2 red parachute and 2 red hand flares and cyalume-type chemical light sticks (red flares compliant with SOLAS)*	MoMu1,2
b)	*watertight hand-held EPFS (Electronic Position-Fixing System) (eg GPS) in at least one of the grab bags carried by a yacht*	MoMu1,2
c)	*SART (Search and Rescue Transponder) in at least one of the grab bags carried by a yacht*	MoMu1,2
d)	*a combined 406MHz/121.5MHz or type "E" EPIRB (see OSR 4.19.1) in at least one of the grab bags carried by a yacht*	MoMu1,2
e)	*water in re-sealable containers or a hand-operated desalinator plus containers for water*	MoMu1,2
f)	*a watertight hand-held marine VHF transceiver plus a spare set of batteries*	MoMu0,1,2
g)	*a watertight flashlight with spare batteries and bulb*	MoMu0,1,2
h)	*dry suits or thermal protective aids or survival bags*	
i)	*second sea anchor for the liferaft (not required if the liferaft has already a spare sea anchor in its pack) (recommended standard ISO 17339) with swivel and >30m line diameter >9.5 mm*	MoMu0,1,2
j)	*two safety tin openers (if appropriate)*	MoMu0,1,2
k)	*first-aid kit including at least 2 tubes of sunscreen. All dressings should be capable of being effectively used in wet conditions. The first-aid kit should be clearly marked and re-sealable*	MoMu0,1,2
l)	*signalling mirror*	MoMu0,1,2
m)	*high-energy food (min 10 000kJ per person recommended for Cat Zero)*	MoMu0,1,2
n)	*nylon string, polythene bags, seasickness tablets (min 6 per person recommended)*	MoMu0,1,2
o)	*watertight hand-held aviation VHF transceiver (if race area warrants)*	MoMu0,1,2

		Category
4.22	**Lifebuoys**	
4.22.1	***The following shall be provided within easy reach of the helmsman and ready for instant use:***	**
a)	a lifebuoy with a self-igniting light and a drogue or a Lifesling with a self-igniting light and without a drogue.	**
	For Categories 0,1,2,3 US SAILING prescribes that the lifebuoy in OSR 4.22.1 a) above shall be a Lifesling (without a drogue), equipped with a self-igniting light within easy reach of the helmsman and ready for instant use. (See Appendix D).	MoMu 0,1,2,3
b)	***In addition to a) above, one lifebuoy within easy reach of the helmsman and ready for instant use, equipped with:***	MoMu 0,1,2
i	a whistle, a drogue, a self-igniting light and	MoMu 0,1,2
ii	a pole and flag. The pole shall be either permanently extended or be capable of being fully automatically extended (not extendable by hand) in less than 20 seconds. It shall be attached to the lifebuoy with 3 m (10 ft) of floating line and is to be of a length and so ballasted that the flag will fly at least 1.8 m (6 ft) off the water.	MoMu 0,1,2
4.22.2	When at least two lifebuoys (and/or Lifeslings) are carried, at least one of them shall depend entirely on permanent (eg foam) buoyancy.	MoMu 0,1,2
4.22.3	Each inflatable lifebuoy and any automatic device (eg pole and flag extended by compressed gas) shall be tested and serviced at intervals in accordance with its manufacturer's instructions.	**
4.22.4	Each lifebuoy or lifesling shall be fitted with marine grade retro-reflective material (4.18).	**
4.22.5	*It is recommended that the colour of each lifebuoy be a safety colour in the yellow-red range.*	**
4.23	**Pyrotechnic and Light Signals**	
4.23.1	Pyrotechnic signals shall be provided conforming to SOLAS LSA Code Chapter III Visual Signals and not older than the stamped expiry date (if any) or if no expiry date stamped , not older than 4 years.	**

TABLE 13

red parachute flares LSA III 3.1	**red hand flares LSA III 3.2**	**orange smoke LSA III 3.3**	**race category**
6	4	2	MoMu0,1
4	4	2	MoMu2,3

		Category
4.24	**Heaving Line**	**
a)	a heaving line shall be provided 15 m - 25 m (50 ft - 75 ft) length readily accessible to cockpit.	**
b)	*the "throwing sock" type is recommended - see Appendix D*	**
	US SAILING prescribes that the heaving line be of 1/4 in. (6 mm) minimum diameter, floating, UV-inhibited and readily accessible to the cockpit.	**
4.25	**Cockpit Knife**	
	A strong, sharp knife, sheathed and securely restrained shall be provided readily accessible from the deck or a cockpit.	**
4.26	**Storm & Heavy Weather Sails**	
4.26.1	*Design*	
a)	*it is strongly recommended that persons in charge consult their designer and sailmaker to decide the most effective size for storm and heavy weather sails. The purpose of these sails is to provide safe propulsion for the yacht in severe weather -they are not intended as part of the racing inventory. The areas below are maxima. Smaller areas are likely to suit some yachts according to their stability and other characteristics.*	**
4.26.2	**High Visibility**	
a)	Every storm jib shall either be of highly-visible coloured material (eg dayglo pink, orange or yellow) or have a highly-visible coloured patch at least 50% of the area of the sail (up to a maximum diameter of 3m) added on each side; and also that a rotating wing mast should have a highly-visible coloured patch on each side. A storm sail purchased after January 2014 shall have the material of the body of the sail a highly-visible colour.	
4.26.3	**Materials**	
a)	aromatic polyamides, carbon and similar fibres shall not be used in a trysail or storm jib but spectra/dyneema and similar materials are permitted.	**
b)	*it is strongly recommended that a heavy weather jib does not contain aromatic polyamides, carbon and similar fibres other than spectra/dyneema.*	**
4.26.4	**The following shall be provided:-**	
a)	sheeting positions on deck for each storm and heavy-weather sail;	**
b)	for each storm or heavy-weather jib, a means to attach the luff to the stay, independent of any luff-groove device. A heavy weather jib shall have the means of attachment readily available. A storm jib shall have the means of attachment permanently attached;	**

		Category
	Storm and heavy weather jib areas shall be calculated as: (0.255 x luff length x (luff perpendicular + 2 x half width))* To apply to sails made in January 2012 and after.	
c)	a storm trysail which shall be capable of being sheeted independently of the boom with trysail area not greater than 17.5% mainsail hoist (P) x mainsail foot length (E). The storm trysail area shall be measured as (0.5 x leech length x shortest distance between tack point and leech). The storm trysail shall have neither headboard nor battens, however a storm trysail is not required in a yacht with a rotating wing mast which can adequately substitute for a trysail. The method of calculating area applies to sails made in January 2012 and after.	MoMu0,1,2
	US SAILING prescribes that a storm trysail shall be capable of being attached to the mast.	MoMu0,1,2
d)	the storm trysail as required by OSR 4.26.4 (c) shall have the yacht's sail number and letter(s) shall be placed on both sides of the trysail (or on a rotating wing mast as substitute for a trysail) in as large a size as practicable;	MoMu0,1,2
e)	a storm jib of area not greater than 5% height of the foretriangle squared, with luff maximum length 65% height of the foretriangle;	MoMu0,1,2
f)	***in addition to the storm jib required by OSR 4.26.4 (e), a heavy-weather jib (or heavy-weather sail in a yacht with no forestay) of area not greater than 13.5% height of the foretriangle squared;***	**
h)	in the case of a yacht with an in-mast furling mainsail, the storm trysail must be capable of being set while the mainsail is furled.	MoMu0,1,2
i)	*A trysail track should allow for the trysail to be hoisted quickly when the mainsail is lowered whether or not the mainsail is stowed on the main boom.*	MoMu0,1,2
	It is strongly recommended that a boat has either a dedicated trysail track permanently installed with the entry point accessible to a person standing on the main deck or coachroof, or a permanently installed stay on which to hank the trysail.	
k)	*It is strongly recommended that an inner forestay is provided either permanently installed or readily set up, on which to set the storm jib.*	MoMu0,1,2

Figure 3

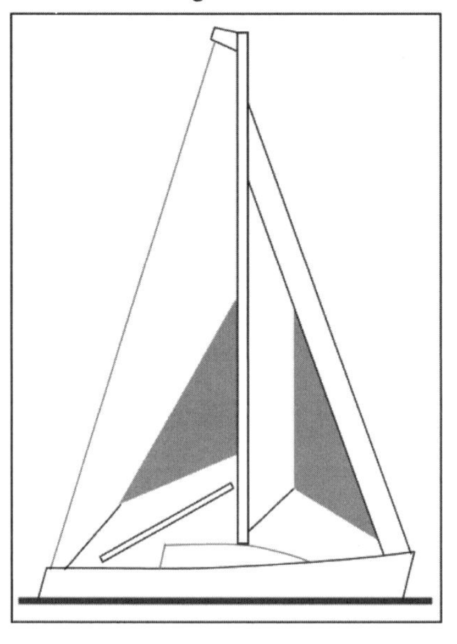

		Category
	In addition, US SAILING prescribes mainsail reefing to reduce the luff by at least 10% for sails built after 1 January 1997.	MoMu 0,1,2,3
4.27	**Drogue, Sea Anchor**	MoMu0,1
4.27.1	*A drogue for deployment over the stern, or alternatively a sea anchor or parachute anchor for deployment over the bow, complete with all gear needed to rig and deploy the sea anchor or drogue, is strongly recommended to withstand long periods in rough conditions (see Appendix F)*	MoMu1
4.28	**Man Overboard Alarm**	
4.28.3	A yacht shall be equipped with an EPFS (e.g. GPS) capable of immediately recording a man overboard position from each helm station (From January 2012)	MoMu1, 2

SECTION 5 - PERSONAL EQUIPMENT

5.01	**Lifejacket**	
	US SAILING prescribes for Categories 0,1,2,and 3: either a lifejacket defined in OSR 5.01.1 (See Note 1), or a USCG approved Type I non-inflatable personal flotation device (PFD), or a USCG approved yoke-type inflatable with 33lb (150N) or greater buoyancy with or without crotch strap, face guard, or buddy line. Each inflatable PFD shall be inflated and inspected annually. Service dates shall be marked on each PFD. It is recommended that all inflatable PFDs be integrated with safety harnesses (see OSR 5.02) (See Note 2).	MoMu 0,1,2,3

		Category
US SAILING Note 1:	***ISO 12402 is not currently approved by the USCG. Boats operating in US waters are not exempt from USCG requirements.***	MoMu 0,1,2,3
US SAILING Note 2:	***Many inflatable PFD's with built-in harnesses are designed for people greater than 5' 5" in height and are potentially dangerous if you are below that height.***	MoMu 0,1,2,3
US SAILING Note 3:	***Inflatable PFDs with the required buoyancy will generally have inflation cylinders containing 33g or more of CO2.***	MoMu 0,1,2,3
US SAILING Note 4:	***"Yoke-type" is defined as a PFD that is designed to keep its wearer face-up and head-up in the water and that provides buoyancy in front of the chest and behind the neck immediately when inflated***	MoMu 0,1,2,3
5.01.1	Each crew member shall have a lifejacket as follows:-	**
a)		**
i	In accordance with ISO 12402 – 3 (Level 150) or equivalent, including EN 396 or UL 1180	**
ii	Lifejackets manufactured after 1 January 2012 shall be in accordance with ISO 12402–3 (Level 150) and shall be fitted with: • an emergency light in accordance with either ISO 12402-8 or SO-LAS LSA code 2.2.3. • a sprayhood in accordance with ISO 12402-8. • a full deck safety harness in accordance with ISO 12401 (ISO 1095) including a crotch or thigh strap (holding down device) as specified in ISO 12401 (ISO 1095). • If of an inflatable type either: (a) automatic, manual and oral inflation or (b) manual and oral inflation	
Notes:	ISO 12402 requires Level 150 lifejackets to be fitted with a mandatory whistle and retro-reflective material. Also, when fitted with a safety harness, ISO 12402 requires that this shall be the full safety harness in accordance with ISO 12401. Any equivalent lifejacket shall have equal requirements. Persons of larger than average build are generally more buoyant than those of average build and so do not require a lifejacket with greater levels of flotation. Wearing a Level 275 lifejacket may hamper entry into liferafts.	
b)	fitted with either a crotch strap(s) / thigh straps or a full safety harness in accordance with ISO 12401,	**
Note:	The function of lifejacket crotch/thigh straps is to hold the buoyancy element down. A crew member before a race should adjust a lifejacket to fit then retain that lifejacket for the duration of the race. Correct adjustment is fundamental to the lifejacket functioning correctly.	
c)	fitted with a lifejacket light in accordance with SOLAS LSA code 2.2.3 (white, >0.75 candelas, >8 hours),	**

		Category
d)	if inflatable have a compressed gas inflation system,	**
e)	if inflatable, regularly checked for gas retention,	**
f)	compatible with the wearer's safety harness,	**
g)	clearly marked with the yacht's or wearer's name,	**
	It is strongly recommended that a lifejacket has:	
j)	*a splashguard / sprayhood See ISO 12402 – 8,*	MoMu 1,2,3,4
k)	*a PLB unit (as with other types of EPIRB, should be properly registered with the appropriate authority)*	MoMu 1,2,3,4
l)	*if of a gas inflatable type, a spare cylinder and if appropriate a spare activation head*	**
	US SAILING prescribes that all personnel on deck shall wear properly fitted personal floatation while starting and finishing. At other times during the race, floatation shall be worn on deck except when the Captain of the boat directs that it may be set aside.	**
5.01.4	The person in charge shall personally check each lifejacket at least once annually.	**
US SAILING Note:	***As is true of all of these regulations, the prescriptions above do not necessarily replace the requirements of other governing authorities.***	**
5.02	**Safety Harness and Safety Lines (Tethers)**	**
5.02.1	Each crew member shall have a harness and safety line that complies with ISO 12401 or equivalent with a safety line not more than 2m in length.	MoMu 0,1,2,3
	Harnesses and safety lines manufactured prior to Jan 2010 shall comply with either ISO 12401 or EN 1095.	MoMu 0,1,2,3
	Harnesses and safety lines manufactured prior to Jan 2001 are not permitted.	
	US Sailing prescribes that harnesses and safety lines manufactured prior to Jan 2001 are not recommended in the U.S.	**
a)	*Warning it is possible for a plain snaphook to disengage from a U bolt if the hook is rotated under load at right-angles to the axis of the U-bolt. For this reason the use of snaphooks with positive locking devices is strongly recommended.*	
5.02.2	At least 30% of the crew shall each, in addition to the above be provided with either:-	MoMu 0,1,2,3
a)	a safety line not more than 1m long, or	MoMu 0,1,2,3

		Category
b)	a mid-point snaphook on a 2m safety line	MoMu 0,1,2,3
5.02.3	A safety line purchased in January 2001 or later shall have a coloured flag embedded in the stitching, to indicate an overload. A line which has been overloaded shall be replaced as a matter of urgency.	MoMu 0,1,2,3
5.02.4	A crew member's lifejacket and harness shall be compatible	MoMu 0,1,2,3
	US SAILING prescribes that the safety harness may be integrated with an inflatable personal floatation device (see OSR 5.01) and recommends that such devices be employed whenever conditions warrant, and always in rough weather, on cold water, or at night, or under conditions of reduced visibility or when sailing short-handed.	MoMu 0,1,2,3
	US SAILING prescribes that safety harnesses and PFD's shall be worn on Category 0 and 1 races from sundown to sun up while on deck.	MoMu0,1
5.02.5	*It is strongly recommended that:-*	MoMu 0,1,2,3
a)	*static safety lines should be securely fastened at work stations;*	MoMu 0,1,2,3
b)	*A harness should be fitted with a crotch strap or thigh straps. Crotch straps or thigh straps together with related fittings and fixtures should be strong enough to lift the wearer from the water.*	MoMu 0,1,2,3
c)	*to draw attention to wear and damage, stitching on harness and safety lines should be of a colour contrasting strongly with the surrounding material;*	MoMu 0,1,2,3
d)	*snaphooks should be of a type which will not self-release from a U-bolt (see OSR 5.02.1(a)) and which can be easily released under load (crew members are reminded that a personal knife may free them from a safety line in emergency);*	MoMu 0,1,2,3
e)	*a crew member before a race should adjust a harness to fit then retain that harness for the duration of the race.*	MoMu 0,1,2,3
5.02.6	*Warning - a safety line and safety harness are not designed to tow a person in the water and it is important that the shortest safety line length possible be used with a harness to minimise or eliminate the risk of a person's torso becoming immersed in water outside the boat, especially when working on the foredeck. 1m safety lines or the midpoint snaphook on a 2m line should be used for this purpose. The diligent use of a properly adjusted safety harness and the shortest safety line practicable is regarded as by far the most effective way of preventing man overboard incidents.preventing man overboard incidents.*	MoMu 0,1,2,3
5.04	**Foul Weather Suits**	
b)	*it is recommended that a foul weather suit should be fitted with marine-grade retro-reflective material, and should have high-visibility colours on its upper parts and sleeve cuffs.See OSR 4.18*	**

		Category
5.07	**Survival Equipment**	
d)	*Attention is drawn to the value of keeping on the person a combined 406MHz/121.5MHz PLB when on deck: this may aid location in a man overboard incident independent of the equipment carried by the parent vessel.*	MoMu 0,1,2
e)	*All PLB units, as with other types of EPIRB, should be properly registered with the appropriate authority.*	MoMu 0,1,2
5.09	***Annual Man-Overboard Practice***	
	US SAILING prescribes that the "Quick-Stop" man-overboard procedure shall be practiced aboard the yacht at least once annually. A certificate of such practice shall be signed by participating crew members and kept aboard the yacht.	**
5.11	***Preventer or Boom Restraining Device***	
	US SAILING recommends that a preventer or boom restraining device should be rigged in such a manner that attachment can be easily and quickly made, with the boom fully extended (running) without leaving the deck or leaning overboard. A process and plan for its use should be part of the crew's training and practice. Recommended for all boats in all categories.	**
	SECTION 6 - TRAINING	
6.01	**At least 30% but not fewer than two members of a crew, including the skipper shall have undertaken training within the five years before the start of the race in both 6.02 topics for theoretical sessions, and 6.03 topics which include practical, hands-on sessions.**	MoMu 1,2
6.01.3	*It is strongly recommended that all crew members should undertake training as in OSR 6.01 at least once every five years*	MoMu 1,2
6.01.4	Except as otherwise provided in the Notice of Race, an in-date certificate gained at an ISAF Approved Offshore Personal Survival Training course shall be accepted by a race organizing authority as evidence of compliance with Special Regulation 6.01. See Appendix G - Model Training Course, for further details.	MoMu 0,1,2
6.02	**Training Topics for Theoretical Sessions**	
6.02.1	care and maintenance of safety equipment	MoMu0,1,2
6.02.2	storm sails	MoMu0,1,2
6.02.3	damage control and repair	MoMu0,1,2
6.02.4	heavy weather - crew routines, boat handling, drogues	MoMu0,1,2
6.02.5	man overboard prevention and recovery	MoMu0,1,2
6.02.6	giving assistance to other craft	MoMu0,1,2

		Category
6.02.7	hypothermia	MoMu0,1,2
6.02.8	SAR organisation and methods	MoMu0,1,2
6.02.9	weather forecasting	MoMu0,1,2
	US SAILING prescribes that training under this regulation (OSR 6.02) shall take place in a program that is approved by US SAILING and that shall require a minimum of 8 hours. Competetitors who are members of other National Governing Bodies may demonstrate that they have completed such training in accordance with the requirements of those organizations.	MoMu0,1,2
6.03	**Training Topics for Practical, Hands-On Sessions**	MoMu0,1,2
6.03.1	liferafts and lifejackets	MoMu0,1,2
6.03.2	fire precautions and use of fire extinguishers	MoMu0,1,2
6.03.3	communications equipment (VHF, GMDSS, satcomms, etc.)	MoMu0,1,2
6.03.4	pyrotechnics and EPIRBs	MoMu0,1,2
	US SAILING prescribes that each skipper in a Category 0 ,1 or 2 race shall ensure that a minimum of 30 percent of the crew have been trained in the use of the boat's equipment, including: liferafts and lifejackets; communications; pyrotechnics; EPIRBs; and fire prevention and fire fighting. A record of this training shall be kept aboard the boat in a manner similar to that required for certifying man-overboard training.	MoMu0,1,2
6.04	***Routine Training On-Board***	
6.04.1	*It is recommended that crews should practice safety routines at reasonable intervals including the drill for man-overboard recovery*	**
6.05	**Medical Training**	
6.05.2	At least two members of the crew	MoMu1
6.05.2	At least one member of the crew	MoMu2
	shall have a first aid certificate completed within the last five years meeting any of the following requirements:	MoMu2
i	A certificate listed on the ISAF website www.sailing.org/specialregs of MNA recognised courses	
US SAILING Note	***MNA recognized First Aid & CPR courses in the U.S. are posted at http://offshore.ussailing.org/SAS/Senior_First_Aid_Certification.htm.***	**
ii	STCW 95 First Aid Training complying with A-VI/1-3 – Elementary First Aid or higher STCW level	
	US SAILING recommends that at least two members of the crew be currently certified in cardiopulmonary resuscitation.	**
6.05.4	*An example model first aid training course is included in Appendix N.*	**

APPENDIX M
HULL CONSTRUCTION STANDARDS (SCANTLINGS)
(Monohulls pre-2010 and Multihulls)

		Category
M.1	A monohull with the earliest of Age or Series Date before the 1 January 2010 shall comply with OSR 3.03.1, 3.03.2 and 3.03.3 or with this appendix. A multihull shall comply with this appendix.	MoMu0,1,2

Table 2 — MoMu0,1,2

LOA	earliest of age or series date	race category	Category
			MoMu0,1,2
all	January 1986 and after	MoMu0,1	
12m (39.4 feet) and over	January 1987 and after	MoMu2	
under 12m (39.4 feet)	January 1988 and after	MoMu2	

		Category
M.2	A yacht defined in the table above shall have been designed built, maintained, modified and repaired in accordance with the requirements of either:	MoMu0,1,2
a)	the EC Recreational Craft Directive for Category A (having obtained the CE mark), or	MoMu0,1,2
b)	the ABS Guide for Building and Classing Offshore Yachts in which case the yacht shall have on board either a certificate of plan approval issued by ABS, or written statements signed by the designer and builder which confirm that they have respectively designed and built the yacht in accordance with the ABS Guide,	MoMu0,1,2
c)	ISO 12215 Category A, with written statements signed by the designer and builder which confirm that they have respectively designed and built the yacht in accordance with the ISO standard,	MoMu0,1,2
d)	except that a race organizer or class rules may accept when that described in (a), (b), or (c) above is not available, the signed statement by a naval architect or other person familiar with the standards listed above that the yacht fulfills the requirements of (a), (b), or (c).	MoMu0,1,2
M.3	Any significant repairs or modifications to the hull, deck, coachroof, keel or appendages, on a yacht defined in table 2 shall be certified by one of the methods above and an appropriate written statement or statements shall be on board.	MoMu0,1,2

ISAF Special Regulations Governing Offshore Racing for Category 3 & 4 Monohulls
Including US SAILING Prescriptions

ISAF Offshore Special Regulations Requirements for Monohull Sailboats

Including US SAILING Prescriptions
www.offshore.ussailing.org
Extract for Race Category 3 and 4 Monohulls
JANUARY 2012 - DECEMBER 2013

US Version 1 - 2012

Because this is an extract not all paragraph numbers will be present

Language & Abbreviations Used

Mo - Monohull
Mu - Multihull
" ** " means the item applies to all types of yacht in all Categories except 5 or 6 for which see Appendix J or L.

A side bar indicates a significant change in 2012

US SAILING extract files are available for individual categories and boat types (monohull and multihull) at http://offshore.ussailing.org/SAS/ISAF_Special_Regulations/Extracts.htm

US SAILING prescriptions are printed in bold, italic letters

ISAF guidance notes and recommendations are printed in italics

The use of the masculine gender shall be taken to mean either gender

SECTION 1 - FUNDAMENTAL AND DEFINITIONS

		Category
1.01	**Purpose and Use**	
1.01.1	It is the purpose of these Special Regulations to establish uniform minimum equipment, accommodation and training standards for monohull and multihull yachts racing offshore. A Proa is excluded from these regulations.	**
1.01.2	These Special Regulations do not replace, but rather supplement, the requirements of governmental authority, the Racing Rules and the rules of Class Associations and Rating Systems. The attention of persons in charge is called to restrictions in the Rules on the location and movement of equipment.	**
1.01.3	These Special Regulations, adopted internationally, are strongly recommended for use by all organizers of offshore races. Race Committees may select the category deemed most suitable for the type of race to be sailed.	**

		Category
1.02	**Responsibility of Person in Charge**	
1.02.1	The safety of a yacht and her crew is the sole and inescapable responsibility of the person in charge who must do his best to ensure that the yacht is fully found, thoroughly seaworthy and manned by an experienced crew who have undergone appropriate training and are physically fit to face bad weather. He must be satisfied as to the soundness of hull, spars, rigging, sails and all gear. He must ensure that all safety equipment is properly maintained and stowed and that the crew know where it is kept and how it is to be used. He shall also nominate a person to take over the responsibilities of the Person in Charge in the event of his incapacitation.	**
1.02.2	Neither the establishment of these Special Regulations, their use by race organizers, nor the inspection of a yacht under these Special Regulations in any way limits or reduces the complete and unlimited responsibility of the person in charge.	**
1.02.3	Decision to race -The responsibility for a yacht's decision to participate in a race or to continue racing is hers alone - RRS Fundamental Rule 4.	**
1.03	**Definitions, Abbreviations, Word Usage**	
1.03.1	Definitions of Terms used in this document	**

TABLE 1	
Age Date	Month/year of first launch
AIS	Automatic Identification Systems
CEN	Comité Européen de Normalisation
CPR	Cardio-Pulmonary Resuscitation
Coaming	includes the transverse after limit of the cockpit over which water would run in the event that when the yacht is floating level the cockpit is flooded or filled to overflowing.
DSC	Digital Selective Calling
EN	European Norm
EPFS	Electronic Position-Fixing System
EPIRB	Emergency Position-Indicating Radio Beacon
FA Station	The transverse station at which the upper corner of the transom meets the sheerline.
Foul-Weather Suit	A foul weather suit is clothing designed to keep the wearer dry and maybe either a jacket and trousers worn together, or a single garment comprising jacket and trousers.
GMDSS	Global Maritime Distress & Safety System

GNSS	Global Navigation Satellite System
GPIRB	EPIRB, with integral GPS position-fixing
ITU	International Telecommunications Union
GPS	Global Positioning System
Hatch	The term hatch includes the entire hatch assembly and also the lid or cover as part of that assembly (the part itself may be described as a hatch).
INMARSAT	This is Inmarsat Global Limited, the private company that provides GMDSS satellite distress and safety communications, plus general communications via voice, fax and data
IMO	International Maritime Organisation
IMSO	The International Mobile Satellite Organisation, the independent, intergovernmental organisation that oversees Inmarsatâs performance of its Public Service Obligations for the GMDSS and reports on these to IMO
ISAF	International Sailing Federation.
ISO	International Standard or International Organization for Standardization.
Lifeline	wire line rigged as guardrail / guardline around the deck
LOA	Length overall not including pulpits, bowsprits, boomkins etc.
LWL	(Length of) loaded waterline
Monohull	Yacht in which the hull depth in any section does not decrease towards the centre-line.
Moveable Ballast	Lead or other material including water which has no practical function in the boat other than to increase weight and/or to influence stability and/or trim and which may be moved transversely but not varied in weight while a boat is racing.
ORC	Offshore Racing Congress (formerly Offshore Racing Council)
OSR	Offshore Special Regulation(s)
Permanently Installed	Means the item is effectively built-in by eg bolting, welding, glassing etc. and may not be removed for or during racing.
PLB	Personal Locator Beacon
Proa	Asymmetric Catamaran
RRS	ISAF - Racing Rules of Sailing
SAR	Search and Rescue
SART	Search and Rescue Transponder
Series Date	Month & Year of first launch of the first yacht of the production series
SOLAS	Safety of Life at Sea Convention

Safety Line	A tether used to connect a safety harness to a strong point
Securely Fastened	Held strongly in place by a method (eg rope lashings, wing-nuts) which will safely retain the fastened object in severe conditions including a 180 degree capsize and allows for the item to be removed and replaced during racing
Static Ballast	Lead or other material including water which has no practical function in the boat other than to increase weight and/or to influence stability and/or trim and which may not be moved or varied in weight while a boat is racing.
Static Safety Line	A safety line (usually shorter than a safety line carried with a harness) kept clipped on at a work-station
Variable Ballast	Water carried for the sole purpose of influencing stability and/or trim and which may be varied in weight and/or moved while a boat is racing.

1.03.2	The words "shall" and "must" are mandatory, and "should" and "may" are permissive.	**
1.03.3	The word "yacht" shall be taken as fully interchangeable with the word "boat".	**

SECTION 2 - APPLICATION & GENERAL REQUIREMENTS

		Category
2.01	**Categories of Events**	
	In many types of race, ranging from trans-oceanic sailed under adverse conditions to short-course day races sailed in protected waters, six categories are established, to provide for differences in the minimum standards of safety and accommodation required for such varying circumstances:	**
2.01.4	**Category 3**	
	Races across open water, most of which is relatively protected or close to shorelines.	MoMu3
2.01.5	**Category 4**	
	Short races, close to shore in relatively warm or protected waters normally held in daylight.	MoMu4
2.02	**Inspection**	
	A yacht may be inspected at any time. If she does not comply with these Special Regulations her entry may be rejected, or she will be liable to disqualification or such other penalty as may be prescribed by the national authority or the race organizers.	**

		Category
2.03	**General Requirements**	
2.03.1	All equipment required by Special Regulations shall:-	
a)	function properly	**
b)	be regularly checked, cleaned and serviced	**
c)	when not in use be stowed in conditions in which deterioration is minimised	**
d)	be readily accessible	**
e)	be of a type, size and capacity suitable and adequate for the intended use and size of the yacht.	**
2.03.2	Heavy items:	
a)	ballast, ballast tanks and associated equipment shall be permanently installed	**
b)	heavy movable items including e.g. batteries, stoves, gas bottles, tanks, toolboxes and anchors and chain shall be securely fastened	**
c)	heavy items for which fixing is not specified in Special Regulations shall be permanently installed or securely fastened, as appropriate	**
2.03.3	When to show navigation lights	**
a)	navigation lights (OSR 3.27) shall be shown as required by the International Regulations for Preventing Collision at Sea, (Part C and Technical Annex 1). All yachts shall exhibit sidelights and a sternlight at the required times.	**

SECTION 3 - STRUCTURAL FEATURES, STABILITY, FIXED EQUIPMENT

		Category
3.01	**Strength of Build, Ballast and Rig**	
	Yachts shall be strongly built, watertight and, particularly with regard to hulls, decks and cabin trunks capable of withstanding solid water and knockdowns. They must be properly rigged and ballasted, be fully seaworthy and must meet the standards set forth herein. Shrouds shall never be disconnected.	**
3.02	**Watertight Integrity of a Hull**	
3.02.1	A hull, including, deck, coach roof, windows, hatches and all other parts, shall form an integral, essentially watertight unit and any openings in it shall be capable of being immediately secured to maintain this integrity.	**

		Category
3.02.2	Centreboard and daggerboard trunks and the like shall not open into the interior of a hull except via a watertight inspection/maintenance hatch of which the opening shall be entirely above the waterline of the yacht floating level in normal trim.	**
3.02.3	A canting keel pivot shall be completely contained within a watertight enclosure which shall comply with OSR 3.02.2. Access pointsÊin the watertight enclosure for control and actuation systems or any other purpose shall comply with OSR 3.02.1.	**
3.02.4	Moveable ballast systems shall be fitted with a manual control and actuation secondary system which shall be capable of controlling the full sailing load of the keel in the event of failure of the primary system. Such failures would include electrical and hydraulic failure and mechanical failure of the components and the structure to which it mounts. The system must be capable of being operational quickly and shall be operable at any angle of heel. It would be desirable if this system was capable of securing the keel on the centreline.	**
3.04	**Stability - Monohulls**	Mo 0,1,2,3,4
3.04.2	A yacht shall be designed and built to resist capsize.	Mo 0,1,2,3,4
3.04.3	*A race organizer should require compliance with a minimum stability or stability/buoyancy index. Attention is drawn to the stability index in the ORC Rules and Regulations.*	Mo 0,1,2,3,4
3.04.4	*Achievement of Design Category B under ISO 12217-2 may be accepted by a race organizer as a guide to general suitability for competition in a Special Regulations Category 3 race.*	Mo3
3.04.5	*Use of the ISO or any other index does not guarantee total safety or total freedom of risk from capsize or sinking.*	Mo 0,1,2,3,4
3.04.6	For boats with moveable or variable ballast the method in OSR 3.04.4 shall apply plus the relevant additional requirement of OSR Appendix K	Mo 0,1,2,3,4
3.04.7	Tanks for variable ballast shall be permanently installed and shall be provided with a system of isolating valves and pump(s) capable of manual operation at any angle of heel. A plan of the plumbing system shall be displayed aboard the boat.	Mo 0,1,2,3,4
3.06	**Exits - Monohulls**	Mo 0,1,2,3,4
3.06.1	Yachts of LOA of 8.5 m (28 ft) and over with age or series date after January 1995 and after shall have at least two exits. At least one exit shall be located forward of the foremost mast except where structural features prevent its installation.	Mo 0,1,2,3,4

		Category
3.06.2	Yachts first launched on or after January 2014 have a hatch with the following minimum clear openings in compliance with ISO 9094:	Mo 0,1,2,3,4
	- Circular shape: diameter 450mm;	
	- Any other shape: minimum dimension of 380mm and minimum area of 0.18m2. The dimension must be large enough to allow for a 380mm diameter circle to be inscribed.	
	The measurement of the minimum clear opening is illustrated in Figure 1.	

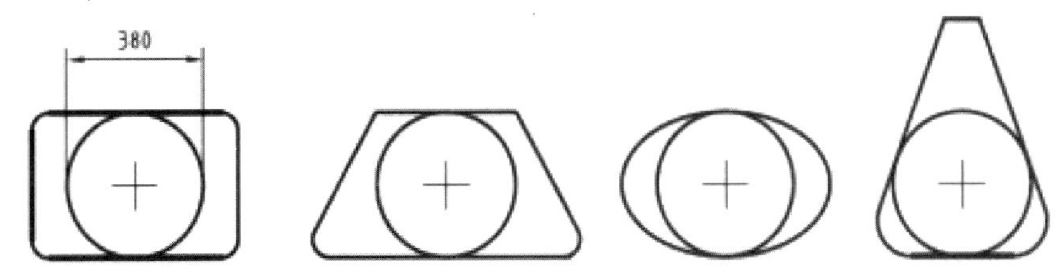

Figure 1 - Measurements of Minimum Clear Opening

3.06.3	*when first launched to January 2014, if possible have each escape hatch in compliance with the dimensions in OSR 3.07.2(a)(ii);*	Mo 0,1,2,3,4
3.08	**Hatches & Companionways**	
3.08.1	No hatch forward of the maximum beam station, other than a hatch in the side of a coachroof, shall open in such a way that the lid or cover moves into the open position towards the interior of the hull (excepting ports having an area of less than 0.071m2 (110 sq in)).	**
3.08.2	A hatch fitted forward of the maximum beam station, located on the side of the coachroof, opening into the interior of the boat, and of area greater than 0.071m2 shall comply with ISO12216 design category A and and be clearly labelled and used in accordance with the following instruction: "NOT TO BE OPENED AT SEA". Attention is drawn to SR 3.02.1	**
3.08.3	A hatch shall be:	
a)	so arranged as to be above the water when the hull is heeled 90 degrees. Hatches over lockers that open to the interior of the vessel shall be included in this requirement. A yacht may have a maximum of four (two on each side of centerline) hatches that do not conform to this requirement, provided that the opening of each is less than 0.071 sq m (110 sq in). Effective for boats of a series begun after January 1, 2009, a written statement signed by the designer or other person who performed the downflooding analysis shall be carried on board. For purposes of this rule the vessel's displacement condition for the analysis shall be the Light Craft Condition LCC (in conformity with 6.3 of the EN ISO 8666 standard and 3.5.1 of the EN ISO12217-2 standard).	Mo 0,1,2,3,4

		Category
b)	permanently attached	**
c)	capable of being firmly shut immediately and remaining firmly shut in a 180 degree capsize (inversion)	**
3.08.4	A companionway hatch shall:	
a)	be fitted with a strong securing arrangement which shall be operable from the exterior and interior including when the yacht is inverted	**
b)	have any blocking devices:	**
i	capable of being retained in position with the hatch open or shut	**
ii	whether or not in position in the hatchway, secured to the yacht (e.g. by lanyard) for the duration of the race, to prevent their being lost overboard	**
iii	permit exit in the event of inversion	**
3.08.5	If the companionway extends below the local sheerline and the boat has a cockpit opening aft to the sea the boat shall comply with one of the following:	Mo 0,1,2,3,4
a)	the companionway sill shall not extend below the local sheerline. Or	Mo 0,1,2,3,4
b)	be in full compliance with all aspects of ISO 11812 to design category A	Mo 0,1,2,3,4
3.08.6	For boats with a cockpit closed aft to the sea where the companionway hatch extends below the local sheerline, the companionway shall be capable of being blocked off up to the level of the local sheerline, provided that the companionway hatch shall continue to give access to the interior with the blocking devices (e.g. washboards) in place	Mo 0,1,2,3,4
3.09	**Cockpits - Attention is Drawn to ISO 11812**	
3.09.1	Cockpits shall be structurally strong, self-draining quickly by gravity at all angles of heel and permanently incorporated as an integral part of the hull.	**
3.09.2	Cockpits must be essentially watertight, that is, all openings to the hull must be capable of being strongly and rigidly secured	**
3.09.3	A bilge pump outlet pipe shall not be connected to a cockpit drain. See OSR 3.09.8 for cockpit drain minimum sizes	**
3.09.4	A cockpit sole shall be at least 2% LWL above LWL (or in IMS yachts first launched before 1/03, at least 2% L above LWL)	**
3.09.5	A bow, lateral, central or stern well shall be considered a cockpit for the purposes of OSR 3.09	**
3.09.6	In cockpits opening aft to the sea structural openings aft shall be not less in area than 50% maximum cockpit depth x maximum cockpit width.	**

		Category
3.09.7	**Cockpit Volume**	
i)	earliest of age or series date before April 1992	
	the total volume of all cockpits below lowest coamings shall not exceed 9% (LWL x maximum beam x freeboard abreast the cockpit).	MoMu 2,3,4
ii)	earliest of age or series date April 1992 and after	
	as above for the appropriate category except that "lowest coamings" shall not include any aft of the FA station and no extension of a cockpit aft of the working deck shall be included in calculation of cockpit volume	**
Note	*IMS-rated boats may instead of the terms LWL, maximum beam, freeboard abreast the cockpit, use the IMS terms L, B and FA.*	**
3.09.8	**Cockpit Drains**	
	See OSR 3.09.1. Cockpit drain cross section area (after allowance for screens if fitted) shall be:-	
a)	in yachts with earliest of age or series date before 1/72 or in any yacht under 8.5m (28ft) LOA - at least that of 2 x 25mm diameter (one inch) unobstructed openings or equivalent	**
b)	in yachts with earliest of age or series date 1/72 and later - at least that of 4 x 20mm diameter (3/4 inch) unobstructed openings or equivalent	**
	US SAILING prescribes that cockpit drains shall be accessible for cleaning.	**
		Category
3.10	**Sea Cocks or Valves**	
	Sea cocks or valves shall be permanently installed on all through-hull openings below the waterline except integral deck scuppers, speed indicators, depth finders and the like, however a means of closing such openings shall be provided.	**
3.11	**Sheet Winches**	
	Sheet winches shall be mounted in such a way that an operator is not required to be substantially below deck.	**
3.12	**Mast Step**	
	The heel of a keel stepped mast shall be securely fastened to the mast step or adjoining structure.	**
3.14	**Pulpits, Stanchions, Lifelines**	
3.14.2	Lifelines required in Special Regulations shall be "taut".	**
a)	As a guide, when a deflecting force of 50 N (5.1 kgf, 11.2 lbf) is applied to a lifeline midway between supports, the lifeline should not deflect more than 50 mm.	**
3.14.3	The following shall be provided:	**

		Category
a)	a bow pulpit with vertical height and openings essentially conforming to Table 7. Bow pulpits may be open but the opening between the pulpit and any part of the boat shall never be greater than 360mm (14.2") (this requirement shall be checked by presenting a 360mm (14.2") circle inside the opening)	Mo 0,1,2,3,4

Figure 2 - Pulpit Opening

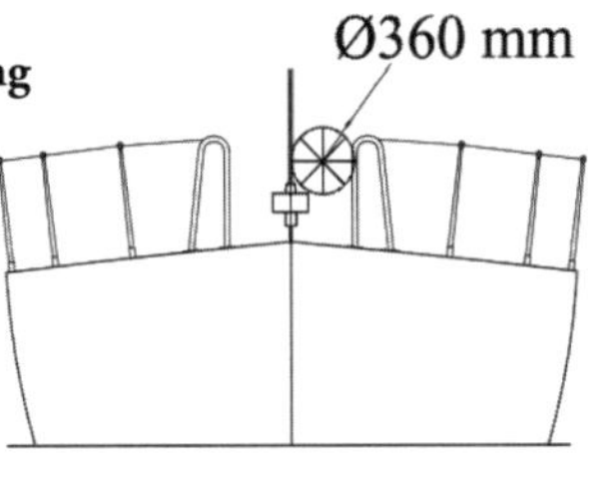

b)	a stern pulpit, or lifelines arranged as an adequate substitute, with vertical openings conforming to Table 7	Mo 0,1,2,3,4
c)	lifelines (guardlines) supported on stanchions, which, with pulpits, shall form an effectively continuous barrier around a working deck for man-overboard prevention. Lifelines shall be permanently supported at intervals of not more than 2.20m (86.6") and shall not pass outboard of supporting stanchions	**
d)	upper rails of pulpits at no less height above the working deck than the upper lifelines as in Table 7.	**
e)	Openable upper rails in bow pulpits shall be secured shut whilst racing	**
f)	Pulpits and stanchions shall be permanently installed. When there are sockets or studs, these shall be through-bolted, bonded or welded. The pulpit(s) and/or stanchions fitted to these shall be mechanically retained without the help of the life-lines. Without sockets or studs, pulpits and/or stanchions shall be through-bolted, bonded or welded.	**
g)	The bases of pulpits and stanchions shall not be further inboard from the edge of the appropriate working deck than 5% of maximum beam or 150 mm (6 in), whichever is greater.	**
h)	Stanchion or pulpit or pushpit bases shall not be situated outboard of a working deck. For the purpose of this rule the base shall be taken to include a sleeve or socket into which the tube is fitted but shall exclude a baseplate which carries fixings into the deck or hull.	**
i)	Provided the complete lifeline enclosure is supported by stanchions and pulpit bases effectively within the working deck, lifeline terminals and support struts may be fixed to a hull aft of the working deck	**
j)	Lifelines need not be fixed to a bow pulpit if they terminate at, or pass through, adequately braced stanchions set inside and overlapping the bow pulpit, provided that the gap between the upper lifeline and the bow pulpit does not exceed 150 mm (6 in).	**

		Category
k)	Lifelines shall be continuous and fixed onlyÊat (or near) the bow and stern. However a bona fide gateÊshall be permitted inÊthe lifelines on each side of a yacht. Except at its end fittings, the movement of a lifeline in a fore-and-aft direction shall not be constrained. Temporary sleeving in 3.14.6 (c) shall not modify tension in the lifeline.	**
l)	Stanchions shall be straight and vertical except that:-	**
i	within the first 50 mm (2 in) from the deck, stanchions shall not be displaced horizontally from the point at which they emerge from the deck or stanchion base by more than 10 mm (3/8 in),and	**
ii	stanchions may be angled to not more than 10 degrees from vertical at any point above 50 mm (2 in) from the deck.	**
m)	*It is strongly recommended that designs also comply to ISO 15085*	**
3.14.5	**Lifeline Height, Vertical Openings, Number of Lifelines**	

TABLE 7 **

LOA	earliest of age/ seriesdate	minimum requirements	Category
under 8.5 m (28 ft)	before January 1992	taut single lifeline at a height of no less than 450 mm (18 in) above the working deck. No vertical opening shall exceed 560 mm (22 in).	**
under 8.5 m (28 ft)	January 1992 and after	as for under 8.5 m(28 ft) in table 7 above, except that when an intermediate lifeline is fitted no vertical opening shall exceed 380 mm (15 in).	**
8.5 m (28 ft) and over	before January 1993	taut double lifeline with upper lifeline at a height of no less than 600 mm (24 in) above the working deck. No vertical opening shall exceed 560 mm (22 in)	**
8.5 m (28 ft) and over	January 1993 and after	as 8.5 m (28 ft) and over in Table 7 above, except that no vertical opening shall exceed 380 mm (15 in).	**
all	all	on yachts with intermediate lifelines the intermediate line shall be not less than 230 mm (9 in) above the working deck	**
		and shall be of the same construction and general arrangements as required for the upper.	

		Category
3.14.6	**Lifeline Minimum Diameters, Required Materials, Specifications**	
a)	Lifelines shall be of :	**
	- stranded stainless steel wire or	**
	- Single-braided High Modulus Polyethylene (HMPE) (Dyneema®/ Spectra® or equivalent) rope	**
	US SAILING note. An article describing the best techniques for using Dyneema line, particularly in the life line application, is posted at http://offshore.ussailing.org/SAS.htm	
b)	The minimum diameter of all lifelines is specified in table 8 below.	**
c)	Stainless steel lifelines shall be uncoated and used without close-fitting sleeving, however, temporary sleeving may be fitted provided it is regularly removed for inspection.	**
d)	*When stainless wire is used, Grade 316 is recommended.*	**
e)	When HMPE (Dyneema®/Spectra®) is used, it shall be spliced in accordance with the manufacturer's recommended procedures.	**
f)	A taut lanyard of synthetic rope may be used to secure lifelines provided the gap it closes does not exceed 100 mm (4 in). This lanyard shall be replaced annually at a minimum.	**
g)	All wire, fittings, anchorage points, fixtures and lanyards shall comprise a lifeline enclosure system which has at all points at least the breaking strength of the required lifeline wire.	**

TABLE 8 **

LOA	minimum wire or rope diameter
under 8.5 m (28ft)	3 mm (1/8 in)
8.5m - 13 m	4 mm (5/32 in)
over 13 m (43 ft)	5 mm (3/16 in)

3.14.7	**Pulpits, Stanchions, Lifelines - Limitations on Materials**	

TABLE 9 **

Earliest of Age or Series Date	detail
before January 1987	carbon fibre is not recommended in stanchions pulpits and lifelines.
January 1987 and after	stanchions, pulpits and lifelines shall not be made of carbon fibre.

		Category
3.17	**Toe Rail or Foot-Stop**	Mo0,1,2,3
3.17.1	A toe rail of minimum height 25 mm (1 in) shall be permanently installed around the foredeck from abreast the mast, except in way of fittings and not further inboard from the edge of the working deck than one third of the local half-beam.	Mo0,1,2,3
3.17.2	The following variations shall apply:-	Mo0,1,2,3

TABLE 10 Mo0.1,2,3

LOA	Earliest of Age or Series Date	minimum requirements	Mo0.1,2,3
any	before January 1981	a toe rail minimum height of 20 mm (3/4 in) is acceptable.	
any	before January 1994	an additional lifeline of minimum height 25 mm (1 in) and maximum height 50 mm (2 in) is acceptable in lieu of a toe rail (but shall not count as an intermediate lifeline).	
any	January 1994 and after	the toe rail shall be fitted as close as practicable to the vertical axis of stanchion bases but not further inboard than 1/3 the local half-beam.	

3.18	**Toilet**	
3.18.2	A toilet, permanently installed or fitted bucket	MoMu3,4
3.19	**Bunks**	
3.19.2	Bunks, permanently installed	**
3.20	**Cooking Facilities**	
3.20.1	A cooking stove, permanently installed or securely fastened with safe accessible fuel shutoff control and capable of being safely operated in a seaway.	MoMu 0,1,2,3
3.21	**Drinking Water Tanks & Drinking Water**	MoMu 0,1,2,3
3.21.1	**Drinking Water Tanks**	MoMu 0,1,2,3
a)	A yacht shall have a permanently installed delivery pump and water tank(s):	MoMu 0,1,2,3
3.21.3	**Emergency Drinking Water**	MoMu 0,1,2,3
a)	At least 9 litres (2 UK gallons, 2.4 US gallons) of drinking water for emergency use shall be provided in a dedicated and sealed container or container(s)	MoMu 1,2,3

		Category
3.22	**Hand Holds**	
	Adequate hand holds shall be fitted below deck so that crew members may move about safely at sea.	**
	A hand hold should be capable of withstanding without rupture a side force of 1500N - attention is drawn to ISO 15085.	
3.23	**Bilge Pumps and Buckets**	
3.23.1	No bilge pump may discharge into a cockpit unless that cockpit opens aft to the sea.	**
3.23.2	Bilge pumps shall not be connected to cockpit drains. (OSR 3.09)	**
3.23.3	Bilge pumps and strum boxes shall be readily accessible for maintenance and for clearing out debris	**
3.23.4	Unless permanently installed, each bilge pump handle shall be provided with a lanyard or catch or similar device to prevent accidental loss	**
3.23.5	The following shall be provided:	
d)	at least one permanently installed manual bilge pump operable with all cockpit seats, hatches and companionways shut	Mo3
e)	one manual bilge pump	Mo4
f)	two buckets of stout construction each with at least 9 litres (2 UK gallons, 2.4 US gallons) capacity. Each bucket to have a lanyard.	**
3.24	**Compass**	
3.24.1	The following shall be provided:-	
a)	a marine magnetic compass, independent of any power supply, permanently installed and correctly adjusted with deviation card, and	**
b)	a magnetic compass independent of any power supply, capable of being used as a steering compass which may be hand-held	MoMu 0,1,2,3
3.25	**Halyards.**	
	No mast shall have less than two halyards, each capable of hoisting a sail.	**
Boom Support	***US SAILING prescribes that some means must exist to prevent the boom from dropping if support from the mainsail and/or halyard fails. Topping lifts or supporting vangs are acceptable for this purpose.***	**
3.27	**Navigation Lights (see OSR 2.03.3)**	
3.27.1	Navigation lights shall be mounted so that they will not be masked by sails or the heeling of the yacht.	**
3.27.2	Navigation lights shall not be mounted below deck level and should be at no less height than immediately under the upper lifeline.	**
3.27.3	Navigation light intensity	

TABLE 11

LOA	Guide to required minimum power rating for an electric bulb in a navigation light	
under 12 m (39.4 ft)	10 W	
12 m (39.4 ft) and above	25 W	

	US SAILING prescribes that in the US compliance with the recommendations of COLREGS shall suffice in satisfying these regulations. COLREGS requirements are as follows;	**

Table 14

LOA	*Light*	*Luminous Intensity*	*Minimum Range of Visibility*
under 39.4 ft	*Side*	*0.9 candelas*	*1 mile*
	Stern	*4.3 candelas*	*2 miles*
39.4 ft and above	*Side*	*4.3 candelas*	*2 miles*
and less than 164 ft	*Stern*	*4.3 candelas*	*2 miles*

		Category
3.27.4	Reserve navigation lights shall be carried having the same minimum specifications as the navigation lights above, with a separable power source, and wiring or supply system essentially separate from that used for the normal navigation lights	MoMu 1,2,3
3.27.5	spare bulbs for navigation lights shall be carried, or for lights not dependent on bulbs, appropriate spares.	**
3.28	**Engines, Generators, Fuel**	
3.28.1	**Propulsion Engines**	**
a)	Engines and associated systems shall be installed in accordance with their manufacturersâ guidelines and shall be of a type, strength, capacity, and installation suitable for the size and intended use of the yacht.	**
b)	An inboard propulsion engine when fitted shall: be provided with a permanently installed exhaust, coolant, and fuel supply systems and fuel tank(s); be securely covered; and have adequate protection from the effects of heavy weather.	**
c)	A propulsion engine required by Special Regulations shall provide a minimum speed in knots of (1.8 x square root of LWL in metres) or (square root of LWL in feet)	MoMu 0,1,2,3

		Category
d)	A propulsion engine shall be provided either as an inboard propulsive engine or as an outboard engine with associated tanks and fuel supply systems, all securely fastened.	Mo3
3.28.2	**Generator**	
	A separate generator for electricity is optional. However, when a separate generator is carried it shall be permanently installed, securely covered, and shall have permanently installed exhaust, cooling and fuel supply systems and fuel tank(s), and have adequate protection from the effects of heavy weather.	**
3.28.3	**Fuel Systems**	
a)	Each fuel tank provided with a shutoff valve. Except for permanently installed linings or liners, a flexible tank is not permitted as a fuel tank.	MoMu 0,1,2,3
b)	The propulsion engine shall have a minimum amount of fuel which may be specified in the Notice of Race but if not, shall be sufficient to be able to meet charging requirements for the duration of the race and to motor at the above minimum speed for at least 8 hours	MoMu 0,1,2,3
3.28.4	**Battery Systems**	
a)	When an electric starter is the only method for starting the engine, the yacht shall have a separate battery, the primary purpose of which is to start the engine	MoMu 0,1,2,3
b)	All rechargeable batteries on board shall be of the sealed type from which liquid electrolyte cannot escape. Other types of battery installed on board at 1/12 may continue in use for the remainder of their service lives.	MoMu 0,1,2,3
3.29	**Communications Equipment, EPFS (Electronic Position-Fixing System), Radar, AIS**	**
	Provision of GMDSS and DSC is unlikely to be mandatory for small craft during the term of the present Special Regulations However it is recommended that persons in charge include these facilities when installing new equipment.	MoMu 0,1,2,3
3.29.1	The following shall be provided:	**
a)	A marine radio transceiver (or if stated in the Notice of Race, an installed satcom terminal), and	MoMu 1,2,3
i	an emergency antenna when the regular antenna depends upon the mast.	MoMu 1,2,3
b)	When the marine radio transceiver is VHF:	MoMu 0,1,2,3
i	it shall have a rated output power of 25W	MoMu 0,1,2,3
ii	it shall have a masthead antenna, and co-axial feeder cable with not more than 40% power loss	MoMu 0,1,2,3

		Category
iii	*the following types and lengths of co-axial feeder cable will meet the requirements of OSR 3.29.1 (b)(ii):*	MoMu 0,1,2,3
a)	*up to 15m (50ft) - type RG8X ("mini 8");*	MoMu 0,1,2,3
b)	*15-28m (50-90ft) - type RG8U;*	MoMu 0,1,2,3
c)	*28-43m (90-140ft) - type 9913F (uses conventional connectors, available from US supplier Belden);*	MoMu 0,1,2,3
d)	*43-70m) 140-230ft - type LMR600 (uses special connectors, available from US supplier Times Microwave).*	MoMu 0,1,2,3
iv	*it should include channel 72 (an international ship-ship channel which, by common use, has become widely accepted as primary choice for ocean racing yachts anywhere in the world)*	MoMu 0,1,2,3
e)	A hand-held marine VHF transceiver, watertight or with a waterproof cover. When not in use to be stowed in a grab bag or emergency container (see OSR 4.21)	MoMu 1,2,3,4
f)	Independent of a main radio transceiver, a radio receiver capable of receiving weather bulletins	**
i)	An EPFS (Electronic Position-Fixing System) (e.g. GPS)	MoMu 0,1,2,3
o)	An AIS Transponder is recommended	MoMu3
3.29.2	*Yachts are reminded that no reflector, active or passive, is a guarantee of detection or tracking by a vessel using radar.*	**
a)	*The attention of persons in charge is drawn to legislation in force or imminent affecting the territorial seas of some countries in which the carriage of an AIS set is or will be mandatory for certain vessels including relatively small craft.*	**

SECTION 4 - PORTABLE EQUIPMENT & SUPPLIES for the yacht
(for water & fuel see OSR 3.21 and OSR 3.28)

		Category
4.01	**Sail Letters & Numbers**	
4.01.1	Yachts which are not in an ISAF International Class or Recognized Class shall comply with RRS 77 and Appendix G as closely as possible, except that sail numbers allotted by a State authority are acceptable .	**
4.01.2	Sail numbers and letters of the size carried on the mainsail must be displayed by alternative means when none of the numbered sails is set.	**
4.03	**Soft Wood Plugs**	

		Category
	Soft wood plugs, tapered and of the appropriate size, shall be attached or stowed adjacent to the appropriate fitting for every through-hull opening.	**
4.04	**Jackstays, Clipping Points and Static Safety Lines**	
4.04.1	The following shall be provided:	
a)	Jackstays:-	MoMu 0,1,2,3
	shall be provided-	
i	attached to through-bolted or welded deck plates or other suitable and strong anchorage fitted on deck, port and starboard of the yacht's centre line to provide secure attachments for safety harness:-	MoMu 0,1,2,3
ii	comprising stainless steel 1 x 19 wire of minimum diameter 5 mm (3/16 in), high modulus polyethylene (such as Dyneema/Spectra) rope or webbing of equivalent strength;	MoMu 0,1,2,3
	US SAILING prescribes that wire jackstays may be of configurations other than 1 X 19.	
iii	which, when made from stainless steel wire shall be uncoated and used without any sleeving;	MoMu 0,1,2,3
iv	*20kN (2,040 kgf or 4,500 lbf) min breaking strain webbing is recommended;*	MoMu 0,1,2,3
4.04.2	**Clipping Points:-**	
	shall be provided-	
a)	attached to through-bolted or welded deck plates or other suitable and strong anchorage points adjacent to stations such as the helm, sheet winches and masts, where crew members work for long periods:-	MoMu 0,1,2,3
b)	which, together with jackstays and static safety lines shall enable a crew member-	MoMu 0,1,2,3
i	to clip on before coming on deck and unclip after going below;	MoMu 0,1,2,3
ii	whilst continuously clipped on, to move readily between the working areas on deck and the cockpit(s) with the minimum of clipping and unclipping operations.	MoMu 0,1,2,3
c)	The provision of clipping points shall enable two-thirds of the crew to be simultaneously clipped on without depending on jackstays	MoMu 0,1,2,3
e)	*Warning - U-bolts as clipping points - see OSR 5.02.1(a)*	
4.05	**Fire Extinguishers**	
	Shall be provided as follows:	
4.05.1	Fire extinguishers, at least two, readily accessible in suitable and different parts of the yacht	**

		Category
4.05.2	Fire Extinguishers, at least two, of minimum 2kgs each of dry powder or equivalent	MoMu 0,1,2,3
4.05.4	A fire blanket adjacent to every cooking device with an open flame	**
4.06	**Anchor(s)**	

TABLE 12

LOA	detail	race category
8.5 m (28 ft) and over	2 anchors together with a suitable combination of chain and rope, all ready for immediate use	MoMu1,2,3
under 8.5 m (28 ft)	1 anchor together with a suitable combination of chain and rope, all ready for immediate use	MoMu1,2,3
any	1 anchor, readily accessible	MoMu4

4.07	**Flashlight(s) and Searchlight(s)**	
4.07.1	The following shall be provided:-	
a)	A watertight, high-powered searchlight, suitable for searching for a person overboard at night and for collision avoidance with spare batteries and bulbs, and	**
b)	a watertight flashlight with spare batteries and bulb	**
4.08	**First Aid Manual and First Aid Kit**	**
4.08.1	A suitable First Aid Manual shall be provided	**
	In the absence of a National Authority's requirement, the latest edition of one of the following is recommended:-	**
b)	*First Aid at Sea, by Douglas Justins and Colin Berry, published by Adlard Coles Nautical,London*	MoMu 2,3,4
c)	*Le Guide de la medecine a distance, by Docteur J Y Chauve, published by Distance Assistance BP33 F-La Baule, cedex, France.*	**
d)	*'PAN-PAN medico a bordo' in Italian edited by Umberto Verna. www.panpan.it*	MoMu 2,3,4
e)	*Skipper's Medical Emergency Handbook by Dr Spike Briggs and Dr Campbell Mackenzie www.msos.org.uk*	**
	US SAILING endorses the above and additionally recommends the following manuals: Advanced First Aid by Peter Eastman, M.D., Cornell Maritime Press and A Comprehensive Guide to Marine Medicine by Eric A. Weiss, M.D. and Michael E. Jacobs, M.D., Adventure Medical Kit.	

		Category
4.08.2	A First Aid Kit shall be provided	**
4.08.3	*The contents and storage of the First Aid Kit should reflect the guidelines of the Manual carried, the likely conditions and duration of the passage, and the number of people aboard the yacht.*	**
4.09	**Foghorn**	
	A foghorn shall be provided	**
4.10	**Radar Reflector**	
4.10.1	A passive Radar Reflector (that is, a Radar Reflector without any power) shall be provided	**
a)	If a radar reflector is:	**
i	*octahedral with triangular plates making up each pocket it must have a minimum diagonal measurement of 456 mm (18in).*	**
ii	*octahederal with circular sector plates making up each pocket it must have a minimum diameter of 304mm (12in).*	**
iii	*not octahedral it must have a documented RCS (radar cross-section) of not less than 10 m2 at 0° elevation and be capable of performance around 360° in azimuth.*	**
	US SAILING prescribes that in the US, radar reflectors shall have a minimum documented "equivalent echoing area" of 6 sq. m. Octahedral reflectors shall have a minimum diameter of 12 inches.	
	The minimum effective height above water is 4.0 m (13 ft).	**
b)	*The passive and active devices referred to in these notes and in 4.10.1 and 4.10.2 above are primarily intended for use in the X (9GHz) band*	**
4.10.2	*The most effective radar response from a yacht may be provided by an RTE (Radar Target Enhancer) which may be on board in addition to the required passive reflector. An RTE should conform to ISO 8729-2:2009. An RTE is strongly recommended.*	MoMu 1,2,3,4
b)	*The display of a passive reflector or the operation of an RTE is for the person in charge to decide according to prevailing conditions.*	**
4.10.3	*When available, a passive radar reflector in compliance with ISO8729-1:2010 will offer improved performance over earlier models and has a size typified by a cylinder of not more than weight 5kg, height 750mm and diameter 300mm.*	**
4.10.4	*S (3GHz) band radar is often used by ships in bad weather to complement X (9GHz) band radar. On S (3GHz) band a passive reflector offers about 1/10 the response obtained on the X (9GHz) band. Unless specifically designed to operate in the S(3GHz) band, an RTE will provide no response at all.*	**
4.11	**Navigation Equipment**	

		Category
4.11.1	Charts	
	Navigational charts (not solely electronic), light list and chart plotting equipment shall be provided	**
4.12	**Safety Equipment Location Chart**	
	A safety equipment location chart in durable waterproof material shall be displayed in the main accommodation where it can best be seen, clearly marked with the location of principal items of safety equipment.	**
4.13	**Echo Sounder or Lead Line**	
4.13.1	An echo sounder or lead line shall be provided	MoMu 1,2,3,4
4.14	**Speedometer or Distance Measuring Instrument (log)**	
	A speedometer or distance measuring instrument (log) shall be provided	MoMu 0,1,2,3
4.15	**Emergency Steering**	
4.15.1	Emergency steering shall be provided as follows:	
a)	except when the principal method of steering is by means of an unbreakable metal tiller, an emergency tiller capable of being fitted to the rudder stock;	MoMu 0,1,2,3
b)	crews must be aware of alternative methods of steering the yacht in any sea condition in the event of rudder loss. At least one method must have been proven to work on board the yacht. An inspector may require that this method be demonstrated.	MoMu 0,1,2,3
4.16	**Tools and Spare Parts**	
	Tools and spare parts, including effective means to quickly disconnect or sever the standing rigging from the hull shall be provided.	**
4.17	**Yacht's name**	
	Yacht's name shall be on miscellaneous buoyant equipment, such as lifejackets, cushions, lifebuoys, lifeslings, grab bags etc.	**
4.18	**Marine grade retro-reflective material**	
	Marine grade retro-reflective material shall be fitted to lifebuoys, lifeslings, liferafts and lifejackets. See OSRs 5.04, 5.08.	**
4.22	**Lifebuoys**	
4.22.1	***The following shall be provided within easy reach of the helmsman and ready for instant use:***	**
a)	a lifebuoy with a self-igniting light and a drogue or a Lifesling with a self-igniting light and without a drogue.	**

		Category
	For Categories 0,1,2,3 US SAILING prescribes that the lifebuoy in OSR 4.22.1 a) above shall be a Lifesling (without a drogue), equipped with a self-igniting light within easy reach of the helmsman and ready for instant use. (See Appendix D).	MoMu 0,1,2,3
	For Category 4, US SAILING prescribes that the lifebuoy must be inherently buoyant.	MoMu4
4.22.3	Each inflatable lifebuoy and any automatic device (eg pole and flag extended by compressed gas) shall be tested and serviced at intervals in accordance with its manufacturer's instructions.	**
4.22.4	Each lifebuoy or lifesling shall be fitted with marine grade retro-reflective material (4.18).	**
4.22.5	*It is recommended that the colour of each lifebuoy be a safety colour in the yellow-red range.*	**
4.23	**Pyrotechnic and Light Signals**	
4.23.1	Pyrotechnic signals shall be provided conforming to SOLAS LSA Code Chapter III Visual Signals and not older than the stamped expiry date (if any) or if no expiry date stamped , not older than 4 years.	**

TABLE 13

red parachute flares LSA III 3.1	*red hand flares LSA III 3.2*	*orange smoke LSA III 3.3*	*race category*
4	4	2	MoMu2,3
	4	2	Mo4

4.24	**Heaving Line**	**
a)	a heaving line shall be provided 15 m - 25 m (50 ft - 75 ft) length readily accessible to cockpit.	**
b)	*the "throwing sock" type is recommended - see Appendix D*	**
	US SAILING prescribes that the heaving line be of 1/4 in. (6 mm) minimum diameter, floating, UV-inhibited and readily accessible to the cockpit.	**
4.25	**Cockpit Knife**	
	A strong, sharp knife, sheathed and securely restrained shall be provided readily accessible from the deck or a cockpit.	**
4.26	**Storm & Heavy Weather Sails**	

		Category
4.26.1	***Design***	
a)	*it is strongly recommended that persons in charge consult their designer and sailmaker to decide the most effective size for storm and heavy weather sails. The purpose of these sails is to provide safe propulsion for the yacht in severe weather -they are not intended as part of the racing inventory. The areas below are maxima. Smaller areas are likely to suit some yachts according to their stability and other characteristics.*	**
4.26.2	**High Visibility**	
a)	Every storm jib shall either be of highly-visible coloured material (eg dayglo pink, orange or yellow) or have a highly-visible coloured patch at least 50% of the area of the sail (up to a maximum diameter of 3m) added on each side; and also that a rotating wing mast should have a highly-visible coloured patch on each side. A storm sail purchased after January 2014 shall have the material of the body of the sail a highly-visible colour.	**
4.26.3	**Materials**	
a)	aromatic polyamides, carbon and similar fibres shall not be used in a trysail or storm jib but spectra/dyneema and similar materials are permitted.	**
b)	*it is strongly recommended that a heavy-weather jib does not contain aromatic polyamides, carbon and similar fibres other than spectra/dyneema.*	**
4.26.4	**The following shall be provided:-**	
a)	sheeting positions on deck for each storm and heavy-weather sail;	**
b)	for each storm or heavy-weather jib, a means to attach the luff to the stay, independent of any luff-groove device. A heavy weather jib shall have the means of attachment readily available. A storm jib shall have the means of attachment permanently attached;	**
	Storm and heavy weather jib areas shall be calculated as: (0.255 x luff length x (luff perpendicular + 2 x half width))* To apply to sails made in January 2012 and after.	
	US SAILING prescribes that a storm trysail shall be capable of being attached to the mast.	MoMu 0,1,2
c)	***when a storm trysail is required by OSR 4.26.4 (g) it shall be capable of being sheeted independently of the boom with trysail area not greater than 17.5% mainsail hoist (P) luff length x mainsail foot length (E). The storm trysail area shall be measured as (0.5 x leech length x shortest distance between tack point and leech). The storm trysail shall have neither headboard nor battens, however a storm trysail is not required in a yacht with a rotating wing mast which can adequately substitute for a trysail. The method of calculating area applies to sails made in January 2012 and after.***	MoMu3

		Category
d)	if a storm trysail is required by OSR 4.26.4 (g) the yacht's sail number and letter(s) shall be placed on both sides of the trysail (or on a rotating wing mast as substitute for a trysail) in as large a size as practicable;	MoMu3,4
f)	***in addition to the storm jib required by OSR 4.26.4 (e), a heavy-weather jib (or heavy-weather sail in a yacht with no forestay) of area not greater than 13.5% height of the foretriangle squared***	**
g)	either a storm trysail as defined in OSR 4.26.4(c), or mainsail reefing to reduce the luff by at least 40%.	MoMu3
	In addition, US SAILING prescribes mainsail reefing to reduce the luff by at least 10% for sails built after 1 January 1997.	MoMu 0,1,2,3

SECTION 5 - PERSONAL EQUIPMENT

		Category
5.01	**Lifejacket**	
	US SAILING prescribes for Categories 0,1,2,and 3: either a life-jacket defined in OSR 5.01.1 (See Note 1), or a USCG approved Type I non-inflatable personal flotation device (PFD), or a USCG approved yoke-type inflatable with 33lb (150N) or greater buoyancy with or without crotch strap, face guard, or buddy line. Each inflatable PFD shall be inflated and inspected annually. Service dates shall be marked on each PFD. It is recommended that all inflatable PFDs be integrated with safety harnesses (see OSR 5.02) (See Note 2).	MoMu 0,1,2,3
	US SAILING Note 1: ISO 12402 is not currently approved by the USCG. Boats operating in US waters are not exempt from USCG requirements.	MoMu 0,1,2,3
	US SAILING Note 2: Many inflatable PFD's with built-in harnesses are designed for people greater than 5' 5" in height and are potentially dangerous if you are below that height.	MoMu 0,1,2,3
	US SAILING Note 3: Inflatable PFDs with the required buoyancy will generally have inflation cylinders containing 33g or more of CO2.	MoMu 0,1,2,3
	US SAILING Note 4: "Yoke-type" is defined as a PFD that is designed to keep its wearer face-up and head-up in the water and that provides buoyancy in front of the chest and behind the neck immediately when inflated	MoMu 0,1,2,3

		Category
5.01.1	Each crew member shall have a lifejacket as follows:-	MoMu 0,1,2,3
a)		
i	In accordance with ISO 12402 - 3 (Level 150) or equivalent, including EN 396 or UL 1180	**
ii	Lifejackets manufactured after 1 January 2012 shall be in accordance with ISO 12402–3 (Level 150) and shall be fitted with:-	**
	• an emergency light in accordance with either ISO 12402-8 or SO LAS LSA code 2.2.3.	
	• a sprayhood in accordance with ISO 12402-8.	
	• a full deck safety harness in accordance with ISO 12401 (ISO 1095) including a crotch or thigh strap (holding down device) as specified in ISO 12401 (ISO 1095).	
	If of an inflatable type either	
a)	automatic, manual and oral inflation or	
b)	manual and oral inflation	
Notes	ISO 12402 requires Level 150 lifejackets to be fitted with a mandatory whistle and retro-reflective material. Also, when fitted with a safety harness, ISO 12402 requires that this shall be the full safety harness in accordance with ISO 12401. Any equivalent lifejacket shall have equal requirements.	
	Persons of larger than average build are generally more buoyant than those of average build and so do not require a lifejacket with greater levels of flotation. Wearing a Level 275 lifejacket may hamper entry into liferafts.	
b)	fitted with either a crotch strap(s) / thigh straps or a full safety harness in accordance with ISO 12401,	
Note	The function of lifejacket crotch/thigh straps is to hold the buoyancy element down. A crew member before a race should adjust a lifejacket to fit then retain that lifejacket for the duration of the race. Correct adjustment is fundamental to the lifejacket functioning correctly.	**
c)	fitted with a lifejacket light in accordance with SOLAS LSA code 2.2.3 (white, >0.75 candelas, >8 hours),	**
d)	if inflatable have a compressed gas inflation system,	**
e)	if inflatable, regularly checked for gas retention,	**

		Category
f)	compatible with the wearer's safety harness,	**
g)	clearly marked with the yacht's or wearer's name,	**
	It is strongly recommended that a lifejacket has:	
j)	*a splashguard / sprayhood See ISO 12402 – 8*	MoMu 1,2,3,4
k)	*a PLB unit (as with other types of EPIRB, should be properly registered with the appropriate authority)*	MoMu 1,2,3,4
l)	*if of a gas inflatable type, a spare cylinder and if appropriate a spare activation head*	MoMu 1,2,3,4
	US SAILING prescribes that all personnel on deck shall wear properly fitted personal floatation while starting and finishing. At other times during the race, floatation shall be worn on deck except when the Captain of the boat directs that it may be set aside.	**
	US SAILING prescribes for Category 4 lifejackets as above or U.S. Coast Guard approved Type III personal floatation devices	MoMu4
5.01.4	The person in charge shall personally check each lifejacket at least once annually.	**
	US SAILING note: As is true of all of these regulations, the prescriptions above do not necessarily replace the requirements of other governing authorities.	**
5.02	**Safety Harness and Safety Lines (Tethers)**	**
5.02.1	Each crew member shall have a harness and safety line that complies with ISO 12401 or equivalent with a safety line not more than 2m in length.	MoMu 0,1,2,3
	Harnesses and safety lines manufactured prior to Jan 2010 shall comply with either ISO 12401 or EN 1095.	MoMu 0,1,2,3
	Harnesses and safety lines manufactured prior to Jan 2001 are not permitted.	
	US SAILING prescribes that harnesses and safety lines manufactured prior to Jan 2001 are not recommended in the U.S.	**
a)	*Warning it is possible for a plain snaphook to disengage from a U bolt if the hook is rotated under load at right-angles to the axis of the U-bolt. For this reason the use of snaphooks with positive locking devices is strongly recommended.*	
5.02.2	At least 30% of the crew shall each, in addition to the above be provided with either:-	MoMu 0,1,2,3
a)	a safety line not more than 1m long, or	MoMu 0,1,2,3
b)	a mid-point snaphook on a 2m safety line	MoMu 0,1,2,3

		Category
5.02.3	A safety line purchased in January 2001 or later shall have a coloured flag embedded in the stitching, to indicate an overload. A line which has been overloaded shall be replaced as a matter of urgency.	MoMu 0,1,2,3
5.02.4	A crew member's lifejacket and harness shall be compatible	MoMu 0,1,2,3
	US SAILING prescribes that the safety harness may be integrated with an inflatable personal floatation device (see OSR 5.01) and recommends that such devices be employed whenever conditions warrant, and always in rough weather, on cold water, or at night, or under conditions of reduced visibility or when sailing short-handed.	MoMu 0,1,2,3
5.02.5	*It is strongly recommended that:-*	MoMu 0,1,2,3
a)	*static safety lines should be securely fastened at work stations;*	MoMu 0,1,2,3
b)	*A harness should be fitted with a crotch strap or thigh straps. Crotch straps or thigh straps together with related fittings and fixtures should be strong enough to lift the wearer from the water.*	MoMu 0,1,2,3
c)	*to draw attention to wear and damage, stitching on harness and safety lines should be of a colour contrasting strongly with the surrounding material;*	MoMu 0,1,2,3
d)	*snaphooks should be of a type which will not self-release from a U-bolt (see OSR 5.02.1(a)) and which can be easily released under load (crew members are reminded that a personal knife may free them from a safety line in emergency);*	MoMu 0,1,2,3
e)	*a crew member before a race should adjust a harness to fit then retain that harness for the duration of the race.*	MoMu 0,1,2,3
5.02.6	*Warning - a safety line and safety harness are not designed to tow a person in the water and it is important that the shortest safety line length possible be used with a harness to minimise or eliminate the risk of a person's torso becoming immersed in water outside the boat, especially when working on the foredeck. 1m safety lines or the midpoint snaphook on a 2m line should be used for this purpose. The diligent use of a properly adjusted safety harness and the shortest safety line practicable is regarded as by far the most effective way of preventing man overboard incidents.preventing man overboard incidents.*	MoMu 0,1,2,3
5.04	**Foul Weather Suits**	
b)	*it is recommended that a foul weather suit should be fitted with marine-grade retro-reflective material, and should have high-visibility colours on its upper parts and sleeve cuffs.See OSR 4.18*	**
5.09	***Annual Man-Overboard Practice***	
	US SAILING prescribes that the "Quick-Stop" man-overboard procedure shall be practiced aboard the yacht at least once annually. A certificate of such practice shall be signed by participating crew members and kept aboard the yacht.	**

		Category
5.11	***Preventer or Boom Restraining Device***	
	US SAILING recommends that a preventer or boom restraining device should be rigged in such a manner that attachment can be easily and quickly made, with the boom fully extended (running) without leaving the deck or leaning overboard. A process and plan for its use should be part of the crew's training and practice. Recommended for all boats in all categories.	**

SECTION 6 - TRAINING

6.04	***Routine Training On-Board***	
6.04.1	*It is recommended that crews should practice safety routines at reasonable intervals including the drill for man-overboard recovery.*	**
	US SAILING Note: MNA recognized First Aid & CPR courses in the U.S. are posted at http://offshore.ussailing.org/SAS/Senior_First_Aid_Certification.htm.	**
	US SAILING recommends that at least two members of the crew be currently certified in cardiopulmonary resuscitation.	**
6.05.3	At least one member of the crew shall be familiar with First Aid procedures, hypothermia, drowning, cardio-pulmonary resuscitation and relevant communications systems.	MoMu3,4
6.05.4	*An example model first aid training course is included in Appendix N.*	**

2012-2013 ISAF OFFSHORE SPECIAL REGULATIONS
with US Sailing Prescriptions
Category 5 for Inshore Races

Category 5 Special Regulations are intended for use in short races, close to shore in relatively warm and protected waters where adequate shelter and/or effective rescue is available all along the course, held in daylight only.

With the exception of recommended item 3.14 pulpits etc. for which see the main body of Special Regulations, all the items relevant to Category 5 are shown in Appendix J.

	Category 5 - Part A Basic **The following regulations shall be observed:-**	

Regulation	Item
1.02	Responsibility of Person in Charge The safety of a yacht and her crew is the sole and inescapable responsibility of the person in charge who must do his best to ensure that the yacht is fully found, thoroughly seaworthy and manned by an experienced crew who have undergone appropriate training and are physically fit to face bad weather. He must be satisfied as to the soundness of hull, spars, rigging, sails and all gear. He must ensure that all safety equipment is properly maintained and stowed and that the crew know where it is kept and how it is to be used. He shall also nominate a person to take over the responsibilities of the Person in Charge in the event of his incapacitation.
2.03.1	suitability of equipment All equipment required by Special Regulations shall:- a) function properly b) be regularly checked, cleaned and serviced c) when not in use be stowed in conditions in which deterioration is minimised d) be readily accessible e) be of a type, size and capacity suitable and adequate for the intended use and size of the yacht.
3.08	hatches & companionways
3.08.1	No hatch forward of the maximum beam station shall open inwards excepting ports having an area of less than 0.071m2 (110 sq in).
3.08.2	A hatch fitted forward of the maximum beam station, located on the side of the coachroof, opening into the interior of the boat ,and of area greater than 0.071m2 shall comply with ISO12216 design category A and and be clearly labelled and used in accordance with the following instruction: "NOT TO BE OPENED AT SEA" Attention is drawn to SR 3.02.1

2012-2013 ISAF OFFSHORE SPECIAL REGULATIONS
with US Sailing Prescriptions
Category 5 for Inshore Races

Regulation	Item
3.08.3	A hatch shall be: a) permanently attached b) capable of being firmly shut immediately, and remaining firmly shut in a 180 degree capsize (inversion) c) and on monohulls so arranged as to be above the water when the hull is heeled 90 degrees. Hatches over lockers that open to the interior of the vessel shall be included in this requirement. A yacht may have a maximum of four (two on each side of centerline) hatches that do not conform to this requirement, provided that the opening of each is less than 0.071 sq m (110 sq in). Effective for boats of a series begun after January 1, 2009, a written statement signed by the designer or other person who performed the downflooding analysis shall be carried on board. For purposes of this rule the vessel's displacement condition for the analysis shall be the Light Craft Condition LCC (in conformity with 6.3 of the EN ISO 8666 standard and 3.5.1 of the EN ISO12217-2 standard). (Monohulls Only)
3.08.4	A companionway hatch shall: (a) be fitted with a strong securing arrangement which shall be operable from the exterior and interior including when the yacht is inverted (b) have any blocking devices: i capable of being retained in position with the hatch open or shut ii whether or not in position in the hatchway, secured to the yacht (e.g. by lanyard) for the duration of the race, to prevent their being lost overboard iii permit exit in the event of inversion
3.08.5	On monohulls if the companionway extends below the local sheerline and the boat has a cockpit opening aft to the sea the boat shall comply with one of the following: a) the companionway sill shall not extend below the local sheerline. Or b) be in full compliance with all aspects of ISO 11812 to design category A
3.08.6	On monohulls with a cockpit closed aft to the sea where the companionway hatch extends below the local sheerline, the companionway shall be capable of being blocked off up to the level of the local sheerline, provided that the companionway hatch shall continue to give access to the interior with the blocking devices (e.g. washboards) in place
3.08.7	On multihulls the companionway hatch extending below the local sheerline and shall comply with either (a) or (b): (a) be capable of being blocked off up to the level of the local sheerline, whilst giving access to the interior with the blocking devices (e.g. washboards) in place with a minimum sill height of 300 mm. (b) A companionway hatch shall be in compliance with ISO 11812 – Watertight cockpits and quick-draining cockpits to design category B
3.09	cockpits
3.09.1	cockpits shall be structurally strong, self-draining quickly by gravity at all angles of heel and permanently incorporated as an integral part of the hull.
3.09.2	cockpits must be essentially watertight, that is, all openings to the hull must be capable of being strongly and rigidly secured

Regulation	Item
3.09.3	a bilge pump outlet pipe or pipes shall not be connected to a cockpit drain
3.09.4	A cockpit sole shall be at least 2% LWL above LWL (or in IMS yachts first launched before 1/03, at least 2% L above LWL)
3.09.5	a bow, lateral, central or stern well shall be considered a cockpit for the purposes of 3.09
3.09.6	In cockpits opening aft to the sea structural openings aft shall be not less in area than 50% maximum cockpit depth x maximum cockpit width
3.09.7	Cockpit volume i) age or series date before 4/92:- the total volume of all cockpits below lowest coamings shall not exceed 9% (LWL x maximum beam x freeboard abreast the cockpit). ii) age or series date 4/92 and after:- as in (i) above except that "lowest coamings" shall not include any aft of the FA station and no extension of a cockpit aft of the working deck shall be included in calculation of cockpit volume iii) IMS-rated boats may use instead instead of LWL, maximum beam, freeboard abreast the cockpit; the IMS terms L, B and FA. **Cockpit drains** Cockpit drain cross section area (after allowance for screens if fitted) shall be:- i) in yachts with earliest of age or series date before 1/72 or in any yacht under 8.5m (28ft) LOA - at least that of 2 x 25mm (one inch) unobstructed openings or equivalent ii) in yachts with earliest of age or series date 1/72 and later - at least that of 4 x 20mm (3/4 inch) unobstructed openings or equivalent
	US SAILING prescribes that cockpit drains shall be accessible for cleaning.
4.01.1	sail numbers Yachts which are not in an ISAF International Class or Recognized Class shall comply with RRS 77 and RRS Appendix G as closely as possible, except that sail numbers allotted by a State authority are acceptable

Category 5 - Part B Portable Equipment

The following shall be provided:

3.23.5 (e)	one manual bilge pump
3.23.5 (f)	one bucket of stout construction with at least 9 litres (2 UK gallons, 2.4 US gallons) capacity plus a lanyard
3.24.1 (b)	one compass (a hand-held is acceptable)
4.05.1	one fire extinguisher required if electrical system, engine or stove on board
4.06.1	one anchor
4.17	yacht's name on buoyant equipment

2012-2013 ISAF OFFSHORE SPECIAL REGULATIONS
with US Sailing Prescriptions
Category 5 for Inshore Races

Regulation	Item
4.22.1 (a)	a lifebuoy with a drogue, or a lifesling without a drogue. Marine grade retro-reflective tape shall be fitted.
4.24	a heaving line shall be provided of length 15m-25m (50ft-75ft) readily accessible to the cockpit or helm
	US SAILING prescribes that the heaving line be of ¼ (6 mm) minimum diameter, floating, UV-inhibited and readily accessible to the cockpit.
5.01.1	each crew member shall have a lifejacket as follows: (a) equipped with a whistle (b) fitted with marine grade retro-reflective tape (d) if inflatable, regularly checked for air retention (e) clearly marked with yacht's or wearer's name
	US SAILING prescribes for Category 5 lifejackets as above or US Coast Guard approved Type III Personal Floatation Devices.
	US SAILING prescribes that all personnel on deck shall wear properly fitted personal floatation while starting and finishing. At other times during the race, floatation shall be worn on deck except when the Captain of the boat directs that it may be set aside.

Category 5 - Part C Recommendations

Regulation	Item
	-see main text of Special Regulations 3.14 etc.
4.01.2	sail numbers for display when sails are down
4.07.1 (a)	a flashlight
4.08.2	a first aid kit
4.11.1	a waterproof chart
4.13	an echo sounder or lead line
4.16	tools and spare parts
4.24	a "throwing sock" type of heaving line - see Appendix D
4.26.9	mainsail reefing to reduce the luff by at least 60%, or a storm trysail as in 4.26.6.
5.01.2	lifejacket equipment or attribute: (a) a lifejacket light in accordance with SOLAS LSA code 2.2.3 (white, >0.75 candelas, > 8 hours) (b) at least 150N buoyancy, arranged to securely suspend an unconscious man face upwards at approximately 45 degrees to the water surface, in accordance with EN396 (ISO 12402) or near equivalent (c) a crotch strap or thigh straps (d) a splashguard: see EN394. (e) if inflatable, supplied with a compressed gas inflation system

2012-2013 ISAF OFFSHORE SPECIAL REGULATIONS
with US Sailing Prescriptions
Category 6 for Inshore Races

CATEGORY 6 SPECIAL REGULATIONS

Category 6 Special Regulations are intended for use in races where:-

- participating boats may not be self-sufficient
- the races are short in duration and close to a single manned shore base, in relatively warm and protected waters, in daylight and good visibility
- participating boats can be observed by race organisers at all times
- safety/rescue boats are available all along the course sufficient to enable any competitor to be returned to the shore base in a timely manner
- safety/rescue boats are of a suitable designed and properly equipped and are manned by adequately trained and competent personnel including, for each race, at least one skilled in first aid

Requirements for Category 6 are:-
Unless otherwise prescribed in Notice of Race and/or Sailing Instructions, where class rules include items of safety such rules shall override the corresponding part of these Regulations.

All equipment required by Special Regulations Category 6 shall:-

- function properly
- be regularly checked, cleaned and serviced
- when not in use be stowed in conditions in which deterioration is minimised
- be readily accessible
- be of a type, size and capacity suitable and adequate for the intended use and size of the boat.

All boats sailing in Category 6 shall be fitted with:-

- A strong point for the attachment of a tow and/or anchor line.

All boats sailing in Category 6 shall carry:-

- A personal flotation device (PFD) for each person aboard to ISO 12402-5 -Level 50 or equivalent

  US SAILING PRESCRIBES FOR Category 6 lifejackets as above or US Coast Guard approved Type III Personal Floatation Devices.
- A knife
- If the hull is not self-draining or is able to carry more than 150 litres of free water, a bucket or bailer of not less than 1 litre capacity
- If a trapeze harness is carried it shall be to ISO DIS 10862
- A paddle or means of propelling the boat when not under sail

ISAF Special Regulations Governing Offshore Racing for Category 1 & 2 Multihulls
Including US SAILING Prescriptions

ISAF Offshore Special Regulations Requirements for Multihull Sailboats

Including US SAILING Prescriptions

www.offshore.ussailing.org

Extract for Race Category 1 and 2 Multihulls

JANUARY 2012 - DECEMBER 2013

US Version 1Mu and 2Mu - 2012

Because this is an extract not all paragraph numbers will be present

Language & Abbreviations Used

Mo - Monohull

Mu - Multihull

" ** " means the item applies to all types of yacht in all Categories except 5 or 6 for which see Appendix J or L.

A side bar indicates a significant change in 2012

US SAILING extract files are available for individual categories and boat types (monohulls and multihulls) at http://offshore.ussailing.org/SAS/ISAF_Special_Regulations/Extracts.htm

US SAILING prescriptions are printed in bold, italic letters

ISAF guidance notes and recommendations are printed in italics

The use of the masculine gender shall be taken to mean either gender

SECTION 1 - FUNDAMENTAL AND DEFINITIONS

		Category
1.01	**Purpose and Use**	
1.01.1	It is the purpose of these Special Regulations to establish uniform minimum equipment, accommodation and training standards for monohull and multihull yachts racing offshore. A Proa is excluded from these regulations.	**
1.01.2	These Special Regulations do not replace, but rather supplement, the requirements of governmental authority, the Racing Rules and the rules of Class Associations and Rating Systems. The attention of persons in charge is called to restrictions in the Rules on the location and movement of equipment.	**
1.01.3	These Special Regulations, adopted internationally, are strongly recommended for use by all organizers of offshore races. Race Committees may select the category deemed most suitable for the type of race to be sailed.	**

SECTION 1 - FUNDAMENTAL AND DEFINITIONS

		Category
1.02	**Responsibility of Person in Charge**	
1.02.1	**The safety of a yacht and her crew is the sole and inescapable responsibility of the person in charge who must do his best to ensure that the yacht is fully found, thoroughly seaworthy and manned by an experienced crew who have undergone appropriate training and are physically fit to face bad weather. He must be satisfied as to the soundness of hull, spars, rigging, sails and all gear. He must ensure that all safety equipment is properly maintained and stowed and that the crew know where it is kept and how it is to be used. He shall also nominate a person to take over the responsibilities of the Person in Charge in the event of his incapacitation.**	**
1.02.2	Neither the establishment of these Special Regulations, their use by race organizers, nor the inspection of a yacht under these Special Regulations in any way limits or reduces the complete and unlimited responsibility of the person in charge.	**
1.02.3	**Decision to race -The responsibility for a yacht's decision to participate in a race or to continue racing is hers alone - RRS Fundamental Rule 4.**	**
1.03	**Definitions, Abbreviations, Word Usage**	
1.03.1	Definitions of Terms used in this document	**

TABLE 1	
Age Date	Month/year of first launch
AIS	Automatic Identification Systems
CEN	Comité Européen de Normalisation
CPR	Cardio-Pulmonary Resuscitation
Coaming	includes the transverse after limit of the cockpit over which water would run in the event that when the yacht is floating level the cockpit is flooded or filled to overflowing.
DSC	Digital Selective Calling
EN	European Norm
EPFS	Electronic Position-Fixing System
EPIRB	Emergency Position-Indicating Radio Beacon
FA Station	The transverse station at which the upper corner of the transom meets the sheerline.

Foul-Weather Suit	A foul weather suit is clothing designed to keep the wearer dry and maybe either a jacket and trousers worn together, or a single garment comprising jacket and trousers.
GMDSS	Global Maritime Distress & Safety System
GNSS	Global Navigation Satellite System
GPIRB	EPIRB, with integral GPS position-fixing
ITU	International Telecommunications Union
GPS	Global Positioning System
Hatch	The term hatch includes the entire hatch assembly and also the lid or cover as part of that assembly (the part itself may be described as a hatch).
INMARSAT	This is Inmarsat Global Limited, the private company that provides GMDSS satellite distress and safety communications, plus general communications via voice, fax and data
IMO	International Maritime Organisation
IMSO	The International Mobile Satellite Organisation, the independent, intergovernmental organisation that oversees Inmarsat's performance of its Public Service Obligations for the GMDSS and reports on these to IMO
ISAF	International Sailing Federation.
ISO	International Standard or International Organization for Standardization.
Lifeline	rope or wire line rigged as guardrail / guardline around the deck
LOA	Length overall not including pulpits, bowsprits, boomkins etc.
LWL	(Length of) loaded waterline
Monohull	Yacht in which the hull depth in any section does not decrease towards the centre-line.
Moveable Ballast	Lead or other material including water which has no practical function in the boat other than to increase weight and/or to influence stability and/or trim and which may be moved transversely but not varied in weight while a boat is racing.
ORC	Offshore Racing Congress (formerly Offshore Racing Council)
OSR	Offshore Special Regulation(s)
Permanently Installed	Means the item is effectively built-in by eg bolting, welding, glassing etc. and may not be removed for or during racing.
PLB	Personal Locator Beacon
Proa	Asymmetric Catamaran
RRS	ISAF - Racing Rules of Sailing
SAR	Search and Rescue

SART	Search and Rescue Transponder
Series Date	Month & Year of first launch of the first yacht of the production series
SOLAS	Safety of Life at Sea Convention
Safety Line	A tether used to connect a safety harness to a strong point
Securely Fastened	Held strongly in place by a method (eg rope lashings, wing-nuts) which will safely retain the fastened object in severe conditions including a 180 degree capsize and allows for the item to be removed and replaced during racing
Static Ballast	Lead or other material including water which has no practical function in the boat other than to increase weight and/or to influence stability and/or trim and which may not be moved or varied in weight while a boat is racing.
Static Safety Line	A safety line (usually shorter than a safety line carried with a harness) kept clipped on at a work-station
Variable Ballast	Water carried for the sole purpose of influencing stability and/or trim and which may be varied in weight and/or moved while a boat is racing.

		Category
1.03.2	The words "shall" and "must" are mandatory, and "should" and "may" are permissive.	**
1.03.3	The word "yacht" shall be taken as fully interchangeable with the word "boat".	**

SECTION 2 - APPLICATION & GENERAL REQUIREMENTS

2.01	**Categories of Events** *In many types of race, ranging from trans-oceanic sailed under adverse conditions to short-course day races sailed in protected waters, six categories are established, to provide for differences in the minimum standards of safety and accommodation required for such varying circumstances:*	**
2.01.2	**Category 1** ***US SAILING prescribes that Category 1 races are of long distance, well offshore, in large unprotected bays, and in waters where large waves, strong currents, or conditions leading to rapid onset of hypothermia are possible, where yachts must be completely self-sufficient for extended periods of time, capable of withstanding heavy storms and prepared to meet serious emergencies without the expectation of outside assistance.***	MoMu1

		Category
2.01.3	**Category 2** ***US SAILING prescribes that Category 2 races are of extended duration along or not far removed from shorelines, where a high degree of self-sufficiency is required of the yachts but with the reasonable probability that outside assistance would be available for aid in the event of serious emergencies.***	MoMu2
2.02	**Inspection** A yacht may be inspected at any time. If she does not comply with these Special Regulations her entry may be rejected, or she will be liable to disqualification or such other penalty as may be prescribed by the national authority or the race organizers.	**
2.03	**General Requirements**	
2.03.1	All equipment required by Special Regulations shall:-	
a)	function properly	**
b)	be regularly checked, cleaned and serviced	**
c)	when not in use be stowed in conditions in which deterioration is minimised	**
d)	be readily accessible	**
e)	be of a type, size and capacity suitable and adequate for the intended use and size of the yacht.	**
2.03.2	Heavy items:	
a)	ballast, ballast tanks and associated equipment shall be permanently installed	**
b)	heavy movable items including e.g. batteries, stoves, gas bottles, tanks, toolboxes and anchors and chain shall be securely fastened	**
c)	heavy items for which fixing is not specified in Special Regulations shall be permanently installed or securely fastened, as appropriate	**
2.03.3	When to show navigation lights	**
a)	navigation lights (OSR 3.27) shall be shown as required by the International Regulations for Preventing Collision at Sea, (Part C and Technical Annex 1). All yachts shall exhibit sidelights and a sternlight at the required times.	**

SECTION 3 - STRUCTURAL FEATURES, STABILITY, FIXED EQUIPMENT

		Category
3.01	**Strength of Build, Ballast and Rig**	
	Yachts shall be strongly built, watertight and, particularly with regard to hulls, decks and cabin trunks capable of withstanding solid water and knockdowns. They must be properly rigged and ballasted, be fully seaworthy and must meet the standards set forth herein. Shrouds shall never be disconnected.	**
3.02	**Watertight Integrity of a Hull**	
3.02.1	A hull, including, deck, coach roof, windows, hatches and all other parts, shall form an integral, essentially watertight unit and any openings in it shall be capable of being immediately secured to maintain this integrity.	**
3.02.2	Centreboard and daggerboard trunks and the like shall not open into the interior of a hull except via a watertight inspection/maintenance hatch of which the opening shall be entirely above the waterline of the yacht floating level in normal trim.	**
3.02.3	A canting keel pivot shall be completely contained within a watertight enclosure which shall comply with OSR 3.02.2. Access points in the watertight enclosure for control and actuation systems or any other purpose shall comply with OSR 3.02.1.	**
3.02.4	Moveable ballast systems shall be fitted with a manual control and actuation secondary system which shall be capable of controlling the full sailing load of the keel in the event of failure of the primary system. Such failures would include electrical and hydraulic failure and mechanical failure of the components and the structure to which it mounts. The system must be capable of being operational quickly and shall be operable at any angle of heel. It would be desirable if this system was capable of securing the keel on the centreline.	**
3.03	**Hull Construction Standards (Scantlings)**	MoMu0,1,2
3.03.4	A multihull shall comply with appendix M to these OSR.	Mu0,1,2
3.05	**Stability and Flotation - Multihulls**	Mu0,1,2,3,4
	Attention is drawn to ISO 12217-2.	Mu0,1,2,3,4
3.05.1	Adequate watertight bulkheads and compartments (which may include permanently installed flotation material) in each hull shall be provided to ensure that a multihull is effectively unsinkable and capable of floating in a stable position with at least half the length of one hull flooded. (see OSR 3.13.2).	Mu0,1,2,3,4
3.05.2	Multihulls built on or after Jan 1999 shall in every hull without accommodation be divided at intervals of not more than 4m (13ft 3”) by one or more transverse watertight bulkheads	Mu0,1,2,3,4

		Category
3.05.3	A yacht shall be designed and built to resist capsize.	Mu0,1,2,3,4
3.07	**Exits and Escape Hatches - Multihulls**	Mu0,1,2,3,4
	Exits	
a)	In a multihull of 8m (26.2ft) LOA and greater, each hull which contains accommodation shall have at least two exits.	Mu0,1,2,3,4
b)	In a multihull of less than 8m (26.2ft) LOA each hull which contains accommodation shall have at least two exits.	Mu0,1,2,3
3.07.2	**Escape Hatches, Underside Clipping Points & Handholds**	
a)	In a multihull of 12m (39.4ft) LOA and greater each hull which contains accommodation shall:-	Mu0,1,2,3,4
i	have an escape hatch for access to and from the hull in the event of an inversion;	Mu0,1,2,3,4
ii	when first launched on or after January 2003 have a minimum clearance diameter through each escape hatch of 450mm or when an escape hatch is not circular, sufficient clearance to allow a crew member to pass through fully clothed;	Mu0,1,2,3,4
iii	*when first launched prior to January 2003, if possible have each escape hatch in compliance with the dimensions in OSR 3.07.2(a)(ii);*	Mu0,1,2,3,4
iv	when the yacht is inverted have each escape hatch above the waterline;	Mu0,1,2,3,4
v	when first launched on or after January 2001 have each escape hatch at or near the midships station;	Mu0,1,2,3,4
vi	in a catamaran first launched on or after January 2003 have each escape hatch on the side nearest the vessel's central axis.	Mu0,1,2,3,4
b)	A trimaran of 12m (39.4ft) LOA and greater first launched on or after 1/03 shall have at least two escape hatches in compliance with the dimensions in OSR 3.07.2(a) (ii)	Mu0,1,2,3,4
c)	Each escape hatch must have been opened both from inside and outside within 6 months prior to an intended race	Mu0,1,2,3,4
d)	A multihull shall have on the underside appropriate handholds/clipping points sufficient for all crew (on a trimaran these shall be around the central hull).	Mu0,1,2,3,4
e)	A catamaran first launched on or after 1/03 with a central nacelle shall have on the underside around the central nacelle, handholds of sufficient capacity to enable all persons on board to hold on and/or clip on securely	Mu0,1,2,3,4

		Category
f)	*In a catamaran with a central nacelle, it is recommended that each hull has an emergency refuge, accessible via a special hatch in the side of the hull nearest the vessel's central axis, which hatch may be opened and closed from the inside and outside*	Mu0,1,2,3,4
3.07.3	A multihull of less than 12m (39.4ft) LOA shall either have escape hatches in compliance with OSR 3.07.2 (a)(b) and (c)or shall comply with OSR 3.07.3 (a) and (b):	Mu2,3,4
a)	each hull which contains accommodation shall have, for the purpose of cutting an escape hatch, appropriate tools kept ready for instant use adjacent to the intended cutting site. Each tool shall be secured to the vessel by a line and a clip, and	Mu2,3,4
b)	in each hull at a station where an emergency hatch may be cut, the cutting line shall be clearly marked both inside and outside with an outline and the words ESCAPE CUT HERE	Mu2,3,4
3.08	**Hatches & Companionways**	
3.08.1	No hatch forward of the maximum beam station, other than a hatch in the side of a coachroof, shall open in such a way that the lid or cover moves into the open position towards the interior of the hull (excepting ports having an area of less than 0.071m2 (110 sq in)).	**
3.08.2	A hatch fitted forward of the maximum beam station, located on the side of the coachroof, opening into the interior of the boat ,and of area greater than 0.071m2 shall comply with ISO12216 design category A and and be clearly labelled and used in accordance with the following instruction: "NOT TO BE OPENED AT SEA" Attention is drawn to SR 3.02.1	**
3.08.3	A hatch shall be:	
b)	permanently attached	**
c)	capable of being firmly shut immediately and remaining firmly shut in a 180 degree capsize (inversion)	**
3.08.4	A companionway hatch shall:	
a)	be fitted with a strong securing arrangement which shall be operable from the exterior and interior including when the yacht is inverted	**
b)	have any blocking devices:	**
i	capable of being retained in position with the hatch open or shut	**
ii	whether or not in position in the hatchway, secured to the yacht (e.g. by lanyard) for the duration of the race, to prevent their being lost overboard	**
iii	permit exit in the event of inversion	**

		Category
3.08.7	A companionway hatch extending below the local sheerline and shall comply with either (a) or (b):	Mu0,1,2,3,4
a)	be capable of being blocked off up to the level of the local sheerline, whilst giving access to the interior with the blocking devices (e.g. wash-boards) in place with a minimum sill height of 300 mm.	Mo0,1,2,3,4
b)		
i	A companionway hatch shall be in compliance with ISO 11812 - Watertight cockpits and quick-draining cockpits to design category A	Mu0,1,2,3
3.09	**Cockpits - Attention is Drawn to ISO 11812**	
3.09.1	Cockpits shall be structurally strong, self-draining quickly by gravity at all angles of heel and permanently incorporated as an integral part of the hull.	**
3.09.2	Cockpits must be essentially watertight, that is, all openings to the hull must be capable of being strongly and rigidly secured	**
3.09.3	A bilge pump outlet pipe shall not be connected to a cockpit drain . See OSR 3.09.8 for cockpit drain minimum sizes	**
3.09.4	A cockpit sole shall be at least 2% LWL above LWL (or in IMS yachts first launched before 1/03, at least 2% L above LWL)	**
3.09.5	A bow, lateral, central or stern well shall be considered a cockpit for the purposes of OSR 3.09	**
3.09.6	In cockpits opening aft to the sea structural openings aft shall be not less in area than 50% maximum cockpit depth x maximum cockpit width.	**
3.09.7	**Cockpit Volume**	
i)	earliest of age or series date before April 1992: the total volume of all cockpits below lowest coamings shall not exceed 6% (LWL x maximum beam x freeboard abreast the cockpit).	MoMu0,1
	the total volume of all cockpits below lowest coamings shall not exceed 9% (LWL x maximum beam x freeboard abreast the cockpit).	MoMu2,3,4
ii)	earliest of age or series date April 1992 and after: as above for the appropriate category except that "lowest coamings" shall not include any aft of the FA station and no extension of a cock-pit aft of the working deck shall be included in calculation of cockpit volume	**
Note	*IMS-rated boats may instead of the terms LWL, maximum beam, free-board abreast the cockpit, use the IMS terms L, B and FA.*	**

		Category
3.09.8	**Cockpit Drains**	
	See OSR 3.09.1. Cockpit drain cross section area (after allowance for screens if fitted) shall be:-	
a)	in yachts with earliest of age or series date before 1/72 or in any yacht under 8.5m (28ft) LOA - at least that of 2 x 25mm diameter (one inch) unobstructed openings or equivalent	**
b)	in yachts with earliest of age or series date 1/72 and later - at least that of 4 x 20mm diameter (3/4 inch) unobstructed openings or equivalent	**
	US SAILING prescribes that cockpit drains shall be accessible for cleaning.	**
3.10	**Sea Cocks or Valves**	
	Sea cocks or valves shall be permanently installed on all through-hull openings below the waterline except integral deck scuppers, speed indicators, depth finders and the like, however a means of closing such openings shall be provided.	**
3.11	**Sheet Winches**	
	Sheet winches shall be mounted in such a way that an operator is not required to be substantially below deck.	**
3.12	**Mast Step**	
	The heel of a keel stepped mast shall be securely fastened to the mast step or adjoining structure.	**
3.13	**Watertight Bulkheads**	
	multihulls also see OSR 3.05	Mu0,1,2,3,4
3.13.1	A hull shall have either a watertight "crash" bulkhead within 15% of LOA from the bow and abaft the forward end of LWL, or permanently installed closed-cell foam buoyancy effectively filling the forward 30% LOA of the hull.	Mo0 Mu0,1,2,3,4
3.13.2	Any required watertight bulkhead shall be strongly built to take a full head of water pressure without allowing any leakage into the adjacent compartment.	Mo0 Mu0,1,2,3,4
3.14	**Pulpits, Stanchions, Lifelines**	
3.14.1	When due to the particular design of a multihull it is impractical to precisely follow Special Regulations regarding pulpits, stanchions, lifelines, the regulations for monohulls shall be followed as closely as possible with the aim of minimising the risk of people falling overboard.	Mu0,1,2,3,4
	US SAILING prescribes that all crew working areas shall be protected by lifelines or jackstays and safety harness attachment points. Lifelines or jackstays with or without safety harness attachment points may be substituted for pulpits.	Mu0,1,2,3,4

		Category
3.14.2	Lifelines required in Special Regulations shall be "taut".	**
a)	*As a guide, when a deflecting force of 50 N (5.1 kgf, 11.2 lbf) is applied to a lifeline midway between supports, the lifeline should not deflect more than 50 mm.*	**
3.14.3	The following shall be provided:	**
c)	lifelines (guardlines) supported on stanchions, which, with pulpits, shall form an effectively continuous barrier around a working deck for man-overboard prevention. Lifelines shall be permanently supported at intervals of not more than 2.20m (86.6") and shall not pass outboard of supporting stanchions	**
d)	upper rails of pulpits at no less height above the working deck than the upper lifelines as in Table 7.	**
e)	Openable upper rails in bow pulpits shall be secured shut whilst racing	**
f)	Pulpits and stanchions shall be permanently installed. When there are sockets or studs, these shall be through-bolted, bonded or welded. The pulpit(s) and/or stanchions fitted to these shall be mechanically retained without the help of the life-lines. Without sockets or studs, pulpits and/or stanchions shall be through-bolted, bonded or welded.	**
g)	The bases of pulpits and stanchions shall not be further inboard from the edge of the appropriate working deck than 5% of maximum beam or 150 mm (6 in), whichever is greater.	**
h)	Stanchion or pulpit or pushpit bases shall not be situated outboard of a working deck. For the purpose of this rule the base shall be taken to include a sleeve or socket into which the tube is fitted but shall exclude a baseplate which carries fixings into the deck or hull.	**
i)	Provided the complete lifeline enclosure is supported by stanchions and pulpit bases effectively within the working deck, lifeline terminals and support struts may be fixed to a hull aft of the working deck	**
j)	Lifelines need not be fixed to a bow pulpit if they terminate at, or pass through, adequately braced stanchions set inside and overlapping the bow pulpit, provided that the gap between the upper lifeline and the bow pulpit does not exceed 150 mm (6 in).	**

		Category
k)	Lifelines shall be continuous and fixed only at (or near) the bow and stern. However a bona fide gate shall be permitted in the lifelines on each side of a yacht. Except at its end fittings, the movement of a lifeline in a fore-and-aft direction shall not be constrained. Temporary sleeving in 3.14.6 (c) shall not modify tension in the lifeline.	**
l)	Stanchions shall be straight and vertical except that:-	**
i	within the first 50 mm (2 in) from the deck, stanchions shall not be displaced horizontally from the point at which they emerge from the deck or stanchion base by more than 10 mm (3/8 in), and	**
ii	stanchions may be angled to not more than 10 degrees from vertical at any point above 50 mm (2 in) from the deck.	**
m)	*It is strongly recommended that designs also comply to ISO 15085*	**
3.14.4	**Special Requirements for Pulpits, Stanchions, Lifelines on Multihulls**	Mu 0,1,2,3,4
	The following shall be provided:-	
a)	on a trimaran - a bow pulpit on the main hull, with lifelines around the main hull supported on stanchions. The lifelines may be interrupted where there are nets or crossbeam wings outboard of the main hull	Mu 0,1,2,3,4
b)	on a trimaran - where a net joins the base of a bow pulpit on the main hull, an additional lifeline from the top of the pulpit to the forward crossbeam at or outboard of the crossbeam mid-point.	Mu 0,1,2,3,4
c)	on a trimaran - at a main or emergency steering position on an outrigger with or without a cockpit, lifelines protecting an arc of 3 meters diameter centred on the steering position. (When measuring between lifelines their taut, undeflected positions shall be taken for this purpose).	Mu 0,1,2,3,4
d)	on a catamaran - lifelines from bow to stern on each hull and transverse lifelines to form an effectively continuous barrier around the working area for man-overboard prevention. The transverse lifelines shall be attached to bow and stern pulpits or superstructure. A webbing, strop or rope (minimum diameter 6mm) shall be rove zig-zag between the transverse lifelines and the net.	Mu 0,1,2,3,4

		Category
3.14.5	**Lifeline Height, Vertical Openings, Number of Lifelines**	

TABLE 7 **

LOA	**earliest of age/ series date**	**minimum requirements**	**Category**
under 8.5 m (28 ft)	before January 1992	taut single lifeline at a height of no less than 450 mm (18 in) above the working deck. No vertical opening shall exceed 560 mm (22 in).	**
under 8.5 m (28 ft)	January 1992 and after	as for under 8.5 m(28 ft) in table 7 above, except that when an intermediate lifeline is fitted no vertical opening shall exceed 380 mm (15 in).	**
8.5 m (28 ft) and over	before January 1993	taut double lifeline with upper lifeline at a height of no less than 600 mm (24 in) above the working deck. No vertical opening shall exceed 560 mm (22 in)	**
8.5 m (28 ft) and over	January 1993 and after	as 8.5 m (28 ft) and over in Table 7 above, except that no vertical opening shall exceed 380 mm (15 in).	**
all	all	on yachts with intermediate lifelines the intermediate line shall be not less than 230 mm (9 in) above the working deck ***and shall be of the same construction and general arrangements as required for the upper.***	**

3.14.6	**Lifeline Minimum Diameters, Required Materials, Specifications**	
a)	Lifelines shall be of : - stranded stainless steel wire or - Single-braided High Modulus Polyethylene (HMPE) (Dyneema®/ Spectra® or equivalent) rope	** ** **
	US SAILING note. An article describing the best techniques for using Dyneema line, particularly in the life line application, is posted at http://offshore.ussailing.org/SAS.htm	
b)	The minimum diameter of all lifelines is specified in table 8 below.	**

		Category
c)	Stainless steel lifelines shall be uncoated and used without close-fitting sleeving, however, temporary sleeving may be fitted provided it is regularly removed for inspection.	**
d)	*When stainless wire is used, Grade 316 is recommended.*	**
e)	When HMPE (Dyneema®/Spectra®) is used, it shall be spliced in accordance with the manufacturer's recommended procedures.	**
f)	A taut lanyard of synthetic rope may be used to secure lifelines provided the gap it closes does not exceed 100 mm (4 in). This lanyard shall be replaced annually at a minimum.	**
g)	All wire, fittings, anchorage points, fixtures and lanyards shall comprise a lifeline enclosure system which has at all points at least the breaking strength of the required lifeline wire.	**

TABLE 8 **

LOA	minimum wire or rope diameter
under 8.5m (28ft)	3 mm (1/8 in)
8.5m - 13m	4 mm (5/32 in)
over 13m (43ft)	5 mm (3/16 in)

3.14.7	Pulpits, Stanchions, Lifelines - Limitations on Materials	

TABLE 9 **

Earliest of Age or Series Date	detail
before January 1987	carbon fibre is not recommended in stanchions pulpits and lifelines.
January 1987 and after	stanchions, pulpits and lifelines shall not be made of carbon fibre.

3.15	**Multihull Nets or Trampolines**	
3.15.1	The word "net" is interchangeable with the word "trampoline"	Mu0,1,2,3,4
	A net shall be:-	Mu0,1,2,3,4
a)	essentially horizontal	Mu0,1,2,3,4
b)	made from durable woven webbing, water permeable fabric, or mesh with openings not larger than 5.08cm (2 inches) in any dimension. Attachment points shall be planned to avoid chafe. The junction between a net and a yacht shall present no risk of foot trapping	Mu0,1,2,3,4
c)	solidly fixed at regular intervals on transverse and longitudinal support lines and shall be fine-stitched to a bolt rope	Mu0,1,2,3,4

		Category
d)	able to carry the full weight of the crew either in normal working conditions at sea or in case of capsize when the yacht is inverted.	Mu0,1,2,3,4
e)	*It is recommended that lines used to tie the nets should be individually tied and not continuously connected to more than four attachment points per connecting line*	Mu0,1,2,3,4
3.15.2	**Trimarans with Double Crossbeams**	
a)	A trimaran with double crossbeams shall have nets on each side covering:-	
b)	the rectangles formed by the crossbeams, central hull and outriggers	Mu0,1,2,3,4
c)	the triangles formed by the aft end of the central pulpit, the mid-point of each forward crossbeam, and the intersection of the crossbeam and the central hull	Mu0,1,2,3,4
d)	the triangles formed by the aftermost part of the cockpit or steering position (whichever is furthest aft), the mid-point of each after crossbeam, and the intersection of the crossbeam and the central hull; except that:-	Mu0,1,2,3,4
e)	the requirement in OSR 3.15.2(d) shall not apply when cockpit coamings and/or lifelines are present which comply with the minimum height requirements in Table 7	Mu0,1,2,3,4
3.15.3	**Trimarans with Single Crossbeams**	
a)	A trimaran with a single crossbeam shall have nets between the central hull and each outrigger:-	Mu0,1,2,3,4
b)	on each side between two straight lines from the intersection of the crossbeam and the outrigger, respectively to the aft end of the pulpit on the central hull, and to the aftermost point of the cockpit or steering position on the central hull (whichever is furthest aft)	Mu0,1,2,3,4
3.16	**Catamarans**	
a)	On a catamaran the total net surface shall be limited:	
b)	laterally by the hulls	Mu0,1,2,3,4
c)	longitudinally by transverse stations through the forestay base, and the aftermost point of the boom lying fore and aft. However, a catamaran with a central nacelle (non-immersed) may satisfy the regulations for a trimaran	Mu0,1,2,3,4

3.18	**Toilet**	
3.18.1	A toilet, permanently installed	MoMu.0,1,2
3.19	**Bunks**	
3.19.2	Bunks, permanently installed	**

		Category
3.20	**Cooking Facilities**	
3.20.1	A cooking stove, permanently installed or securely fastened with safe accessible fuel shutoff control and capable of being safely operated in a seaway.	MoMu. 0,1,2,3
3.21	**Drinking Water Tanks & Drinking Water**	MoMu. 0,1,2,3
3.21.1	**Drinking Water Tanks**	MoMu. 0,1,2,3
a)	A yacht shall have a permanently installed delivery pump and water tank(s):	MoMu. 0,1,2,3
ii	dividing the water supply into at least two compartments	MoMu1
3.21.3	**Emergency Drinking Water**	MoMu. 0,1,2,3
a)	At least 9 litres (2 UK gallons, 2.4 US gallons) of drinking water for emergency use shall be provided in a dedicated and sealed container or container(s)	MoMu. 1,2,3
3.22	**Hand Holds**	
	Adequate hand holds shall be fitted below deck so that crew members may move about safely at sea.	**
	A hand hold should be capable of withstanding without rupture a side force of 1500N - attention is drawn to ISO 15085.	
3.23	**Bilge Pumps and Buckets**	
3.23.1	No bilge pump may discharge into a cockpit unless that cockpit opens aft to the sea.	**
3.23.2	Bilge pumps shall not be connected to cockpit drains. (OSR 3.09)	**
3.23.3	Bilge pumps and strum boxes shall be readily accessible for maintenance and for clearing out debris	**
3.23.4	Unless permanently installed, each bilge pump handle shall be provided with a lanyard or catch or similar device to prevent accidental loss	**
3.23.5	The following shall be provided:	
b)	one permanently installed manual bilge pump either above or below deck. The pump shall be operable with all cockpit seats, hatches and companionways shut and shall have a permanently installed discharge pipe.	Mu0,1,2
c)	multihulls shall have provision to pump out all watertight compartments (except those filled with impermeable buoyancy).	Mu0,1,2,3,4
f)	two buckets of stout construction each with at least 9 litres (2 UK gallons, 2.4 US gallons) capacity. Each bucket to have a lanyard.	**

		Category
3.24	**Compass**	
3.24.1	The following shall be provided:-	
a)	a marine magnetic compass, independent of any power supply, permanently installed and correctly adjusted with deviation card, and	**
b)	a magnetic compass independent of any power supply, capable of being used as a steering compass which may be hand-held	MoMu 0,1,2,3
3.25	**Halyards.**	
	No mast shall have less than two halyards, each capable of hoisting a sail.	**
Boom Support	***US SAILING prescribes that some means must exist to prevent the boom from dropping if support from the mainsail and/or halyard fails. Topping lifts or supporting vangs are acceptable for this purpose.***	**
3.27	**Navigation Lights (see OSR 2.03.3)**	
3.27.1	Navigation lights shall be mounted so that they will not be masked by sails or the heeling of the yacht.	**
3.27.2	Navigation lights shall not be mounted below deck level and should be at no less height than immediately under the upper lifeline.	**
3.27.3	Navigation light intensity	

TABLE 11

LOA	**Guide to required minimum power rating for an electric bulb in a navigation light**	
under 12 m (39.4 ft)	10 W	
12 m (39.4 ft) and above	25 W	

	US SAILING prescribes that in the US compliance with the recommendations of COLREGS shall suffice in satisfying these regulations. COLREGS requirements are as follows;	**

Table 14

LOA	*Light*	*Luminous Intensity*	*Minimum Range of Visibility*
under 39.4 ft	*Side*	*0.9 candelas*	*1 mile*
	Stern	*4.3 candelas*	*2 miles*
39.4 ft and above	*Side*	*4.3 candelas*	*2 miles*
and less than 164 ft	*Stern*	*4.3 candelas*	*2 miles*

		Category
3.27.4	Reserve navigation lights shall be carried having the same minimum specifications as the navigation lights above, with a separable power source, and wiring or supply system essentially separate from that used for the normal navigation lights	MoMu. 0,1,2,3
3.27.5	spare bulbs for navigation lights shall be carried, or for lights not dependent on bulbs, appropriate spares.	**
3.28	**Engines, Generators, Fuel**	
3.28.1	**Propulsion Engines**	**
a)	Engines and associated systems shall be installed in accordance with their manufacturers' guidelines and shall be of a type, strength, capacity, and installation suitable for the size and intended use of the yacht.	**
b)	An inboard propulsion engine when fitted shall: be provided with a permanently installed exhaust, coolant, and fuel supply systems and fuel tank(s); be securely covered; and have adequate protection from the effects of heavy weather.	**
c)	A propulsion engine required by Special Regulations shall provide a minimum speed in knots of (1.8 x square root of LWL in metres) or (square root of LWL in feet)	MoMu. 0,1,2,3
f)	Boats of less than 12.0 m hull length may be provided with an inboard propulsion engine, or an outboard engine together with permanently installed fuel supply systems and fuel tank(s) may be used as an alternative.	Mu1,2,3
3.28.2	**Generator**	
	A separate generator for electricity is optional. However, when a separate generator is carried it shall be permanently installed, securely covered, and shall have permanently installed exhaust, cooling and fuel supply systems and fuel tank(s), and have adequate protection from the effects of heavy weather.	**
3.28.3	**Fuel Systems**	
a)	Each fuel tank provided with a shutoff valve. Except for permanently installed linings or liners, a flexible tank is not permitted as a fuel tank.	MoMu. 0,1,2,3
b)	The propulsion engine shall have a minimum amount of fuel which may be specified in the Notice of Race but if not, shall be sufficient to be able to meet charging requirements for the duration of the race and to motor at the above minimum speed for at least 8 hours	MoMu. 0,1,2,3
3.28.4	**Battery Systems**	
a)	When an electric starter is the only method for starting the engine, the yacht shall have a separate battery, the primary purpose of which is to start the engine	MoMu. 0,1,2,3

		Category
b)	All rechargeable batteries on board shall be of the sealed type from which liquid electrolyte cannot escape. Other types of battery installed on board at 1/12 may continue in use for the remainder of their service lives.	MoMu. 0,1,2,3
3.29	**Communications Equipment, EPFS (Electronic Position-Fixing System), Radar, AIS**	**
	Provision of GMDSS and DSC is unlikely to be mandatory for small craft during the term of the present Special Regulations However it is recommended that persons in charge include these facilities when installing new equipment.	MoMu. 0,1,2,3
3.29.1	The following shall be provided:	**
a)	A marine radio transceiver (or if stated in the Notice of Race, an installed satcom terminal), and	MoMu. 0,1,2,3
i	an emergency antenna when the regular antenna depends upon the mast.	MoMu0,1,2,3
b)	When the marine radio transceiver is VHF:	MoMu0,1,2,3
i	it shall have a rated output power of 25W	MoMu0,1,2,3
ii	it shall have a masthead antenna, and co-axial feeder cable with not more than 40% power loss	MoMu. 0,1,2,3
iii	*the following types and lengths of co-axial feeder cable will meet the requirements of OSR 3.29.1 (b)(ii): (a) up to 15m (50ft) - type RG8X ("mini 8"); (b) 15-28m (50-90ft) - type RG8U; (c) 28-43m (90-140ft) - type 9913F (uses conventional connectors, available from US supplier Belden); (d) 43-70m) 140-230ft - type LMR600 (uses special connectors, available from US supplier Times Microwave).*	MoMu. 0,1,2,3
iv	*it should include channel 72 (an international ship-ship channel which, by common use, has become widely accepted as primary choice for ocean racing yachts anywhere in the world)*	MoMu. 0,1,2,3
e)	A hand-held marine VHF transceiver, watertight or with a waterproof cover. When not in use to be stowed in a grab bag or emergency container (see OSR 4.21)	MoMu. 1,2,3,4
f)	Independent of a main radio transceiver, a radio receiver capable of receiving weather bulletins	**
i)	An EPFS (Electronic Position-Fixing System) (e.g. GPS)	MoMu0,1,2,3
n)	An AIS Transponder	MoMu1,2
3.29.2	*Yachts are reminded that no reflector, active or passive, is a guarantee of detection or tracking by a vessel using radar.*	**
a)	*The attention of persons in charge is drawn to legislation in force or imminent affecting the territorial seas of some countries in which the carriage of an AIS set is or will be mandatory for certain vessels including relatively small craft.*	**

SECTION 4 - PORTABLE EQUIPMENT & SUPPLIES for the yacht
(for water & fuel see OSR 3.21 and OSR 3.28)

		Category
4.01	**Sail Letters & Numbers**	
4.01.1	Yachts which are not in an ISAF International Class or Recognized Class shall comply with RRS 77 and Appendix G as closely as possible, except that sail numbers allotted by a State authority are acceptable .	**
4.01.2	Sail numbers and letters of the size carried on the mainsail must be displayed by alternative means when none of the numbered sails is set.	**
4.02	***Hull marking (colour blaze)***	Mo0,1 Mu0,1,2,3,4
4.02.1	To assist in SAR location:-	
b)	*Each yacht is recommended to show at least 1 m^2 of fluorescent pink or orange or yellow colour as far as possible in a single area on the coachroof and/or deck where it can best be seen*	MoMu1
4.02.2	Multihulls shall show on the underside, where they can be seen when inverted, an solid area of highly-visible colour (e.g. Day-Glo pink, orange, or yellow) of at least 1m^2	Mu0,1,2,3,4
4.02.3	*Each yacht is recommended to show on each underwater appendage an area of highly-visible colour*	MoMu0,1
4.03	**Soft Wood Plugs**	
	Soft wood plugs, tapered and of the appropriate size, shall be attached or stowed adjacent to the appropriate fitting for every through-hull opening.	**
4.04	**Jackstays, Clipping Points and Static Safety Lines**	
4.04.1	The following shall be provided:	
a)	Jackstays:-	MoMu0,1,2,3
	shall be provided-	
i	attached to through-bolted or welded deck plates or other suitable and strong anchorage fitted on deck, port and starboard of the yacht's centre line to provide secure attachments for safety harness:-	MoMu0,1,2,3
ii	comprising stainless steel 1 x 19 wire of minimum diameter 5 mm (3/16 in), high modulus polyethylene (such as Dyneema/Spectra) rope or webbing of equivalent strength;	MoMu0,1,2,3
	US SAILING prescribes that wire jackstays (jacklines) may be of configurations other than 1 X 19.	

		Category
iii	which, when made from stainless steel wire shall be uncoated and used without any sleeving;	MoMu0,1,2,3
iv	*20kN (2,040 kgf or 4500 lbf) min breaking strain webbing is recommended;*	MoMu0,1,2,3
v	*at least two of which should be fitted on the underside of a multihull in case of inversion.*	Mu0,1,2,3
4.04.2	**Clipping Points:-**	
	shall be provided-	
a)	attached to through-bolted or welded deck plates or other suitable and strong anchorage points adjacent to stations such as the helm, sheet winches and masts, where crew members work for long periods:-	MoMu 0,1,2,3
b)	which, together with jackstays and static safety lines shall enable a crew member-	MoMu0,1,2,3
i	to clip on before coming on deck and unclip after going below;	MoMu0,1,2,3
ii	whilst continuously clipped on, to move readily between the working areas on deck and the cockpit(s) with the minimum of clipping and unclipping operations.	MoMu 0,1,2,3
c)	The provision of clipping points shall enable two-thirds of the crew to be simultaneously clipped on without depending on jackstays	MoMu 0,1,2,3
d)	In a trimaran with a rudder on the outrigger, adequate clipping points shall be provided that are not part of the deck gear or the steering mechanism, in order that the steering mechanism can be reached by a crew member whilst clipped on.	Mu 0,1,2,3
e)	*Warning - U-bolts as clipping points - see OSR 5.02.1(a)*	
4.05	**Fire Extinguishers**	
	Shall be provided as follows:	
4.05.1	Fire extinguishers, at least two, readily accessible in suitable and different parts of the yacht	**
4.05.2	Fire Extinguishers, at least two, of minimum 2kgs each of dry powder or equivalent	MoMu0,1,2,3
4.05.4	A fire blanket adjacent to every cooking device with an open flame	**
4.06	**Anchor(s)**	
4.06.1	An anchor or anchors shall be carried according to the table below:	**

TABLE 12 **

LOA	detail	race category
8.5 m (28 ft) and over	2 anchors together with a suitable combination of chain and rope, all ready for immediate use	MoMu1,2,3
under 8.5 m (28 ft)	1 anchor together with a suitable combination of chain and rope, all ready for immediate use	MoMu1,2,3

		Category
4.07	**Flashlight(s) and Searchlight(s)**	
4.07.1	The following shall be provided:-	
a)	A watertight, high-powered searchlight, suitable for searching for a person overboard at night and for collision avoidance with spare batteries and bulbs, and	**
b)	a watertight flashlight with spare batteries and bulb	**
4.08	**First Aid Manual and First Aid Kit**	**
4.08.1	A suitable First Aid Manual shall be provided	**
	In the absence of a National Authority's requirement, the latest edition of one of the following is recommended:-	**
a)	*International Medical Guide for Ships, World Health Organisation, Geneva*	MoMu0,1
c)	*Le Guide de la medecine a distance, by Docteur J Y Chauve, published by Distance Assistance BP33 F-La Baule, cedex, France.*	**
d)	*PAN-PAN medico bordo' in Italian edited by Umberto Verna, www.panpan.it*	MoMu2,3,4
e)	*Skipper's Medical Emergency Handbook by Dr Spike Briggs and Dr Campbell Mackenzie www.msos.org.uk*	**
	US SAILING endorses the above and additionally recommends the following manuals: Advanced First Aid by Peter Eastman, M.D., Cornell Maritime Press and A Comprehensive Guide to Marine Medicine by Eric A. Weiss, M.D. and Michael E. Jacobs, M.D., Adventure Medical Kit.	**
4.08.2	A First Aid Kit shall be provided	**
4.08.3	*The contents and storage of the First Aid Kit should reflect the guidelines of the Manual carried, the likely conditions and duration of the passage, and the number of people aboard the yacht.*	**
4.09	**Foghorn**	
	A foghorn shall be provided	**
4.10	**Radar Reflector**	
4.10.1	A passive Radar Reflector (that is, a Radar Reflector without any power) shall be provided	**
a)	If a radar reflector is:	**
i	octahedral with triangular plates making up each pocket it must have a minimum diagonal measurement of 456 mm (18in).	**
ii	octahederal with circular sector plates making up each pocket it must have a minimum diameter of 304mm (12in).	**
iii	not octahedral it must have a documented RCS (radar cross-section) of not less than 10 m2 at 0° elevation and be capable of performance around 360° in azimuth.	**

		Category
	US SAILING prescribes that in the US, radar reflectors shall have a minimum documented "equivalent echoing area" of 6 sq. m. Octahedral reflectors shall have a minimum diameter of 12 inches.	**
	The minimum effective height above water is 4.0 m (13 ft).	**
b)	*The passive and active devices referred to in these notes and in 4.10.1 and 4.10.2 above are primarily intended for use in the X (9GHz) band*	**
4.10.2	*The most effective radar response from a yacht may be provided by an RTE (Radar Target Enhancer) which may be on board in addition to the required passive reflector. An RTE should conform to ISO 8729-2:2009. An RTE is strongly recommended.*	MoMu 1,2,3,4
b)	*The display of a passive reflector or the operation of an RTE is for the person in charge to decide according to prevailing conditions.*	**
4.10.3	*When available, a passive radar reflector in compliance with ISO8729-1:2010 will offer improved performance over earlier models and has a size typified by a cylinder of not more than weight 5kg, height 750mm and diameter 300mm.*	**
4.10.4	*S (3GHz) band radar is often used by ships in bad weather to complement X (9GHz) band radar. On S (3GHz) band a passive reflector offers about 1/10 the response obtained on the X (9GHz) band. Unless specifically designed to operate in the S(3GHz) band, an RTE will provide no response at all.*	**
4.11	**Navigation Equipment**	
4.11.1	Charts	
	Navigational charts (not solely electronic), light list and chart plotting equipment shall be provided	**
4.11.2	*Reserve Navigation System*	
	Navigators are recommended to carry a sextant with suitable tables and a timepiece or an adequate reserve navigation system so that total reliance is not placed on dead-reckoning and a single form of EPFS (Electronic Position-Fixing System) (see Volpe Report at www.navcen.uscg.gov/archive/2001/Oct/FinalReport-v4.6.pdf)	MoMu0,1
4.12	**Safety Equipment Location Chart**	
	A safety equipment location chart in durable waterproof material shall be displayed in the main accommodation where it can best be seen, clearly marked with the location of principal items of safety equipment.	**
4.13	**Echo Sounder or Lead Line**	
4.13.1	An echo sounder or lead line shall be provided	MoMu 1,2,3,4
4.13	**Echo Sounder or Lead Line**	
4.13.1	An echo sounder or lead line shall be provided	MoMu 1,2,3,4

		Category
4.14	**Speedometer or Distance Measuring Instrument (log)**	
	A speedometer or distance measuring instrument (log) shall be provided	MoMu0,1,2,3
4.15	**Emergency Steering**	
4.15.1	Emergency steering shall be provided as follows:	
a)	except when the principal method of steering is by means of an unbreakable metal tiller, an emergency tiller capable of being fitted to the rudder stock;	MoMu 0,1,2,3
b)	crews must be aware of alternative methods of steering the yacht in any sea condition in the event of rudder loss. At least one method must have been proven to work on board the yacht. An inspector may require that this method be demonstrated.	MoMu 0,1,2,3
4.16	**Tools and Spare Parts**	
	Tools and spare parts, including effective means to quickly disconnect or sever the standing rigging from the hull shall be provided.	**
4.17	**Yacht's name**	
	Yacht's name shall be on miscellaneous buoyant equipment, such as lifejackets, cushions, lifebuoys, lifeslings, grab bags etc.	**
4.18	**Marine grade retro-reflective material**	
	Marine grade retro-reflective material shall be fitted to lifebuoys, lifeslings, liferafts and lifejackets. See OSRs 5.04, 5.08.	**
4.14	**EPIRBs**	
4.19.1	A 406 MHz EPIRB shall be provided	MoMu1,2
b)	*It is recommended that a 406 MHz EPIRB should include an internal GPS, and also a 121.5MHz transmitter for local homing.*	MoMu 0,1,2
c)	Every 406 MHz EPIRB shall be properly registered with the appropriate authority.	MoMu 0,1,2
d)	Every ship's 406 MHz EPIRB shall be water and manually activated.	MoMu0,1,2
e)	*EPIRBs should be tested in accordance with manufacturer's instructions when first commissioned and then at least annually.*	MoMu 0,1,2
f)	*A list of registration numbers of 406 EPIRBs should be notified to event organizers and kept available for immediate use.*	MoMu 0,1,2
g)	*Consideration should be given to the provision of a locator device (eg an "Argos" beacon) operating on non - SAR frequencies, to aid salvage if a yacht is abandoned.*	MoMu 0,1,2
h)	*Beacons with only 121.5MHz are no longer recommended for distress alerting. Satellite processing of 121.5 MHz is being phased out. 121.5MHz will continue to be used for local homing by on-board D/F systems and for local homing by SAR units. Type "E" EPIRBs are no longer supported and should be replaced immediately.*	MoMu 0,1,2

		Category
i)	*See OSR 3.29.1(e) for on-board D/F and OSR 5.07.1(b) for personal EPIRBs (PLBs)*	MoMu0
	US SAILING requires the use of 406 EPIRBs (with or without GPS input), as USCG advises that rescue efforts will be launched immediately upon receipt of a distress signal from these units. USCG also advises that some PLB and INMARSAT "E" transmissions are not monitored by U.S. Rescue Coordination Centers and that slight delays are likely to occur while the commercial ground stations forward an alert to the USCG.	MoMu 0,1,2
4.20	**Liferafts**	MoMu 0,1,2
4.20.1	**Liferaft Construction and Packed Equipment**	
4.20.2	Liferaft(s) shall be provided capable of carrying the whole crew when each liferaft shall comply with either:-	MoMu1,2
a)	Liferafts shall comply with SOLAS LSA code 1997 Chapter IV or later version except that they are acceptable with a capacity of 4 persons and may be packed in a valise. A SOLAS liferaft shall contain at least a SOLAS "A" pack or	MoMu1,2
b)	***for liferafts manufactured prior to January 2003 (1/06 in the U.S.) OSR Appendix A part I (ORC), or***	MoMu1,2
c)	OSR Appendix A part II (ISAF) when, unless otherwise specified by a race organizer, the floor shall include thermal insulation, or	MoMu1,2
d)	ISO 9650 Part I Type I Group A (ISO) when each liferaft shall contain at least a Pack 2 (<24h) and	MoMu1,2
i	shall have a semi-rigid boarding ramp, and	MoMu1,2
ii	shall be so arranged that any high-pressure hose shall not impede the boarding process, and	MoMu1,2
iii	shall have a topping-up means provided for any inflatable boarding ramp, and	MoMu1,2
iv	when the liferaft is designed with a single ballast pocket this shall be accepted provided the liferaft otherwise complies with ISO 9650 and meets a suitable test of ballast pocket strength devised by the manufacturer and	MoMu1,2
v	compliance with OSR 4.20.2 (d) i-iv shall be indicated on the liferaft certificate.	MoMu1,2
	US SAILING recommends that liferafts be equipped with insulated floors for events that take place in waters of less than 68 deg F (20deg C).	MoMu1,2
	US SAILING prescribes that liferafts shall be equipped with canopies.	MoMu1,2

		Category
4.20.3	**Liferaft Packing and Stowage**	MoMu0,1,2
	A Liferaft shall be either:-	MoMu0,1,2
a)	packed in a transportable rigid container or canister and stowed on the working deck or in the cockpit, or:-	MoMu 0,1,2
b)	packed in a transportable rigid container or canister or in a valise and stowed in a purpose-built rigid compartment containing liferaft(s) only and opening into or adjacent to the cockpit or working deck, or through a transom, provided that:-	MoMu 0,1,2
i	each compartment is watertight or self-draining (self-draining compartments will be counted as part of the cockpit volume except when entirely above working deck level or when draining independently overboard from a transom stowage - see OSR 3.09) and-	MoMu 0,1,2
ii	the cover of each compartment is capable of being easily opened under water pressure, and-	MoMu 0,1,2
iii	the compartment is designed and built to allow a liferaft to be removed and launched quickly and easily, or-	MoMu 0,1,2
iv	in a yacht with age or series date before June 2001, a liferaft may be packed in a valise not exceeding 40kg securely stowed below deck adjacent to a companionway.	MoMu 1,2
v	Liferaft stowage on a multihull shall be such that each liferaft may be readily removed and launched whether or not the yacht is inverted.	Mu 0,1,2
c)	The end of each liferaft painter should be permanently made fast to a strong point on board the yacht.	MoMu 0,1,2
4.20.4	**Liferaft Launching**	MoMu0,1,2
a)	Each raft shall be capable of being got to the lifelines or launched within 15 seconds.	MoMu 0,1,2
b)	*Each liferaft of more than 40kg weight should be stowed in such a way that the liferaft can be dragged or slid into the sea without significant lifting*	MoMu 0,1,2
4.20.5	**Liferaft Servicing and Inspection**	MoMu0,1,2
	IMPORTANT NOTICE Recent evidence has shown that packaged liferafts are vulnerable to serious damage when dropped (eg from a boat onto a marina pontoon) or when subjected to the weight of a crew member or heavy object (eg an anchor). Damage can be caused internally by the weight of the heavy steel CO2 bottle abrading or splitting neighbouring layers of buoyancy tube material. ISAF has instituted an investigation into this effect and as an interim measure requires that every valise-packed liferaft shall have an annual certificate of servicing. A liferaft should be taken for servicing if there is any sign of damage or deterioration (including on the underside of the pack). Persons in charge should insist on great care in handling liferafts and apply the rules NO STEP and DO NOT DROP UNLESS LAUNCHING INTO THE SEA.	MoMu 0,1,2

		Category
a)	Certificates or copies, of servicing and/or inspection shall be kept on board the yacht. Every SOLAS liferaft and every valise-packed liferaft shall have a valid annual certificate of new or serviced status from the manufacturer or his approved service station.	MoMu 0,1,2
b)	A liferaft built to OSR Appendix A part I ("ORC") packed in a rigid container or canister shall either be serviced annually or may, when the manufacturer so specifies, be inspected annually (not necessarily unpacked) provided the yacht has on board written confirmation from the manufacturer's approved service station stating that the inspection was satisfactory.	MoMu 0,1,2
c)	A liferaft built to OSR Appendix A part II ("ISAF") packed in a rigid container or canister shall either be serviced annually or may, when the manufacturer so specifies, have its first service no longer than 3 years after commissioning and its second service no longer than 2 years after the first. Subsequent services shall be at intervals of not more than 12 months.	MoMu 1,2
d)	A liferaft built to ISO 9650 Part 1 Type Group A, packed in a rigid container or canister shall be serviced in accordance with the manufacturer's instructions but NOT less frequently than every three years	MoMu 1,2
e)	A liferaft built to ISO 9650 Part 1 Type Group A packed in a valise shall be inspected annually by an approved manufacturer's agent and serviced in accordance with the manufacturer's instructions but NOT less frequently than every three years.	MoMu 1,2
f)	Liferaft servicing certificates shall state the specification that the liferaft was built to. See OSR 4.20.2	MoMu 1,2
4.21.2	***Grab Bags to Accompany Liferafts***	
a)	*A yacht is recommended to have for each liferaft, a grab bag with the following minimum contents. A grab bag should have inherent flotation, at least 0.1 m^2 area of fluorescent orange colour on the outside, should be marked with the name of the yacht, and should have a lanyard and clip.*	MoMu 0,1,2
b)	*Note: it is not intended to duplicate in a grab bag items required by other OSRs to be on board the yacht - these recommendations cover only the stowage of those items*	MoMu 0,1,2
4.21.3	***Grab Bag Recommended Contents***	
a)	*2 red parachute and 2 red hand flares and cyalume-type chemical light sticks (red flares compliant with SOLAS)*	MoMu1,2
b)	*watertight hand-held EPFS (Electronic Position-Fixing System) (eg GPS) in at least one of the grab bags carried by a yacht*	MoMu1,2
c)	*SART (Search and Rescue Transponder) in at least one of the grab bags carried by a yacht*	MoMu1,2
d)	*a combined 406MHz/121.5MHz or type "E" EPIRB (see OSR 4.19.1) in at least one of the grab bags carried by a yacht*	MoMu1,2

		Category
e)	*water in re-sealable containers or a hand-operated desalinator plus containers for water*	MoMu1,2
f)	*a watertight hand-held marine VHF transceiver plus a spare set of batteries*	MoMu0,1,2
g)	*a watertight flashlight with spare batteries and bulb*	MoMu0,1,2
h)	*dry suits or thermal protective aids or survival bags*	
i)	*second sea anchor for the liferaft (not required if the liferaft has already a spare sea anchor in its pack) (recommended standard ISO 17339) with swivel and >30m line diameter >9.5 mm*	MoMu0,1,2
j)	*two safety tin openers (if appropriate)*	MoMu0,1,2
k)	*first-aid kit including at least 2 tubes of sunscreen. All dressings should be capable of being effectively used in wet conditions. The first-aid kit should be clearly marked and re-sealable*	MoMu0,1,2
l)	*signalling mirror*	MoMu0,1,2
m)	*high-energy food (min 10 000kJ per person recommended for Cat Zero)*	MoMu0,1,2
n)	*nylon string, polythene bags, seasickness tablets (min 6 per person recommended)*	MoMu0,1,2
o)	*watertight hand-held aviation VHF transceiver (if race area warrants)*	MoMu0,1,2
4.22	**Lifebuoys**	
4.22.1	***The following shall be provided within easy reach of the helmsman and ready for instant use:***	**
a)	a lifebuoy with a self-igniting light and a drogue or a Lifesling with a self-igniting light and without a drogue.	**
	For Categories 0,1,2,3 US SAILING prescribes that the lifebuoy in OSR 4.22.1 a) above shall be a Lifesling (without a drogue), equipped with a self-igniting light within easy reach of the helmsman and ready for instant use. (See Appendix D).	MoMu 0,1,2,3
b)	***In addition to a) above, one lifebuoy within easy reach of the helmsman and ready for instant use, equipped with:***	MoMu 0,1,2
i	a whistle, a drogue, a self-igniting light and	MoMu 0,1,2
ii	a pole and flag. The pole shall be either permanently extended or be capable of being fully automatically extended (not extendable by hand) in less than 20 seconds. It shall be attached to the lifebuoy with 3 m (10 ft) of floating line and is to be of a length and so ballasted that the flag will fly at least 1.8 m (6 ft) off the water.	MoMu 0,1,2
4.22.2	When at least two lifebuoys (and/or Lifeslings) are carried, at least one of them shall depend entirely on permanent (eg foam) buoyancy.	MoMu 0,1,2

		Category
4.22.3	Each inflatable lifebuoy and any automatic device (eg pole and flag extended by compressed gas) shall be tested and serviced at intervals in accordance with its manufacturer's instructions.	**
4.22.4	Each lifebuoy or lifesling shall be fitted with marine grade retro-reflective material (4.18).	**
4.22.5	*It is recommended that the colour of each lifebuoy be a safety colour in the yellow-red range.*	**
4.23	**Pyrotechnic and Light Signals**	
4.22.5	Pyrotechnic signals shall be provided conforming to SOLAS LSA Code Chapter III Visual Signals and not older than the stamped expiry date (if any) or if no expiry date stamped , not older than 4 years.	**

TABLE 13

red parachute flares LSA III 3.1	red hand flares LSA III 3.2	orange smoke LSA III 3.3	race category
6	4	2	MoMu0,1
4	4	2	MoMu2,3

4.24	**Heaving Line**	**
a)	a heaving line shall be provided 15 m - 25 m (50 ft - 75 ft) length readily accessible to cockpit.	**
b)	*the "throwing sock" type is recommended - see Appendix D*	**
	US SAILING prescribes that the heaving line be of 1/4 in. (6 mm) minimum diameter, floating, UV-inhibited and readily accessible to the cockpit.	**
4.25	**Cockpit Knife**	
	A strong, sharp knife, sheathed and securely restrained shall be provided readily accessible from the deck or a cockpit.	**
4.26	**Storm & Heavy Weather Sails**	
4.26.1	*Design*	
a)	***it is strongly recommended that persons in charge consult their designer and sailmaker to decide the most effective size for storm and heavy weather sails. The purpose of these sails is to provide safe propulsion for the yacht in severe weather -they are not intended as part of the racing inventory. The areas below are maxima. Smaller areas are likely to suit some yachts according to their stability and other characteristics.***	**

		Category
4.26.2	**High Visibility**	
a)	Every storm jib shall either be of highly-visible coloured material (eg dayglo pink, orange or yellow) or have a highly-visible coloured patch at least 50% of the area of the sail (up to a maximum diameter of 3m) added on each side; and also that a rotating wing mast should have a highly-visible coloured patch on each side. A storm sail purchased after January 2014 shall have the material of the body of the sail a highly-visible colour.	
4.26.3	**Materials**	
a)	aromatic polyamides, carbon and similar fibres shall not be used in a trysail or storm jib but spectra/dyneema and similar materials are permitted.	**
b)	*it is strongly recommended that a heavy-weather jib does not contain aromatic polyamides, carbon and similar fibres other than spectra/dyneema.*	**
4.26.4	**The following shall be provided:-**	
a)	sheeting positions on deck for each storm and heavy-weather sail;	**
b)	for each storm or heavy-weather jib, a means to attach the luff to the stay, independent of any luff-groove device. A heavy weather jib shall have the means of attachment readily available. A storm jib shall have the means of attachment permanently attached;	**
	Storm and heavy weather jib areas shall be calculated as: (0.255 x luff length x (luff perpendicular + 2 x half width))* To apply to sails made in January 2012 and after.	
c)	a storm trysail which shall be capable of being sheeted independently of the boom with trysail area not greater than 17.5% mainsail hoist (P) x mainsail foot length (E). The storm trysail area shall be measured as (0.5 x leech length x shortest distance between tack point and leech). The storm trysail shall have neither headboard nor battens, however a storm trysail is not required in a yacht with a rotating wing mast which can adequately substitute for a trysail. The method of calculating area applies to sails made in January 2012 and after.	MoMu0,1,2
	US SAILING prescribes that a storm trysail shall be capable of being attached to the mast.	MoMu0,1,2
d)	the storm trysail as required by OSR 4.26.4 (c) shall have the yacht's sail number and letter(s) shall be placed on both sides of the trysail (or on a rotating wing mast as substitute for a trysail) in as large a size as practicable;	MoMu0,1,2
e)	a storm jib of area not greater than 5% height of the foretriangle squared, with luff maximum length 65% height of the foretriangle;	MoMu0,1,2
f)	***in addition to the storm jib required by OSR 4.26.4 (e), a heavy-weather jib (or heavy-weather sail in a yacht with no forestay) of area not greater than 13.5% height of the foretriangle squared;***	**

		Category
g)	either a storm trysail as defined in OSR 4.26.4(c), or mainsail reefing to reduce the luff by at least 40%	Mu2
h)	in the case of a yacht with an in-mast furling mainsail, the storm trysail must be capable of being set while the mainsail is furled.	MoMu0,1,2
i)	*A trysail track should allow for the trysail to be hoisted quickly when the mainsail is lowered whether or not the mainsail is stowed on the main boom.*	MoMu0,1,2
	It is strongly recommended that a boat has either a dedicated trysail track permanently installed with the entry point accessible to a person standing on the main deck or coachroof, or a permanently installed stay on which to hank the trysail.	
k)	*It is strongly recommended that an inner forestay is provided either permanently installed or readily set up, on which to set the storm jib.*	MoMu0,1,2
	In addition, US SAILING prescribes mainsail reefing to reduce the luff by at least 10% for sails built after 1 January 1997.	MoMu 0,1,2,3

Figure 3

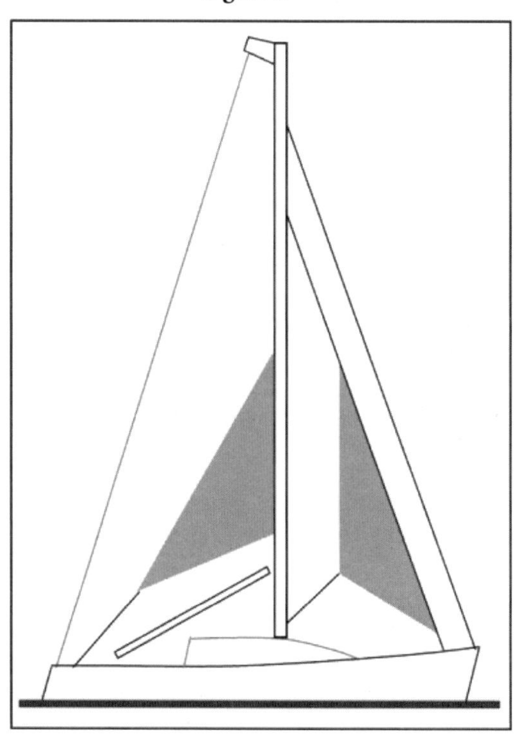

		Category
4.27	**Drogue, Sea Anchor**	MoMu0,1
4.27.1	*A drogue for deployment over the stern, or alternatively a sea anchor or parachute anchor for deployment over the bow, complete with all gear needed to rig and deploy the sea anchor or drogue, is strongly recommended to withstand long periods in rough conditions (see Appendix F)*	MoMu1
4.28	**Man Overboard Alarm**	
4.28.3	A yacht shall be equipped with an EPFS (e.g. GPS) capable of immediately recording a man overboard position from each helm station (From January 2012)	MoMu1, 2

SECTION 5 - PERSONAL EQUIPMENT

5.01	**Lifejacket**	
	US SAILING prescribes for Categories 0,1,2,and 3: either a lifejacket defined in OSR 5.01.1 (See Note 1), or a USCG approved Type I non-inflatable personal flotation device (PFD), or a USCG approved yoke-type inflatable with 33lb (150N) or greater buoyancy with or without crotch strap, face guard, or buddy line. Each inflatable PFD shall be inflated and inspected annually. Service dates shall be marked on each PFD. It is recommended that all inflatable PFDs be integrated with safety harnesses (see OSR 5.02) (See Note 2).	MoMu 0,1,2,3
US SAILING Note 1:	***ISO 12402 is not currently approved by the USCG. Boats operating in US waters are not exempt from USCG requirements.***	MoMu 0,1,2,3
US SAILING Note 2:	***Many inflatable PFD's with built-in harnesses are designed for people greater than 5' 5" in height and are potentially dangerous if you are below that height.***	MoMu 0,1,2,3
US SAILING Note 3:	***Inflatable PFDs with the required buoyancy will generally have inflation cylinders containing 33g or more of CO2.***	MoMu 0,1,2,3
US SAILING Note 4:	***"Yoke-type" is defined as a PFD that is designed to keep its wearer face-up and head-up in the water and that provides buoyancy in front of the chest and behind the neck immediately when inflated***	MoMu 0,1,2,3
5.01.1	Each crew member shall have a lifejacket as follows:-	**
a)		**
i	In accordance with ISO 12402 – 3 (Level 150) or equivalent, including EN 396 or UL 1180	**

		Category
ii	Lifejackets manufactured after 1 January 2012 shall be in accordance with ISO 12402–3 (Level 150) and shall be fitted with: • an emergency light in accordance with either ISO 12402-8 or SOLAS LSA code 2.2.3. • a sprayhood in accordance with ISO 12402-8. • a full deck safety harness in accordance with ISO 12401 (ISO 1095) including a crotch or thigh strap (holding down device) as specified in ISO 12401 (ISO 1095). • If of an inflatable type either: (a) automatic, manual and oral inflation or (b) manual and oral inflation	
Notes:	ISO 12402 requires Level 150 lifejackets to be fitted with a mandatory whistle and retro-reflective material. Also, when fitted with a safety harness, ISO 12402 requires that this shall be the full safety harness in accordance with ISO 12401. Any equivalent lifejacket shall have equal requirements. Persons of larger than average build are generally more buoyant than those of average build and so do not require a lifejacket with greater levels of flotation. Wearing a Level 275 lifejacket may hamper entry into liferafts.	
b)	fitted with either a crotch strap(s) / thigh straps or a full safety harness in accordance with ISO 12401,	**
Note:	The function of lifejacket crotch/thigh straps is to hold the buoyancy element down. A crew member before a race should adjust a lifejacket to fit then retain that lifejacket for the duration of the race. Correct adjustment is fundamental to the lifejacket functioning correctly.	
c)	fitted with a lifejacket light in accordance with SOLAS LSA code 2.2.3 (white, >0.75 candelas, >8 hours),	**
d)	if inflatable have a compressed gas inflation system,	**
e)	if inflatable, regularly checked for gas retention,	**
f)	compatible with the wearer's safety harness,	**
g)	clearly marked with the yacht's or wearer's name,	**
	It is strongly recommended that a lifejacket has:	
j)	*a splashguard / sprayhood See ISO 12402 – 8,*	MoMu 1,2,3,4
k)	*a PLB unit (as with other types of EPIRB, should be properly registered with the appropriate authority)*	MoMu 1,2,3,4
l)	*if of a gas inflatable type, a spare cylinder and if appropriate a spare activation head*	**
	US SAILING prescribes that all personnel on deck shall wear properly fitted personal floatation while starting and finishing. At other times during the race, floatation shall be worn on deck except when the Captain of the boat directs that it may be set aside.	MoMu 1,2,3,4

		Category
5.01.4	The person in charge shall personally check each lifejacket at least once annually.	**
US SAILING Note:	***As is true of all of these regulations, the prescriptions above do not necessarily replace the requirements of other governing authorities.***	**
5.02	**Safety Harness and Safety Lines (Tethers)**	**
5.02.1	Each crew member shall have a harness and safety line that complies with ISO 12401 or equivalent with a safety line not more than 2m in length.	MoMu 0,1,2,3
	Harnesses and safety lines manufactured prior to Jan 2010 shall comply with either ISO 12401 or EN 1095.	MoMu 0,1,2,3
	Harnesses and safety lines manufactured prior to Jan 2001 are not permitted.	
	US Sailing prescribes that harnesses and safety lines manufactured prior to Jan 2001 are not recommended in the U.S.	**
a)	*Warning it is possible for a plain snaphook to disengage from a U bolt if the hook is rotated under load at right-angles to the axis of the U-bolt. For this reason the use of snaphooks with positive locking devices is strongly recommended.*	
5.02.2	At least 30% of the crew shall each, in addition to the above be provided with either:-	MoMu 0,1,2,3
a)	a safety line not more than 1m long, or	MoMu 0,1,2,3
b)	a mid-point snaphook on a 2m safety line	MoMu 0,1,2,3
5.02.3	A safety line purchased in January 2001 or later shall have a coloured flag embedded in the stitching, to indicate an overload. A line which has been overloaded shall be replaced as a matter of urgency.	MoMu 0,1,2,3
5.02.4	A crew member's lifejacket and harness shall be compatible	MoMu 0,1,2,3
	US SAILING prescribes that the safety harness may be integrated with an inflatable personal floatation device (see OSR 5.01) and recommends that such devices be employed whenever conditions warrant, and always in rough weather, on cold water, or at night, or under conditions of reduced visibility or when sailing short-handed.	MoMu 0,1,2,3
	US SAILING prescribes that safety harnesses and PFD's shall be worn on Category 0 and 1 races from sundown to sun up while on deck.	MoMu0,1
5.02.5	It is strongly recommended that:-	MoMu 0,1,2,3
a)	static safety lines should be securely fastened at work stations;	MoMu 0,1,2,3

		Category
b)	A harness should be fitted with a crotch strap or thigh straps. Crotch straps or thigh straps together with related fittings and fixtures should be strong enough to lift the wearer from the water.	MoMu 0,1,2,3
c)	to draw attention to wear and damage, stitching on harness and safety lines should be of a colour contrasting strongly with the surrounding material;	MoMu 0,1,2,3
d)	snaphooks should be of a type which will not self-release from a U-bolt (see OSR 5.02.1(a)) and which can be easily released under load (crew members are reminded that a personal knife may free them from a safety line in emergency);	MoMu 0,1,2,3
e)	a crew member before a race should adjust a harness to fit then retain that harness for the duration of the race.	MoMu 0,1,2,3
5.02.6	Warning - a safety line and safety harness are not designed to tow a person in the water and it is important that the shortest safety line length possible be used with a harness to minimise or eliminate the risk of a person's torso becoming immersed in water outside the boat, especially when working on the foredeck. 1m safety lines or the midpoint snaphook on a 2m line should be used for this purpose. The diligent use of a properly adjusted safety harness and the shortest safety line practicable is regarded as by far the most effective way of preventing man overboard incidents.preventing man overboard incidents.	**
5.04	**Foul Weather Suits**	
b)	*it is recommended that a foul weather suit should be fitted with marine-grade retro-reflective material, and should have high-visibility colours on its upper parts and sleeve cuffs.See OSR 4.18*	**
5.07	**Survival Equipment**	
d)	*Attention is drawn to the value of keeping on the person a combined 406MHz/121.5MHz PLB when on deck: this may aid location in a man overboard incident independent of the equipment carried by the parent vessel.*	MoMu 0,1,2
e)	*All PLB units, as with other types of EPIRB, should be properly registered with the appropriate authority.*	MoMu 0,1,2
5.07.2	*It is strongly recommended that an immersion suit should be supplied to each crew member in a multihull in conditions where there is a potential for hypothermia*	Mu 1,2,3,4
	US SAILING prescribes that an immersion suit as specified above for each crew member is strongly recommended above latitude 30.	Mu1,2
5.09	***Annual Man-Overboard Practice***	

		Category
	US SAILING prescribes that the "Quick-Stop" man-overboard procedure shall be practiced aboard the yacht at least once annually. A certificate of such practice shall be signed by participating crew members and kept aboard the yacht.	**
5.11	***Preventer or Boom Restraining Device***	
	US SAILING recommends that a preventer or boom restraining device should be rigged in such a manner that attachment can be easily and quickly made, with the boom fully extended (running) without leaving the deck or leaning overboard. A process and plan for its use should be part of the crew's training and practice. Recommended for all boats in all categories.	**
	SECTION 6 - TRAINING	
6.01	**At least 30% but not fewer than two members of a crew, including the skipper shall have undertaken training within the five years before the start of the race in both 6.02 topics for theoretical sessions, and 6.03 topics which include practical, hands-on sessions.**	MoMu 1,2
6.01.3	*It is strongly recommended that all crew members should undertake training as in OSR 6.01 at least once every five years*	MoMu 1,2
6.01.4	Except as otherwise provided in the Notice of Race, an in-date certificate gained at an ISAF Approved Offshore Personal Survival Training course shall be accepted by a race organizing authority as evidence of compliance with Special Regulation 6.01. See Appendix G - Model Training Course, for further details.	MoMu 0,1,2
6.02	**Training Topics for Theoretical Sessions**	
6.02.1	care and maintenance of safety equipment	MoMu0,1,2
6.02.2	storm sails	MoMu0,1,2
6.02.3	damage control and repair	MoMu0,1,2
6.02.4	heavy weather - crew routines, boat handling, drogues	MoMu0,1,2
6.02.5	man overboard prevention and recovery	MoMu0,1,2
6.02.6	giving assistance to other craft	MoMu0,1,2
6.02.7	hypothermia	MoMu0,1,2
6.02.8	SAR organisation and methods	MoMu0,1,2
6.02.9	weather forecasting	MoMu0,1,2
	US SAILING prescribes that training under this regulation (OSR 6.02) shall take place in a program that is approved by US SAILING and that shall require a minimum of 8 hours. Competetitors who are members of other National Governing Bodies may demonstrate that they have completed such training in accordance with the requirements of those organizations.	MoMu0,1,2

		Category
6.03	**Training Topics for Practical, Hands-On Sessions**	MoMu0,1,2
6.03.1	liferafts and lifejackets	MoMu0,1,2
6.03.2	fire precautions and use of fire extinguishers	MoMu0,1,2
6.03.3	communications equipment (VHF, GMDSS, satcomms, etc.)	MoMu0,1,2
6.03.4	pyrotechnics and EPIRBs	MoMu0,1,2
	US SAILING prescribes that each skipper in a Category 0 ,1 or 2 race shall ensure that a minimum of 30 percent of the crew have been trained in the use of the boat's equipment, including: liferafts and lifejackets; communications; pyrotechnics; EPIRBs; and fire prevention and fire fighting. A record of this training shall be kept aboard the boat in a manner similar to that required for certifying man-overboard training.	MoMu0,1,2
6.04	***Routine Training On-Board***	
6.04.1	*It is recommended that crews should practice safety routines at reasonable intervals including the drill for man-overboard recovery*	**
6.05	**Medical Training**	
6.05.2	At least two members of the crew	MoMu1
	At least one member of the crew	MoMu2
	shall have a first aid certificate completed within the last five years meeting any of the following requirements:	
i	A certificate listed on the ISAF website www.sailing.org/specialregs of MNA recognised courses	
US SAILING Note	***MNA recogized First Aid & CPR courses in the U.S. are posted at http://offshore.ussailing.org/SAS/Senior_First_Aid_Certification.htm.***	**
ii	STCW 95 First Aid Training complying with A-VI/1-3 – Elementary First Aid or higher STCW level	
	US SAILING recommends that at least two members of the crew be currently certified in cardiopulmonary resuscitation.	**
6.05.4	*An example model first aid training course is included in Appendix N.*	**

APPENDIX M
HULL CONSTRUCTION STANDARDS (SCANTLINGS)
(Monohulls pre-2010 and Multihulls)

		Category
M.1	A monohull with the earliest of Age or Series Date before the 1 January 2010 shall comply with OSR 3.03.1, 3.03.2 and 3.03.3 or with this appendix. A multihull shall comply with this appendix.	MoMu0,1,2
	Table 2	MoMu0,1,2

LOA	earliest of age or series date	race category
all	January 1986 and after	MoMu0,1
12m (39.4 feet) and over	January 1987 and after	MoMu2
under 12m (39.4 feet)	January 1988 and after	MoMu2

(Category: MoMu0,1,2)

M.2	A yacht defined in the table above shall have been designed built, maintained, modified and repaired in accordance with the requirements of either:	MoMu0,1,2
a)	the EC Recreational Craft Directive for Category A (having obtained the CE mark), or	MoMu0,1,2
b)	the ABS Guide for Building and Classing Offshore Yachts in which case the yacht shall have on board either a certificate of plan approval issued by ABS, or written statements signed by the designer and builder which confirm that they have respectively designed and built the yacht in accordance with the ABS Guide,	MoMu0,1,2
c)	ISO 12215 Category A, with written statements signed by the designer and builder which confirm that they have respectively designed and built the yacht in accordance with the ISO standard,	MoMu0,1,2
d)	except that a race organizer or class rules may accept when that described in (a), (b), or (c) above is not available, the signed statement by a naval architect or other person familiar with the standards listed above that the yacht fulfills the requirements of (a), (b), or (c).	MoMu0,1,2
M.3	Any significant repairs or modifications to the hull, deck, coachroof, keel or appendages, on a yacht defined in table 2 shall be certified by one of the methods above and an appropriate written statement or statements shall be on board.	MoMu0,1,2

ISAF Offshore Special Regulations Requirements for Multihull Sailboats

Including US SAILING Prescriptions

www.offshore.ussailing.org

Extract for Race Category 3 and 4 Multihulls

JANUARY 2012 - DECEMBER 2013

US Version 3Mu and 4Mu - 2012

Because this is an extract not all paragraph numbers will be present

Language & Abbreviations Used

Mo - Monohull

Mu - Multihull

" ** " means the item applies to all types of yacht in all Categories except 5 or 6 for which see Appendix J or L.

A side bar indicates a significant change in 2012

US SAILING extract files are available for individual categories and boat types (monohulls and multihulls) at http://offshore.ussailing.org/SAS/ISAF_Special_Regulations/Extracts.htm

US SAILING prescriptions are printed in bold, italic letters

ISAF guidance notes and recommendations are printed in italics

The use of the masculine gender shall be taken to mean either gender

SECTION 1 - FUNDAMENTAL AND DEFINITIONS

		Category
1.01	**Purpose and Use**	
1.01.1	It is the purpose of these Special Regulations to establish uniform minimum equipment, accommodation and training standards for monohull and multihull yachts racing offshore. A Proa is excluded from these regulations.	**
1.01.2	These Special Regulations do not replace, but rather supplement, the requirements of governmental authority, the Racing Rules and the rules of Class Associations and Rating Systems. The attention of persons in charge is called to restrictions in the Rules on the location and movement of equipment.	**
1.01.3	These Special Regulations, adopted internationally, are strongly recommended for use by all organizers of offshore races. Race Committees may select the category deemed most suitable for the type of race to be sailed.	**

		Category
1.02	**Responsibility of Person in Charge**	
1.02.1	The safety of a yacht and her crew is the sole and inescapable responsibility of the person in charge who must do his best to ensure that the yacht is fully found, thoroughly seaworthy and manned by an experienced crew who have undergone appropriate training and are physically fit to face bad weather. He must be satisfied as to the soundness of hull, spars, rigging, sails and all gear. He must ensure that all safety equipment is properly maintained and stowed and that the crew know where it is kept and how it is to be used. He shall also nominate a person to take over the responsibilities of the Person in Charge in the event of his incapacitation.	**
1.02.2	Neither the establishment of these Special Regulations, their use by race organizers, nor the inspection of a yacht under these Special Regulations in any way limits or reduces the complete and unlimited responsibility of the person in charge.	**
1.02.3	**Decision to race -The responsibility for a yacht's decision to participate in a race or to continue racing is hers alone - RRS Fundamental Rule 4.**	**
1.03	**Definitions, Abbreviations, Word Usage**	
1.03.1	Definitions of Terms used in this document	**

TABLE 1	
Age Date	Month/year of first launch
AIS	Automatic Identification Systems
CEN	Comité Européen de Normalisation
CPR	Cardio-Pulmonary Resuscitation
Coaming	includes the transverse after limit of the cockpit over which water would run in the event that when the yacht is floating level the cockpit is flooded or filled to overflowing.
DSC	Digital Selective Calling
EN	European Norm
EPFS	Electronic Position-Fixing System
EPIRB	Emergency Position-Indicating Radio Beacon
FA Station	The transverse station at which the upper corner of the transom meets the sheerline.
Foul-Weather Suit	A foul weather suit is clothing designed to keep the wearer dry and maybe either a jacket and trousers worn together, or a single garment comprising jacket and trousers.

GMDSS	Global Maritime Distress & Safety System
GNSS	Global Navigation Satellite System
GPIRB	EPIRB, with integral GPS position-fixing
ITU	International Telecommunications Union
GPS	Global Positioning System
Hatch	The term hatch includes the entire hatch assembly and also the lid or cover as part of that assembly (the part itself may be described as a hatch).
INMARSAT	This is Inmarsat Global Limited, the private company that provides GMDSS satellite distress and safety communications, plus general communications via voice, fax and data
IMO	International Maritime Organisation
IMSO	The International Mobile Satellite Organisation, the independent, intergovernmental organisation that oversees Inmarsatâs performance of its Public Service Obligations for the GMDSS and reports on these to IMO
ISAF	International Sailing Federation.
ISO	International Standard or International Organization for Standardization.
Lifeline	wire line rigged as guardrail / guardline around the deck
LOA	Length overall not including pulpits, bowsprits, boomkins etc.
LWL	(Length of) loaded waterline
Monohull	Yacht in which the hull depth in any section does not decrease towards the centre-line.
Moveable Ballast	Lead or other material including water which has no practical function in the boat other than to increase weight and/or to influence stability and/or trim and which may be moved transversely but not varied in weight while a boat is racing.
ORC	Offshore Racing Congress (formerly Offshore Racing Council)
OSR	Offshore Special Regulation(s)
Permanently Installed	Means the item is effectively built-in by eg bolting, welding, glassing etc. and may not be removed for or during racing.
PLB	Personal Locator Beacon
Proa	Asymmetric Catamaran
RRS	ISAF - Racing Rules of Sailing
SAR	Search and Rescue
SART	Search and Rescue Transponder
Series Date	Month & Year of first launch of the first yacht of the production series

SOLAS	Safety of Life at Sea Convention
Safety Line	A tether used to connect a safety harness to a strong point
Securely Fastened	Held strongly in place by a method (eg rope lashings, wing-nuts) which will safely retain the fastened object in severe conditions including a 180 degree capsize and allows for the item to be removed and replaced during racing
Static Ballast	Lead or other material including water which has no practical function in the boat other than to increase weight and/or to influence stability and/or trim and which may not be moved or varied in weight while a boat is racing.
Static Safety Line	A safety line (usually shorter than a safety line carried with a harness) kept clipped on at a work-station
Variable Ballast	Water carried for the sole purpose of influencing stability and/or trim and which may be varied in weight and/or moved while a boat is racing.

		Category
1.03.2	The words "shall" and "must" are mandatory, and "should" and "may" are permissive.	**
1.03.3	The word "yacht" shall be taken as fully interchangeable with the word "boat".	**
SECTION 2 - APPLICATION & GENERAL REQUIREMENTS		
2.01	**Categories of Events**	
	In many types of race, ranging from trans-oceanic sailed under adverse conditions to short-course day races sailed in protected waters, six categories are established, to provide for differences in the minimum standards of safety and accommodation required for such varying circumstances:	**
2.01.4	**Category 3**	
	Races across open water, most of which is relatively protected or close to shorelines.	MoMu3
2.01.5	**Category 4**	
	Short races, close to shore in relatively warm or protected waters normally held in daylight.	MoMu4
2.02	**Inspection**	
	A yacht may be inspected at any time. If she does not comply with these Special Regulations her entry may be rejected, or she will be liable to disqualification or such other penalty as may be prescribed by the national authority or the race organizers.	**
2.03	**General Requirements**	

		Category
2.03.1	All equipment required by Special Regulations shall:-	
a)	function properly	**
b)	be regularly checked, cleaned and serviced	**
c)	when not in use be stowed in conditions in which deterioration is minimised	**
d)	be readily accessible	**
e)	be of a type, size and capacity suitable and adequate for the intended use and size of the yacht.	**
2.03.2	Heavy items:	
a)	ballast, ballast tanks and associated equipment shall be permanently installed	**
b)	heavy movable items including e.g. batteries, stoves, gas bottles, tanks, toolboxes and anchors and chain shall be securely fastened	**
c)	heavy items for which fixing is not specified in Special Regulations shall be permanently installed or securely fastened, as appropriate	**
2.03.3	When to show navigation lights	**
a)	navigation lights (OSR 3.27) shall be shown as required by the International Regulations for Preventing Collision at Sea, (Part C and Technical Annex 1). All yachts shall exhibit sidelights and a sternlight at the required times.	**
	SECTION 3 - STRUCTURAL FEATURES, STABILITY, FIXED EQUIPMENT	
3.01	**Strength of Build, Ballast and Rig**	
	Yachts shall be strongly built, watertight and, particularly with regard to hulls, decks and cabin trunks capable of withstanding solid water and knockdowns. They must be properly rigged and ballasted, be fully seaworthy and must meet the standards set forth herein. Shrouds shall never be disconnected.	**
3.02	**Watertight Integrity of a Hull**	
3.02.1	A hull, including, deck, coach roof, windows, hatches and all other parts, shall form an integral, essentially watertight unit and any openings in it shall be capable of being immediately secured to maintain this integrity.	**
3.02.2	Centreboard and daggerboard trunks and the like shall not open into the interior of a hull except via a watertight inspection/maintenance hatch of which the opening shall be entirely above the waterline of the yacht floating level in normal trim.	**

		Category
3.02.3	A canting keel pivot shall be completely contained within a watertight enclosure which shall comply with OSR 3.02.2. Access pointsÊin the watertight enclosure for control and actuation systems or any other purpose shall comply with OSR 3.02.1.	**
3.02.4	Moveable ballast systems shall be fitted with a manual control and actuation secondary system which shall be capable of controlling the full sailing load of the keel in the event of failure of the primary system. Such failures would include electrical and hydraulic failure and mechanical failure of the components and the structure to which it mounts. The system must be capable of being operational quickly and shall be operable at any angle of heel. It would be desirable if this system was capable of securing the keel on the centreline.	**
3.05	**Stability and Flotation - Multihulls**	Mu0,1,2,3,4
	Attention is drawn to ISO 12217-2.	Mu0,1,2,3,4
3.05.1	Adequate watertight bulkheads and compartments (which may include permanently installed flotation material) in each hull shall be provided to ensure that a multihull is effectively unsinkable and capable of floating in a stable position with at least half the length of one hull flooded. (see OSR 3.13.2).	Mu0,1,2,3,4
3.05.2	Multihulls built on or after Jan 1999 shall in every hull without accommodation be divided at intervals of not more than 4m (13ft 3") by one or more transverse watertight bulkheads	Mu0,1,2,3,4
3.05.3	A yacht shall be designed and built to resist capsize.	Mu0,1,2,3,4
3.07	**Exits and Escape Hatches - Multihulls**	Mu0,1,2,3,4
3.07.1	Exits	
a)	In a multihull of 8m (26.2ft) LOA and greater, each hull which contains accommodation shall have at least two exits.	Mu0,1,2,3,4
b)	In a multihull of less than 8m (26.2ft) LOA each hull which contains accommodation shall have at least two exits.	Mu0,1,2,3
3.07.2	**Escape Hatches, Underside Clipping Points & Handholds**	
a)	In a multihull of 12m (39.4ft) LOA and greater each hull which contains accommodation shall:-	Mu0,1,2,3,4
i	have an escape hatch for access to and from the hull in the event of an inversion;	Mu0,1,2,3,4
ii	when first launched on or after January 2003 have a minimum clearance diameter through each escape hatch of 450mm or when an escape hatch is not circular, sufficient clearance to allow a crew member to pass through fully clothed;	Mu0,1,2,3,4
iii	*when first launched prior to January 2003, if possible have each escape hatch in compliance with the dimensions in OSR 3.07.2(a)(ii);*	Mu0,1,2,3,4

		Category
iv	when the yacht is inverted have each escape hatch above the waterline;	Mu0,1,2,3,4
v	when first launched on or after January 2001 have each escape hatch at or near the midships station;	Mu0,1,2,3,4
vi	in a catamaran first launched on or after January 2003 have each escape hatch on the side nearest the vessel's central axis.	Mu0,1,2,3,4
b)	A trimaran of 12m (39.4ft) LOA and greater first launched on or after 1/03 shall have at least two escape hatches in compliance with the dimensions in OSR 3.07.2(a) (ii)	Mu0,1,2,3,4
c)	Each escape hatch must have been opened both from inside and outside within 6 months prior to an intended race	Mu0,1,2,3,4
d)	A multihull shall have on the underside appropriate handholds/clipping points sufficient for all crew (on a trimaran these shall be around the central hull).	Mu0,1,2,3,4
e)	A catamaran first launched on or after 1/03 with a central nacelle shall have on the underside around the central nacelle, handholds of sufficient capacity to enable all persons on board to hold on and/or clip on securely	Mu0,1,2,3,4
f)	In a catamaran with a central nacelle, it is recommended that each hull has an emergency refuge, accessible via a special hatch in the side of the hull nearest the vessel's central axis, which hatch may be opened and closed from the inside and outside	Mu0,1,2,3,4
3.07.3	A multihull of less than 12m (39.4ft) shall either have escape hatches in compliance with OSR 3.07.2 (a),(b) and (c) or shall comply with OSR 3.07.3 (a) and (b).	Mu2,3,4
a)	each hull which contains accommodation shall have, for the purpose of cutting an escape hatch, appropriate tools kept ready for instant use adjacent to the intended cutting site. Each tool shall be secured to the vessel by a line and a clip, and	Mu2,3,4
b)	in each hull at a station where an emergency hatch may be cut, the cutting line shall be clearly marked both inside and outside with an outline and the words ESCAPE CUT HERE	Mu2,3,4
3.08	**Hatches & Companionways**	
3.08.1	No hatch forward of the maximum beam station, other than a hatch in the side of a coachroof, shall open in such a way that the lid or cover moves into the open position towards the interior of the hull (excepting ports having an area of less than 0.071m2 (110 sq in)).	**
3.08.2	A hatch fitted forward of the maximum beam station, located on the side of the coachroof, opening into the interior of the boat, and of area greater than 0.071m2 shall comply with ISO12216 design category A and and be clearly labelled and used in accordance with the following instruction: "NOT TO BE OPENED AT SEA". Attention is drawn to SR 3.02.1	**

		Category
3.08.3	A hatch shall be:	
b)	permanently attached	**
c)	capable of being firmly shut immediately and remaining firmly shut in a 180 degree capsize (inversion)	**
3.08.4	A companionway hatch shall:	
a)	be fitted with a strong securing arrangement which shall be operable from the exterior and interior including when the yacht is inverted	**
b)	have any blocking devices:	**
i	capable of being retained in position with the hatch open or shut	**
ii	whether or not in position in the hatchway, secured to the yacht (e.g. by lanyard) for the duration of the race, to prevent their being lost overboard	**
iii	permit exit in the event of inversion	**
3.08.7	A companionway hatch extending below the local sheerline and shall comply with either (a) or (b):	Mu 0,1,2,3,4
a)	be capable of being blocked off up to the level of the local sheerline, whilst giving access to the interior with the blocking devices (e.g. wash-boards) in place with a minimum sill height of 300 mm.	Mu 0,1,2,3,4
b)		
i	A companionway hatch shall be in compliance with ISO 11812 – Watertight cockpits and quick-draining cockpits to design category A	Mu 0,1,2,3
ii	A companionway hatch shall be in compliance with ISO 11812 – Watertight cockpits and quick-draining cockpits to design category B	Mu4
3.09	**Cockpits - Attention is Drawn to ISO 11812**	
3.09.1	Cockpits shall be structurally strong, self-draining quickly by gravity at all angles of heel and permanently incorporated as an integral part of the hull.	**
3.09.2	Cockpits must be essentially watertight, that is, all openings to the hull must be capable of being strongly and rigidly secured	**
3.09.3	A bilge pump outlet pipe shall not be connected to a cockpit drain. See OSR 3.09.8 for cockpit drain minimum sizes	**
3.09.4	A cockpit sole shall be at least 2% LWL above LWL (or in IMS yachts first launched before 1/03, at least 2% L above LWL)	**
3.09.5	A bow, lateral, central or stern well shall be considered a cockpit for the purposes of OSR 3.09	**
3.09.6	In cockpits opening aft to the sea structural openings aft shall be not less in area than 50% maximum cockpit depth x maximum cockpit width.	**

		Category
3.09.7	**Cockpit Volume**	
i)	earliest of age or series date before April 1992	
	the total volume of all cockpits below lowest coamings shall not exceed 9% (LWL x maximum beam x freeboard abreast the cockpit).	MoMu 2,3,4
ii)	earliest of age or series date April 1992 and after	
	as above for the appropriate category except that "lowest coamings" shall not include any aft of the FA station and no extension of a cockpit aft of the working deck shall be included in calculation of cockpit volume	**
	IMS-rated boats may instead of the terms LWL, maximum beam, freeboard abreast the cockpit, use the IMS terms L, B and FA.	**
3.09.8	**Cockpit Drains**	
	See OSR 3.09.1. Cockpit drain cross section area (after allowance for screens if fitted) shall be:-	
a)	in yachts with earliest of age or series date before 1/72 or in any yacht under 8.5m (28ft) LOA - at least that of 2 x 25mm diameter (one inch) unobstructed openings or equivalent	**
b)	in yachts with earliest of age or series date 1/72 and later - at least that of 4 x 20mm diameter (3/4 inch) unobstructed openings or equivalent	**
	US SAILING prescribes that cockpit drains shall be accessible for cleaning.	**
3.10	**Sea Cocks or Valves**	
	Sea cocks or valves shall be permanently installed on all through-hull openings below the waterline except integral deck scuppers, speed indicators, depth finders and the like, however a means of closing such openings shall be provided.	**
3.11	**Sheet Winches**	
	Sheet winches shall be mounted in such a way that an operator is not required to be substantially below deck.	**
3.12	**Mast Step**	
	The heel of a keel stepped mast shall be securely fastened to the mast step or adjoining structure.	**
3.13	**Watertight Bulkheads**	
	multihulls also see OSR 3.05	Mu0,1,2,3,4
3.13.1	A hull shall have either a watertight "crash" bulkhead within 15% of LOA from the bow and abaft the forward end of LWL, or permanently installed closed-cell foam buoyancy effectively filling the forward 30% LOA of the hull.	Mo0 Mu 0,1,2,3,4
3.13.2	Any required watertight bulkhead shall be strongly built to take a full head of water pressure without allowing any leakage into the adjacent compartment.	Mo0 Mu 0,1,2,3,4

		Category
3.14	**Pulpits, Stanchions, Lifelines**	
3.14.1	When due to the particular design of a multihull it is impractical to precisely follow Special Regulations regarding pulpits, stanchions, lifelines, the regulations for monohulls shall be followed as closely as possible with the aim of minimising the risk of people falling overboard.	Mu 0,1,2,3,4
	US SAILING prescribes that all crew working areas shall be protected by lifelines or jackstays and safety harness attachment points. Lifelines or jackstays with or without safety harness attachment points may be substituted for pulpits	Mu 0,1,2,3,4
3.14.2	Lifelines required in Special Regulations shall be "taut".	**
a)	*As a guide, when a deflecting force of 50 N (5.1 kgf, 11.2 lbf) is applied to a lifeline midway between supports, the lifeline should not deflect more than 50 mm.*	**
3.14.3	The following shall be provided:	**
c)	lifelines (guardlines) supported on stanchions, which, with pulpits, shall form an effectively continuous barrier around a working deck for man-overboard prevention. Lifelines shall be permanently supported at intervals of not more than 2.20m (86.6") and shall not pass outboard of supporting stanchions	**
d)	upper rails of pulpits at no less height above the working deck than the upper lifelines as in Table 7.	**
e)	Openable upper rails in bow pulpits shall be secured shut whilst racing	**
f)	Pulpits and stanchions shall be permanently installed. When there are sockets or studs, these shall be through-bolted, bonded or welded. The pulpit(s) and/or stanchions fitted to these shall be mechanically retained without the help of the life-lines. Without sockets or studs, pulpits and/or stanchions shall be through-bolted, bonded or welded.	**
g)	The bases of pulpits and stanchions shall not be further inboard from the edge of the appropriate working deck than 5% of maximum beam or 150 mm (6 in), whichever is greater.	**
h)	Stanchion or pulpit or pushpit bases shall not be situated outboard of a working deck. For the purpose of this rule the base shall be taken to include a sleeve or socket into which the tube is fitted but shall exclude a baseplate which carries fixings into the deck or hull.	**
i)	Provided the complete lifeline enclosure is supported by stanchions and pulpit bases effectively within the working deck, lifeline terminals and support struts may be fixed to a hull aft of the working deck	**
j)	Lifelines need not be fixed to a bow pulpit if they terminate at, or pass through, adequately braced stanchions set inside and overlapping the bow pulpit, provided that the gap between the upper lifeline and the bow pulpit does not exceed 150 mm (6 in).	**

		Category
k)	Lifelines shall be continuous and fixed onlyÊat (or near) the bow and stern. However a bona fide gateÊshall be permitted inÊthe lifelines on each side of a yacht. Except at its end fittings, the movement of a lifeline in a fore-and-aft direction shall not be constrained. Temporary sleeving in 3.14.6 (c) shall not modify tension in the lifeline.	**
l)	Stanchions shall be straight and vertical except that:-	**
i	within the first 50 mm (2 in) from the deck, stanchions shall not be displaced horizontally from the point at which they emerge from the deck or stanchion base by more than 10 mm (3/8 in),and	**
ii	stanchions may be angled to not more than 10 degrees from vertical at any point above 50 mm (2 in) from the deck.	**
m)	*It is strongly recommended that designs also comply to ISO 15085*	**
3.14.4	**Special Requirements for Pulpits, Stanchions, Lifelines on Multihulls**	
	The following shall be provided:-	
a)	on a trimaran - a bow pulpit on the main hull, with lifelines around the main hull supported on stanchions. The lifelines may be interrupted where there are nets or crossbeam wings outboard of the main hull	Mu0,1,2,3,4
b)	on a trimaran - where a net joins the base of a bow pulpit on the main hull, an additional lifeline from the top of the pulpit to the forward crossbeam at or outboard of the crossbeam mid-point.	Mu0,1,2,3,4
c)	on a trimaran - at a main or emergency steering position on an outrigger with or without a cockpit, lifelines protecting an arc of 3 meters diameter centred on the steering position. (When measuring between lifelines their taut, undeflected positions shall be taken for this purpose).	Mu0,1,2,3,4
d)	on a catamaran - lifelines from bow to stern on each hull and transverse lifelines to form an effectively continuous barrier around the working area for man-overboard prevention. The transverse lifelines shall be attached to bow and stern pulpits or superstructure. A webbing, strop or rope (minimum diameter 6mm) shall be rove zig-zag between the transverse lifelines and the net.	Mu0,1,2,3,4

		Category
3.14.5	**Lifeline Height, Vertical Openings, Number of Lifelines**	

TABLE 7 **

LOA	earliest of age/ seriesdate	minimum requirements	Category
under 8.5 m (28 ft)	before January 1992	taut single lifeline at a height of no less than 450 mm (18 in) above the working deck. No vertical opening shall exceed 560 mm (22 in).	**
under 8.5 m (28 ft)	January 1992 and after	as for under 8.5 m(28 ft) in table 7 above, except that when an intermediate lifeline is fitted no vertical opening shall exceed 380 mm (15 in).	**
8.5 m (28 ft) and over	before January 1993	taut double lifeline with upper lifeline at a height of no less than 600 mm (24 in) above the working deck. No vertical opening shall exceed 560 mm (22 in)	**
8.5 m (28 ft) and over	January 1993 and after	as 8.5 m (28 ft) and over in Table 7 above, except that no vertical opening shall exceed 380 mm (15 in).	**
all	all	on yachts with intermediate lifelines the intermediate line shall be not less than 230 mm (9 in) above the working deck	**
		and shall be of the same construction and general arrangements as required for the upper.	

3.14.6	**Lifeline Minimum Diameters, Required Materials, Specifications**	
a)	Lifelines shall be of :	**
	- stranded stainless steel wire or	**
	- Single-braided High Modulus Polyethylene (HMPE) (Dyneema®/ Spectra® or equivalent) rope	**
	US SAILING note. An article describing the best techniques for using Dyneema line, particularly in the life line application, is posted at http://offshore.ussailing.org/SAS.htm	
b)	The minimum diameter of all lifelines is specified in table 8 below.	**

		Category
c)	Stainless steel lifelines shall be uncoated and used without close-fitting sleeving, however, temporary sleeving may be fitted provided it is regularly removed for inspection.	**
d)	*When stainless wire is used, Grade 316 is recommended.*	**
e)	When HMPE (Dyneema®/Spectra®) is used, it shall be spliced in accordance with the manufacturer's recommended procedures.	**
f)	A taut lanyard of synthetic rope may be used to secure lifelines provided the gap it closes does not exceed 100 mm (4 in). This lanyard shall be replaced annually at a minimum.	**
g)	All wire, fittings, anchorage points, fixtures and lanyards shall comprise a lifeline enclosure system which has at all points at least the breaking strength of the required lifeline wire.	**

TABLE 8 **

LOA	minimum wire or rope diameter
under 8.5 m (28ft)	3 mm (1/8 in)
8.5m - 13 m	4 mm (5/32 in)
over 13 m (43 ft)	5 mm (3/16 in)

3.14.7	Pulpits, Stanchions, Lifelines - Limitations on Materials	

TABLE 9 **

Earliest of Age or Series Date	detail
before January 1987	carbon fibre is not recommended in stanchions pulpits and lifelines.
January 1987 and after	stanchions, pulpits and lifelines shall not be made of carbon fibre.

3.15	Multihull Nets or Trampolines	
3.15.1	The word "net" is interchangeable with the word "trampoline"	Mu0,1,2,3,4
	A net shall be:-	Mu0,1,2,3,4
a)	essentially horizontal	Mu0,1,2,3,4
b)	made from durable woven webbing, water permeable fabric, or mesh with openings not larger than 5.08cm (2 inches) in any dimension. Attachment points shall be planned to avoid chafe. The junction between a net and a yacht shall present no risk of foot trapping	Mu0,1,2,3,4

		Category
c)	solidly fixed at regular intervals on transverse and longitudinal support lines and shall be fine-stitched to a bolt rope	Mu0,1,2,3,4
d)	able to carry the full weight of the crew either in normal working conditions at sea or in case of capsize when the yacht is inverted.	Mu0,1,2,3,4
e)	*It is recommended that lines used to tie the nets should be individually tied and not continuously connected to more than four attachment points per connecting line*	Mu0,1,2,3,4
3.15.2	**Trimarans with Double Crossbeams**	
a)	A trimaran with double crossbeams shall have nets on each side covering:-	
b)	the rectangles formed by the crossbeams, central hull and outriggers	Mu0,1,2,3,4
c)	the triangles formed by the aft end of the central pulpit, the mid-point of each forward crossbeam, and the intersection of the crossbeam and the central hull	Mu0,1,2,3,4
d)	the triangles formed by the aftermost part of the cockpit or steering position (whichever is furthest aft), the mid-point of each after crossbeam, and the intersection of the crossbeam and the central hull; except that:-	Mu0,1,2,3,4
e)	the requirement in OSR 3.15.2(d) shall not apply when cockpit coamings and/or lifelines are present which comply with the minimum height requirements in Table 7	Mu0,1,2,3,4
3.15.3	**Trimarans with Single Crossbeams**	
a)	A trimaran with a single crossbeam shall have nets between the central hull and each outrigger:-	Mu0,1,2,3,4
b)	on each side between two straight lines from the intersection of the crossbeam and the outrigger, respectively to the aft end of the pulpit on the central hull, and to the aftermost point of the cockpit or steering position on the central hull (whichever is furthest aft)	Mu0,1,2,3,4
3.16	**Catamarans**	
a)	On a catamaran the total net surface shall be limited:	
b)	laterally by the hulls	Mu0,1,2,3,4
c)	longitudinally by transverse stations through the forestay base, and the aftermost point of the boom lying fore and aft. However, a catamaran with a central nacelle (non-immersed) may satisfy the regulations for a trimaran	Mu0,1,2,3,4
3.18	**Toilet**	
3.18.2	A toilet, permanently installed or fitted bucket	MoMu3,4
3.19	**Bunks**	
3.19.2	Bunks, permanently installed	**
3.20	**Cooking Facilities**	

		Category
3.20.1	A cooking stove, permanently installed or securely fastened with safe accessible fuel shutoff control and capable of being safely operated in a seaway.	MoMu 0,1,2,3
3.21	**Drinking Water Tanks & Drinking Water**	MoMu 0,1,2,3
3.21.1	**Drinking Water Tanks**	MoMu 0,1,2,3
a)	A yacht shall have a permanently installed delivery pump and water tank(s):	MoMu 0,1,2,3
3.21.3	**Emergency Drinking Water**	MoMu 0,1,2,3
a)	At least 9 litres (2 UK gallons, 2.4 US gallons) of drinking water for emergency use shall be provided in a dedicated and sealed container or container(s)	MoMu 1,2,3
3.22	**Hand Holds**	
	Adequate hand holds shall be fitted below deck so that crew members may move about safely at sea.	**
	A hand hold should be capable of withstanding without rupture a side force of 1500N - attention is drawn to ISO 15085.	
3.23	**Bilge Pumps and Buckets**	
3.23.1	No bilge pump may discharge into a cockpit unless that cockpit opens aft to the sea.	**
3.23.2	Bilge pumps shall not be connected to cockpit drains. (OSR 3.09)	**
3.23.3	Bilge pumps and strum boxes shall be readily accessible for maintenance and for clearing out debris	**
3.23.4	Unless permanently installed, each bilge pump handle shall be provided with a lanyard or catch or similar device to prevent accidental loss	**
3.23.5	The following shall be provided:	
c)	multihulls shall have provision to pump out all watertight compartments (except those filled with impermeable buoyancy).	Mu0,1,2,3,4
f)	two buckets of stout construction each with at least 9 litres (2 UK gallons, 2.4 US gallons) capacity. Each bucket to have a lanyard.	**
3.24	**Compass**	
3.24.1	The following shall be provided:-	
a)	a marine magnetic compass, independent of any power supply, permanently installed and correctly adjusted with deviation card, and	**
b)	a magnetic compass independent of any power supply, capable of being used as a steering compass which may be hand-held	MoMu 0,1,2,3

		Category
3.25	**Halyards.**	
	No mast shall have less than two halyards, each capable of hoisting a sail.	**
Boom Support	***US SAILING prescribes that some means must exist to prevent the boom from dropping if support from the mainsail and/or halyard fails. Topping lifts or supporting vangs are acceptable for this purpose.***	**
3.27	**Navigation Lights (see OSR 2.03.3)**	
3.27.1	Navigation lights shall be mounted so that they will not be masked by sails or the heeling of the yacht.	**
3.27.2	Navigation lights shall not be mounted below deck level and should be at no less height than immediately under the upper lifeline.	**
3.27.3	Navigation light intensity	

TABLE 11

LOA	**Guide to required minimum power rating for an electric bulb in a navigation light**	
under 12 m (39.4 ft)	10 W	
12 m (39.4 ft) and above	25 W	

	US SAILING prescribes that in the US compliance with the recommendations of COLREGS shall suffice in satisfying these regulations. COLREGS requirements are as follows;	**

Table 14

LOA	*Light*	*Luminous Intensity*	*Minimum Range of Visibility*
under 39.4 ft	*Side*	*0.9 candelas*	*1 mile*
	Stern	*4.3 candelas*	*2 miles*
39.4 ft and above	*Side*	*4.3 candelas*	*2 miles*
and less than 164 ft	*Stern*	*4.3 candelas*	*2 miles*

3.27.4	Reserve navigation lights shall be carried having the same minimum specifications as the navigation lights above, with a separable power source, and wiring or supply system essentially separate from that used for the normal navigation lights	MoMu 1,2,3
3.27.5	spare bulbs for navigation lights shall be carried, or for lights not dependent on bulbs, appropriate spares.	**

		Category
3.28	**Engines, Generators, Fuel**	
3.28.1	**Propulsion Engines**	**
a)	Engines and associated systems shall be installed in accordance with their manufacturersâ guidelines and shall be of a type, strength, capacity, and installation suitable for the size and intended use of the yacht.	**
b)	An inboard propulsion engine when fitted shall: be provided with a permanently installed exhaust, coolant, and fuel supply systems and fuel tank(s); be securely covered; and have adequate protection from the effects of heavy weather.	**
c)	A propulsion engine required by Special Regulations shall provide a minimum speed in knots of (1.8 x square root of LWL in metres) or (square root of LWL in feet)	MoMu 0,1,2,3
f)	Boats of less than 12.0 m hull length may be provided with an inboard propulsion engine, or an outboard engine together with permanently installed fuel supply systems and fuel tank(s) may be used as an alternative.	Mu1,2,3
3.28.2	**Generator**	
	A separate generator for electricity is optional. However, when a separate generator is carried it shall be permanently installed, securely covered, and shall have permanently installed exhaust, cooling and fuel supply systems and fuel tank(s), and have adequate protection from the effects of heavy weather.	**
3.28.3	**Fuel Systems**	
a)	Each fuel tank provided with a shutoff valve. Except for permanently installed linings or liners, a flexible tank is not permitted as a fuel tank.	MoMu 0,1,2,3
b)	The propulsion engine shall have a minimum amount of fuel which may be specified in the Notice of Race but if not, shall be sufficient to be able to meet charging requirements for the duration of the race and to motor at the above minimum speed for at least 8 hours	MoMu 0,1,2,3
3.28.4	**Battery Systems**	
a)	When an electric starter is the only method for starting the engine, the yacht shall have a separate battery, the primary purpose of which is to start the engine	MoMu 0,1,2,3
b)	All rechargeable batteries on board shall be of the sealed type from which liquid electrolyte cannot escape. Other types of battery installed on board at 1/12 may continue in use for the remainder of their service lives.	MoMu 0,1,2,3
3.29	**Communications Equipment, EPFS (Electronic Position-Fixing System), Radar, AIS**	**
	Provision of GMDSS and DSC is unlikely to be mandatory for small craft during the term of the present Special Regulations However it is recommended that persons in charge include these facilities when installing new equipment.	MoMu 0,1,2,3

		Category
3.29.1	The following shall be provided:	**
a)	A marine radio transceiver (or if stated in the Notice of Race, an installed satcom terminal), and	MoMu 1,2,3
i	an emergency antenna when the regular antenna depends upon the mast.	MoMu 1,2,3
b)	When the marine radio transceiver is VHF:	MoMu 0,1,2,3
i	it shall have a rated output power of 25W	MoMu 0,1,2,3
ii	it shall have a masthead antenna, and co-axial feeder cable with not more than 40% power loss	MoMu 0,1,2,3
iii	*the following types and lengths of co-axial feeder cable will meet the requirements of OSR 3.29.1 (b)(ii):*	MoMu 0,1,2,3
a)	*up to 15m (50ft) - type RG8X ("mini 8");*	MoMu 0,1,2,3
b)	*15-28m (50-90ft) - type RG8U;*	MoMu 0,1,2,3
c)	*28-43m (90-140ft) - type 9913F (uses conventional connectors, available from US supplier Belden);*	MoMu 0,1,2,3
d)	*43-70m) 140-230ft - type LMR600 (uses special connectors, available from US supplier Times Microwave).*	MoMu 0,1,2,3
iv	*it should include channel 72 (an international ship-ship channel which, by common use, has become widely accepted as primary choice for ocean racing yachts anywhere in the world)*	MoMu 0,1,2,3
e)	A hand-held marine VHF transceiver, watertight or with a waterproof cover. When not in use to be stowed in a grab bag or emergency container (see OSR 4.21)	MoMu 1,2,3,4
f)	Independent of a main radio transceiver, a radio receiver capable of receiving weather bulletins	**
i)	An EPFS (Electronic Position-Fixing System) (e.g. GPS)	MoMu 0,1,2,3
o)	An AIS Transponder is recommended	MoMu3
3.29.2	*Yachts are reminded that no reflector, active or passive, is a guarantee of detection or tracking by a vessel using radar.*	**
a)	*The attention of persons in charge is drawn to legislation in force or imminent affecting the territorial seas of some countries in which the carriage of an AIS set is or will be mandatory for certain vessels including relatively small craft.*	**

SECTION 4 - PORTABLE EQUIPMENT & SUPPLIES for the yacht (for water & fuel see OSR 3.21 and OSR 3.28)

		Category
4.01	**Sail Letters & Numbers**	
4.01.1	Yachts which are not in an ISAF International Class or Recognized Class shall comply with RRS 77 and Appendix G as closely as possible, except that sail numbers allotted by a State authority are acceptable .	**
4.01.2	Sail numbers and letters of the size carried on the mainsail must be displayed by alternative means when none of the numbered sails is set.	**
4.02	***Hull marking (colour blaze)***	Mo0,1 Mu0,1,2,3,4
4.02.1	To assist in SAR location:-	
4.02.2	Multihulls shall show on the underside, where they can be seen when inverted, an solid area of highly-visible colour (e.g. Day-Glo pink, orange, or yellow) of at least 1m^2	Mu0,1,2,3,4
4.03	**Soft Wood Plugs**	
	Soft wood plugs, tapered and of the appropriate size, shall be attached or stowed adjacent to the appropriate fitting for every through-hull opening.	**
4.04	**Jackstays, Clipping Points and Static Safety Lines**	
4.04.1	The following shall be provided:	
a)	Jackstays:-	MoMu 0,1,2,3
	shall be provided-	
i	attached to through-bolted or welded deck plates or other suitable and strong anchorage fitted on deck, port and starboard of the yacht's centre line to provide secure attachments for safety harness:-	MoMu 0,1,2,3
ii	comprising stainless steel 1 x 19 wire of minimum diameter 5 mm (3/16 in), high modulus polyethylene (such as Dyneema/Spectra) rope or webbing of equivalent strength;	MoMu 0,1,2,3
	US SAILING prescribes that wire jackstays may be of configurations other than 1 X 19.	
iii	which, when made from stainless steel wire shall be uncoated and used without any sleeving;	MoMu 0,1,2,3
iv	*20kN (2,040 kgf or 4,500 lbf) min breaking strain webbing is recommended;*	MoMu 0,1,2,3
v	*at least two of which should be fitted on the underside of a multihull in case of inversion.*	Mu 0,1,2,3

		Category
4.04.2	**Clipping Points:-**	
	shall be provided-	
a)	attached to through-bolted or welded deck plates or other suitable and strong anchorage points adjacent to stations such as the helm, sheet winches and masts, where crew members work for long periods:-	MoMu 0,1,2,3
b)	which, together with jackstays and static safety lines shall enable a crew member-	MoMu 0,1,2,3
i	to clip on before coming on deck and unclip after going below;	MoMu 0,1,2,3
ii	whilst continuously clipped on, to move readily between the working areas on deck and the cockpit(s) with the minimum of clipping and unclipping operations.	MoMu 0,1,2,3
c)	The provision of clipping points shall enable two-thirds of the crew to be simultaneously clipped on without depending on jackstays	MoMu 0,1,2,3
d)	In a trimaran with a rudder on the outrigger, adequate clipping points shall be provided that are not part of the deck gear or the steering mechanism, in order that the steering mechanism can be reached by a crew member whilst clipped on.	Mu 0,1,2,3
e)	*Warning - U-bolts as clipping points - see OSR 5.02.1(a)*	
4.05	**Fire Extinguishers**	
	Shall be provided as follows:	
4.05.1	Fire extinguishers, at least two, readily accessible in suitable and different parts of the yacht	**
4.05.2	Fire Extinguishers, at least two, of minimum 2kgs each of dry powder or equivalent	MoMu 0,1,2,3
4.05.4	A fire blanket adjacent to every cooking device with an open flame	**
4.06	**Anchor(s)**	
4.06.1	An anchor or anchors shall be carried according to the table below:	**

TABLE 12 **

LOA	Detail	Race Category
8.5 m (28 ft) and over	2 anchors together with a suitable combination of chain and rope, all ready for immediate use	MoMu1,2,3
under 8.5 m (28 ft)	1 anchor together with a suitable combination of chain and rope, all ready for immediate use	MoMu1,2,3
any	1 anchor, readily accessible	MoMu4

		Category
4.07	**Flashlight(s) and Searchlight(s)**	
4.07.1	The following shall be provided:-	
a)	A watertight, high-powered searchlight, suitable for searching for a person overboard at night and for collision avoidance with spare batteries and bulbs, and	**
b)	a watertight flashlight with spare batteries and bulb	**
c)	for Mu3,4 the watertight flashlight in OSR 4.07.1 (b) shall be stowed in the grab bag or emergency container	Mu3,4
4.08	**First Aid Manual and First Aid Kit**	**
4.08.1	A suitable First Aid Manual shall be provided	**
	In the absence of a National Authority's requirement, the latest edition of one of the following is recommended:-	**
b)	*First Aid at Sea, by Douglas Justins and Colin Berry, published by Adlard Coles Nautical,London*	MoMu 2,3,4
c)	*Le Guide de la medecine a distance, by Docteur J Y Chauve, published by Distance Assistance BP33 F-La Baule, cedex, France.*	**
d)	*'PAN-PAN medico a bordo' in Italian edited by Umberto Verna. www.panpan.it*	MoMu 2,3,4
e)	*Skipper's Medical Emergency Handbook by Dr Spike Briggs and Dr Campbell Mackenzie www.msos.org.uk*	**
	US SAILING endorses the above and additionally recommends the following manuals: Advanced First Aid by Peter Eastman, M.D., Cornell Maritime Press and A Comprehensive Guide to Marine Medicine by Eric A. Weiss, M.D. and Michael E. Jacobs, M.D., Adventure Medical Kit.	
4.08.2	A First Aid Kit shall be provided	**
4.08.3	*The contents and storage of the First Aid Kit should reflect the guidelines of the Manual carried, the likely conditions and duration of the passage, and the number of people aboard the yacht.*	**
4.09	**Foghorn**	
	A foghorn shall be provided	**
4.10	**Radar Reflector**	
4.10.1	A passive Radar Reflector (that is, a Radar Reflector without any power) shall be provided	**
a)	If a radar reflector is:	**
i	*octahedral with triangular plates making up each pocket it must have a minimum diagonal measurement of 456 mm (18in).*	**

		Category
ii	*octahederal with circular sector plates making up each pocket it must have a minimum diameter of 304mm (12in).*	**
iii	*not octahedral it must have a documented RCS (radar cross-section) of not less than 10 m2 at 0° elevation and be capable of performance around 360° in azimuth.*	**
	US SAILING prescribes that in the US, radar reflectors shall have a minimum documented "equivalent echoing area" of 6 sq. m. Octahedral reflectors shall have a minimum diameter of 12 inches.	
	The minimum effective height above water is 4.0 m (13 ft).	**
b)	*The passive and active devices referred to in these notes and in 4.10.1 and 4.10.2 above are primarily intended for use in the X (9GHz) band*	**
4.10.2	*The most effective radar response from a yacht may be provided by an RTE (Radar Target Enhancer) which may be on board in addition to the required passive reflector. An RTE should conform to ISO 8729-2:2009. An RTE is strongly recommended.*	MoMu 1,2,3,4
b)	*The display of a passive reflector or the operation of an RTE is for the person in charge to decide according to prevailing conditions.*	**
4.10.3	*When available, a passive radar reflector in compliance with ISO8729-1:2010 will offer improved performance over earlier models and has a size typified by a cylinder of not more than weight 5kg, height 750mm and diameter 300mm.*	**
4.10.4	*S (3GHz) band radar is often used by ships in bad weather to complement X (9GHz) band radar. On S (3GHz) band a passive reflector offers about 1/10 the response obtained on the X (9GHz) band. Unless specifically designed to operate in the S(3GHz) band, an RTE will provide no response at all.*	**
4.11	**Navigation Equipment**	
4.11.1	Charts	
	Navigational charts (not solely electronic), light list and chart plotting equipment shall be provided	**
4.12	**Safety Equipment Location Chart**	
	A safety equipment location chart in durable waterproof material shall be displayed in the main accommodation where it can best be seen, clearly marked with the location of principal items of safety equipment.	**
4.13	**Echo Sounder or Lead Line**	
4.13.1	An echo sounder or lead line shall be provided	MoMu 1,2,3,4
4.14	**Speedometer or Distance Measuring Instrument (log)**	
	A speedometer or distance measuring instrument (log) shall be provided	MoMu 0,1,2,3
4.15	**Emergency Steering**	

		Category
4.15.1	Emergency steering shall be provided as follows:	
a)	except when the principal method of steering is by means of an unbreakable metal tiller, an emergency tiller capable of being fitted to the rudder stock;	MoMu 0,1,2,3
b)	crews must be aware of alternative methods of steering the yacht in any sea condition in the event of rudder loss. At least one method must have been proven to work on board the yacht. An inspector may require that this method be demonstrated.	MoMu 0,1,2,3
4.16	**Tools and Spare Parts**	
	Tools and spare parts, including effective means to quickly disconnect or sever the standing rigging from the hull shall be provided.	**
4.17	**Yacht's name**	
	Yacht's name shall be on miscellaneous buoyant equipment, such as lifejackets, cushions, lifebuoys, lifeslings, grab bags etc.	**
4.18	**Marine grade retro-reflective material**	
	Marine grade retro-reflective material shall be fitted to lifebuoys, lifeslings, liferafts and lifejackets. See OSRs 5.04, 5.08.	**
4.21	**Grab Bags**	
4.21.1	**Grab Bag or Emergency Container for Multihulls Without Liferafts**	Mu3,4
a)	A multihull without a liferaft shall have, readily accessible whether or not the yacht is inverted, either a watertight compartment or a grab bag with the following minimum contents. A grab bag shall have inherent flotation, at least 0.1 m^2 area of fluorescent orange colour on the outside, shall be marked with the name of the yacht, and shall have a lanyard and clip.	Mu3,4
b)	*Note: it is not intended to duplicate in a grab bag etc. items required by other OSRs to be on board the yacht - this regulation covers only the stowage of those items*	Mu3,4
c)	a watertight hand-held marine VHF transceiver plus a spare set of batteries	Mu3,4
d)	a watertight flashlight with spare batteries and bulb	Mu3,4
e)	2 red parachute and 3 red hand flares	Mu3,4
f)	a watertight strobe light with spare batteries	Mu3,4
g)	a knife	Mu3,4
4.22	**Lifebuoys**	
4.22.1	***The following shall be provided within easy reach of the helmsman and ready for instant use:***	**
a)	a lifebuoy with a self-igniting light and a drogue or a Lifesling with a self-igniting light and without a drogue.	**

		Category
	For Categories 0,1,2,3 US SAILING prescribes that the lifebuoy in OSR 4.22.1 a) above shall be a Lifesling (without a drogue), equipped with a self-igniting light within easy reach of the helmsman and ready for instant use. (See Appendix D).	MoMu 0,1,2,3
	For Category 4, US SAILING prescribes that the lifebuoy must be inherently buoyant.	MoMu4
4.22.3	Each inflatable lifebuoy and any automatic device (eg pole and flag extended by compressed gas) shall be tested and serviced at intervals in accordance with its manufacturer's instructions.	**
4.22.4	Each lifebuoy or lifesling shall be fitted with marine grade retro-reflective material (4.18).	**
4.22.5	*It is recommended that the colour of each lifebuoy be a safety colour in the yellow-red range.*	**
4.23	**Pyrotechnic and Light Signals**	
4.23.1	Pyrotechnic signals shall be provided conforming to SOLAS LSA Code Chapter III Visual Signals and not older than the stamped expiry date (if any) or if no expiry date stamped , not older than 4 years.	**

TABLE 13

red parachute flares LSA III 3.1	red hand flares LSA III 3.2	orange smoke LSA III 3.3	race category
4	4	2	MoMu2,3
	4	2	Mo4
2	4	2	Mu4

4.24	**Heaving Line**	**
a)	a heaving line shall be provided 15 m - 25 m (50 ft - 75 ft) length readily accessible to cockpit.	**
b)	*the "throwing sock" type is recommended - see Appendix D*	**
	US SAILING prescribes that the heaving line be of 1/4 in. (6 mm) minimum diameter, floating, UV-inhibited and readily accessible to the cockpit.	**
4.25	**Cockpit Knife**	
	A strong, sharp knife, sheathed and securely restrained shall be provided readily accessible from the deck or a cockpit.	**
4.26	**Storm & Heavy Weather Sails**	
4.26.1	***Design***	

		Category
a)	*it is strongly recommended that persons in charge consult their designer and sailmaker to decide the most effective size for storm and heavy weather sails. The purpose of these sails is to provide safe propulsion for the yacht in severe weather -they are not intended as part of the racing inventory. The areas below are maxima. Smaller areas are likely to suit some yachts according to their stability and other characteristics.*	**
4.26.2	**High Visibility**	
a)	Every storm jib shall either be of highly-visible coloured material (eg dayglo pink, orange or yellow) or have a highly-visible coloured patch at least 50% of the area of the sail (up to a maximum diameter of 3m) added on each side; and also that a rotating wing mast should have a highly-visible coloured patch on each side. A storm sail purchased after January 2014 shall have the material of the body of the sail a highly-visible colour.	**
4.26.3	**Materials**	
a)	aromatic polyamides, carbon and similar fibres shall not be used in a trysail or storm jib but spectra/dyneema and similar materials are permitted.	**
b)	*it is strongly recommended that a heavy-weather jib does not contain aromatic polyamides, carbon and similar fibres other than spectra/dyneema.*	**
4.26.4	**The following shall be provided:-**	
a)	sheeting positions on deck for each storm and heavy-weather sail;	**
b)	for each storm or heavy-weather jib, a means to attach the luff to the stay, independent of any luff-groove device. A heavy weather jib shall have the means of attachment readily available. A storm jib shall have the means of attachment permanently attached;	**
	Storm and heavy weather jib areas shall be calculated as: (0.255 x luff length x (luff perpendicular + 2 x half width))* To apply to sails made in January 2012 and after.	
c)	when a storm trysail is required by OSR 4.26.4 (g) it shall be capable of being sheeted independently of the boom with trysail area not greater than 17.5% mainsail hoist (P) luff length x mainsail foot length (E). The storm trysail area shall be measured as (0.5 x leech length x shortest distance between tack point and leech). The storm trysail shall have neither headboard nor battens, however a storm trysail is not required in a yacht with a rotating wing mast which can adequately substitute for a trysail. The method of calculating area applies to sails made in January 2012 and after.	MoMu3
d)	if a storm trysail is required by OSR 4.26.4 (g) the yacht's sail number and letter(s) shall be placed on both sides of the trysail (or on a rotating wing mast as substitute for a trysail) in as large a size as practicable;	MoMu3,4

		Category
f)	***in addition to the storm jib required by OSR 4.26.4 (e), a heavy-weather jib (or heavy-weather sail in a yacht with no forestay) of area not greater than 13.5% height of the foretriangle squared***	**
g)	either a storm trysail as defined in OSR 4.26.4(c), or mainsail reefing to reduce the luff by at least 40%.	MoMu3,4
	In addition, US SAILING prescribes mainsail reefing to reduce the luff by at least 10% for sails built after 1 January 1997.	MoMu 0,1,2,3

SECTION 5 - PERSONAL EQUIPMENT

		Category
5.01	**Lifejacket**	
	US SAILING prescribes for Categories 0,1,2,and 3: either a life-jacket defined in OSR 5.01.1 (See Note 1), or a USCG approved Type I non-inflatable personal flotation device (PFD), or a USCG approved yoke-type inflatable with 33lb (150N) or greater buoy-ancy with or without crotch strap, face guard, or buddy line. Each inflatable PFD shall be inflated and inspected annually. Service dates shall be marked on each PFD. It is recommended that all inflatable PFDs be integrated with safety harnesses (see OSR 5.02) (See Note 2).	MoMu 0,1,2,3
	US SAILING Note 1: ISO 12402 is not currently approved by the USCG. Boats operating in US waters are not exempt from USCG requirements.	MoMu 0,1,2,3
	US SAILING Note 2: Many inflatable PFD's with built-in har-nesses are designed for people greater than 5' 5" in height and are potentially dangerous if you are below that height.	MoMu 0,1,2,3
	US SAILING Note 3: Inflatable PFDs with the required buoyancy will generally have inflation cylinders containing 33g or more of CO2.	MoMu 0,1,2,3
	US SAILING Note 4: "Yoke-type" is defined as a PFD that is designed to keep its wearer face-up and head-up in the water and that provides buoyancy in front of the chest and behind the neck im-mediately when inflated	MoMu 0,1,2,3
5.01.1	Each crew member shall have a lifejacket as follows:-	MoMu 0,1,2,3
a)		
i	In accordance with ISO 12402 - 3 (Level 150) or equivalent, including EN 396 or UL 1180	**
ii	Lifejackets manufactured after 1 January 2012 shall be in accordance with ISO 12402–3 (Level 150) and shall be fitted with:-	**

		Category
	• an emergency light in accordance with either ISO 12402-8 or SO LAS LSA code 2.2.3.	
	• a sprayhood in accordance with ISO 12402-8.	
	• a full deck safety harness in accordance with ISO 12401 (ISO 1095) including a crotch or thigh strap (holding down device) as specified in ISO 12401 (ISO 1095).	
	If of an inflatable type either	
a)	automatic, manual and oral inflation or	
b)	manual and oral inflation	
Notes	ISO 12402 requires Level 150 lifejackets to be fitted with a mandatory whistle and retro-reflective material. Also, when fitted with a safety harness, ISO 12402 requires that this shall be the full safety harness in accordance with ISO 12401. Any equivalent lifejacket shall have equal requirements.	
	Persons of larger than average build are generally more buoyant than those of average build and so do not require a lifejacket with greater levels of flotation. Wearing a Level 275 lifejacket may hamper entry into liferafts.	
b)	fitted with either a crotch strap(s) / thigh straps or a full safety harness in accordance with ISO 12401,	**
Note	The function of lifejacket crotch/thigh straps is to hold the buoyancy element down. A crew member before a race should adjust a lifejacket to fit then retain that lifejacket for the duration of the race. Correct adjustment is fundamental to the lifejacket functioning correctly.	
c)	fitted with a lifejacket light in accordance with SOLAS LSA code 2.2.3 (white, >0.75 candelas, >8 hours),	**
d)	if inflatable have a compressed gas inflation system,	**
e)	if inflatable, regularly checked for gas retention,	**
f)	compatible with the wearer's safety harness,	**
g)	clearly marked with the yacht's or wearer's name,	**
	It is strongly recommended that a lifejacket has:	
j)	*a splashguard / sprayhood See ISO 12402 – 8*	MoMu 1,2,3,4
k)	*a PLB unit (as with other types of EPIRB, should be properly registered with the appropriate authority)*	MoMu 1,2,3,4
l)	*if of a gas inflatable type, a spare cylinder and if appropriate a spare activation head*	MoMu 1,2,3,4

		Category
	US SAILING prescribes that all personnel on deck shall wear properly fitted personal floatation while starting and finishing. At other times during the race, floatation shall be worn on deck except when the Captain of the boat directs that it may be set aside.	MoMu 1,2,3,4
	US SAILING prescribes for Category 4 lifejackets as above or U.S. Coast Guard approved Type III personal floatation devices	MoMu4
5.01.4	The person in charge shall personally check each lifejacket at least once annually.	**
	US SAILING note: As is true of all of these regulations, the prescriptions above do not necessarily replace the requirements of other governing authorities.	**
5.02	**Safety Harness and Safety Lines (Tethers)**	**
5.02.1	Each crew member shall have a harness and safety line that complies with ISO 12401 or equivalent with a safety line not more than 2m in length.	MoMu 0,1,2,3
	Harnesses and safety lines manufactured prior to Jan 2010 shall comply with either ISO 12401 or EN 1095.	
	Harnesses and safety lines manufactured prior to Jan 2001 are not permitted.	
	US SAILING prescribes that harnesses and safety lines manufactured prior to Jan 2001 are not recommended in the U.S.	**
a)	*Warning it is possible for a plain snaphook to disengage from a U bolt if the hook is rotated under load at right-angles to the axis of the U-bolt. For this reason the use of snaphooks with positive locking devices is strongly recommended.*	
5.02.2	At least 30% of the crew shall each, in addition to the above be provided with either:-	MoMu 0,1,2,3
a)	a safety line not more than 1m long, or	MoMu 0,1,2,3
b)	a mid-point snaphook on a 2m safety line	MoMu 0,1,2,3
5.02.3	A safety line purchased in January 2001 or later shall have a coloured flag embedded in the stitching, to indicate an overload. A line which has been overloaded shall be replaced as a matter of urgency.	MoMu 0,1,2,3
5.02.4	A crew member's lifejacket and harness shall be compatible	MoMu 0,1,2,3
	US SAILING prescribes that the safety harness may be integrated with an inflatable personal floatation device (see OSR 5.01) and recommends that such devices be employed whenever conditions warrant, and always in rough weather, on cold water, or at night, or under conditions of reduced visibility or when sailing short-handed.	MoMu 0,1,2,3

		Category
5.02.5	*It is strongly recommended that:-*	MoMu0,1,2,3
a)	*static safety lines should be securely fastened at work stations;*	MoMu0,1,2,3
b)	*A harness should be fitted with a crotch strap or thigh straps. Crotch straps or thigh straps together with related fittings and fixtures should be strong enough to lift the wearer from the water.*	MoMu 0,1,2,3
c)	*to draw attention to wear and damage, stitching on harness and safety lines should be of a colour contrasting strongly with the surrounding material;*	MoMu 0,1,2,3
d)	*snaphooks should be of a type which will not self-release from a U-bolt (see OSR 5.02.1(a)) and which can be easily released under load (crew members are reminded that a personal knife may free them from a safety line in emergency);*	MoMu 0,1,2,3
e)	*a crew member before a race should adjust a harness to fit then retain that harness for the duration of the race.*	MoMu 0,1,2,3
5.02.6	*Warning - a safety line and safety harness are not designed to tow a person in the water and it is important that the shortest safety line length possible be used with a harness to minimise or eliminate the risk of a person's torso becoming immersed in water outside the boat, especially when working on the foredeck. 1m safety lines or the midpoint snaphook on a 2m line should be used for this purpose. The diligent use of a properly adjusted safety harness and the shortest safety line practicable is regarded as by far the most effective way of preventing man overboard incidents.preventing man overboard incidents.*	MoMu 0,1,2,3
5.04	**Foul Weather Suits**	
b)	*it is recommended that a foul weather suit should be fitted with marine-grade retro-reflective material, and should have high-visibility colours on its upper parts and sleeve cuffs.See OSR 4.18*	**
5.07	**Survival Equipment**	
5.07.2	*It is strongly recommended that an immersion suit should be supplied to each crew member in a multihull in conditions where there is a potential for hypothermia*	Mu 1,2,3,4
5.09	***Annual Man-Overboard Practice***	
	US SAILING prescribes that the "Quick-Stop" man-overboard procedure shall be practiced aboard the yacht at least once annually. A certificate of such practice shall be signed by participating crew members and kept aboard the yacht.	**
5.11	***Preventer or Boom Restraining Device***	
	US SAILING recommends that a preventer or boom restraining device should be rigged in such a manner that attachment can be easily and quickly made, with the boom fully extended (running) without leaving the deck or leaning overboard. A process and plan for its use should be part of the crew's training and practice. Recommended for all boats in all categories.	**

SECTION 6 - TRAINING

		Category
6.04	***Routine Training On-Board***	
6.04.1	*It is recommended that crews should practice safety routines at reasonable intervals including the drill for man-overboard recovery.*	**
	US SAILING Note: MNA recognized First Aid & CPR courses in the U.S. are posted at http://offshore.ussailing.org/SAS/Senior_First_Aid_Certification.htm.	**
	US SAILING recommends that at least two members of the crew be currently certified in cardiopulmonary resuscitation.	**
6.05.3	At least one member of the crew shall be familiar with First Aid procedures, hypothermia, drowning, cardio-pulmonary resuscitation and relevant communications systems.	MoMu3,4
6.05.4	*An example model first aid training course is included in Appendix N.*	**

APPENDIX A part I
Minimum Specifications for Yachtsmen's Liferafts
for liferafts manufactured prior to 1/03 *(1/06 in the U.S.)*
Appendix A does not cover liferafts intended for category 0 races

1.0 General design
Liferaft(s) capable of carrying the whole crew shall meet the following requirements:

a) Stowage - see Special Regulation 4.20.2

b) Must be designed and used solely for saving life at sea

c) The liferaft shall be so constructed that, when fully inflated and floating with the cover uppermost, it shall be stable in a seaway

d) The construction of the liferaft shall include a canopy or cover, which shall unless specified by the national Authority or Notice of Race automatically be set in place when the liferaft is inflated. This cover shall be capable of protecting the occupants against injury from exposure, and means shall be provided for collecting rain. The cover of the liferaft shall be of a highly visible colour.

e) The liferaft shall be fitted with a painter line and shall have a lifeline becketed round the outside. A lifeline shall also be fitted round the inside of the liferaft

f) The liferaft shall be capable of being readily righted by one person if it inflates in an inverted position

g) The liferaft shall be fitted at each opening with efficient means to enable persons in the water to climb on board

h) The liferaft shall be contained in a valise or other container, so constructed as to be capable of withstanding hard wear under conditions met with at sea. The liferaft in its valise or other container shall be inherently buoyant

i) The buoyancy of the liferaft shall be so arranged as to achieve a division into an even number of separate compartments, half of which shall be capable of supporting out of the water the number of persons which the liferaft is fit to accommodate, without reducing the total supporting area.

j) The number of persons which an inflatable liferaft shall be permitted to accommodate shall be equal to:-

   i) the greatest whole number obtained by dividing by 0.096 the volume, measured in cubic metres of the main buoyancy tubes (which for this purpose shall include neither the arches nor the thwarts if fitted) when inflated, or

   ii) the greatest whole number obtained by dividing by 3720 the area measured in square centimetres of the floor (which for this purpose may include the thwart or thwarts if fitted) of the liferaft when inflated whichever number shall the less

k) The floor of the liferaft shall be waterproof and unless otherwise prescribed by a National Authority or Notice of Race, shall be capable of being sufficiently insulated against the cold either:-

i) by means of one or more compartments which the occupants can inflate if they so desire, or which inflate automatically and can be deflated and re-inflated by the occupants; or

ii) by other equally efficient means not dependent on inflation

2.0 Equipment

a) one buoyant rescue quoit, attached to at least 30 metres of buoyant line

b) one safety knife and one bailer

c) two sponges

d) one sea anchor or drogue permanently attached to the liferaft (compliance with ISO 17339 or equivalent is recommended)

e) two paddles

f) one repair outfit capable of repairing punctures in buoyancy compartments

g) one topping-up pump or bellows

h) one waterproof electric torch

i) three hand-held red distress flare signals in accordance with SOLAS regulation 36

j) six anti-seasickness tablets for each person which the liferaft is deemed fit to accommodate

k) instructions on a plastic sheet on how to survive in the liferaft

l) the liferaft shall be inflated by a gas which is not injurious to the occupants and the inflation shall take place automatically either on the pulling of a line or by some other equally simple and efficient method. Means shall be provided whereby a topping-up pump or bellows may be used to maintain pressure

3.0 Marking of liferafts

3.1 Each liferaft shall be clearly marked with the yacht's name or sail number or identification code on:-

a) the canopy

b) the bottom

c) the valise or container

d) the certificate

3.2 Numbers and letters on the liferaft shall be as large as possible and in a strongly contrasting colour. Marine grade retro-reflective material shall be appropriately fitted to every raft.

APPENDIX A part II

Appendix A does not cover liferafts intended for category 0 races

The ISAF liferaft

The ISAF liferaft specification (OSR Appendix A part II) was published in 2002 pending completion of ISO standard 9650 and served the offshore community well.

As ISO 9650 is now widely available ISAF is following previously-established policy to promote the ISO standard as its primary reference. It is the intention of ISAF that the ISAF specification will continue to be an acceptable alternative although manufacturers may choose to no longer market products under the ISAF name. The complete ISAF liferaft specification is at www.sailing.org/specialregs

Please refer to the text of Special Regulations for further details.

Chairman Special Regulations Liferaft Working Party
November 2007

APPENDIX B
A Guide to ISO and other standards

Application and Development Policy
Whenever possible a relevant ISO Standard, CEN Norm, SOLAS regulation or other internationally-recognised standard is called up by OSR. Changes and developments in international standards are reviewed by the Special Regulations sub Committee and may replace part of Special Regulations. Significant changes will when possible affect new yachts and/or new equipment only.

ISO
ISO, the International Organization for Standardization is a world-wide federation of national standards bodies (ISO member bodies). The work of preparing International Standards is normally carried out through ISO Technical Committees. Each member body interested in a subject for which a Technical Committee has been established has the right to be represented on that committee. International organisations governmental and non-governmental, including eg ISAF, take part in the work. Copies of International Standards may be obtained from a national standards body.

The following International Standards (or Draft Standards) are mentioned in Special Regulations:-

ISO standard	Subject	Special Regulation
8729-1	marine radar reflectors	4.10
8729-2	marine radar reflectors	4.10
9650	liferafts	Appendix A Part II
11812	watertight & quick draining cockpits	3.09
12401	deck safety harness (also published as EN 1095)	5.02
12402	Personal Flotation Devices	5.01
12215	hull construction standards	3.03
12217-2	assessment of stability and buoyancy	3.04.4, 3.05
15085	guardlines (lifelines) trampolines, nets, stanchions, hooking points	3.14, 3.15
17339	sea anchors	4.27

CEN

CEN standards (Norms) are developed in Europe by CEN (European Committee for Standardization – Committée Européen de Normalisation) which publishes ENs (European Norms) and which works closely with ISO. In OSR the following are mentioned:-

EN standard	Subject	Special Regulation
394,399	lifejacket accessories	5.01
396	lifejackets	5.01
1095	deck safety harness (also published as ISO 12401)	5.02
1913-1-3	immersion suits	5.07

ABS

ABS Guide for Building and Classing Offshore Yachts. This Guide to scantlings (construction standards) was originally published by ABS (American Bureau of Shipping) in co-operation with the Offshore Racing Council. A plan approval service formerly offered by ABS has been discontinued. However, copies of the Guide are available from the ISAF office. Designers and builders may provide written statements to confirm that they have designed and built a yacht in accordance with the original Guide or ABS-approved derivatives (see OSR Appendix M).

RCD

The RCD (Recreational Craft Directive) is published with the authority of the EC under which "notified bodies" may approve construction standards of yachts which may then be entitled to display a CE mark permitting sale in the EC (see OSR 3.03 and Appendix M).

SOLAS

The SOLAS (Safety of Life At Sea) Convention is published by IMO (International Maritime Organisation) at which ISAF has Consultative Status. SOLAS Chapter III, Regulation 3, 10 refers to the LSA (Life Saving Appliances) Code (published as a separate booklet) to which OSR makes the following references:-

LSA Code	Subject	Special Regulation
Chapter III, 3.1, 3.2, 3.3	Flares (pyrotechnics)	4.23
Chapter II, 2.2.3	Lifejacket lights	5.01
Chapter IV, 4	Liferafts	4.20
Chapter II, 2.3	Immersion suits	5.07.1
Chapter II, 2.5	Thermal protective aids	Appendix A Part II

Addresses

CEN Central Secretariat,
rue de Stassart 36,
B-1050 Brussels,
Belgium
tel +32 2 550 08 11
fax +32 2 550 08 19
www.cenorm.be

ISO Central Secretariat,
1 rue de Varembé,
Case Postale 56,
CH-1211 Genéve 20,
Switzerland
email: central@isocs.iso.ch
tel +41 22 749 01 11
fax + 41 22 733 34 30
www.iso.org

IMO International Maritime Organization,
4 Albert Embankment,
London EC1 7SR,
Great Britain
email: info@imo.org
tel +44 207 735 7611
fax +44 207 587 3210
www.imo.org

APPENDIX C
Standard Inspection Card

- Please note that this appendix is not comprehensive but only a guide for use by Race Organisers. Add items as appropriate. A copy of the card should be given to the yacht in advance.
- **PERSON IN CHARGE** please prepare the boat and sign the card.
- **INSPECTORS** mark each item with a tick or cross in the check box. Write an additional report if necessary. Show the card to the person in charge and return card with report to the Race Committee as soon as possible.

YACHT ____________________

Sail No ____________________

Number of crew this race ____________________

Liferaft total capacity ____________________

IMPORTANT inspection is carried out only as a guide. An inspector cannot limit or reduce the complete and unlimited responsibility of the owner and the person in charge.

"I hereby declare that I am the owner or person in charge and that I have read and understood Special Regulations and in particular 1.02.1, 1.02.2, and 1.02.3 (Responsibility of Person in Charge)"

Signed ____________________

Printed Name ____________________

Date ____________________

BELOW DECK
On one or more berths show the following:-

	Special Regs	Completed Inspection / Comment
How many safety harness and lines?	5.02.2	
Coloured flags in new harness lines?	5.02	
How many extra safety harness lines?	5.02.2	
How many lifejackets?	5.02	
Foghorn	4.09	
Flashlight + spare batteries and bulbs	4.07.1(b)	
Hi-powered flashlight/spotlight + appropriate spares	4.07.1(a)	
rigging cutters	4.16	
first aid kit and manual	4.08	
2 stout buckets	3.23	
2 fire extinguishers	4.05	
is keel-stepped mast heel restrained?	3.12	
engine permanently installed and securely covered?	3.28.1	
heavy-weather jib (if not rigged on deck-see below)	4.26.4(b), (f)	
stowage chart with location of principal items of safety equipment	4.12	
heavy movable objects securely fastened in place?	2.03.2	

BELOW DECK also show the following:-

How many valid liferaft certificate(s)?	4.20	
in date liferaft certificate(s)?	4.20	
rating certificate(s) signed by owner?		
rating certificate(s) expiry date(s)?		
radar reflector data sheet (if not 18" octahedral) declaring at least 10m2 RCS	4.10	
charts (not solely electronic)	4.11	
Structural requirement conformity	3.03.	
Stability requirement conformity	3.04.	
406MHz EPIRB - identity number?	4.19	
serviced?	4.19	
Statement(s) of training completed by how many crew?	6.01	

ON DECK

block companionway hatch shut	3.08.3(b)	
show retaining device connected to washboard(s)	3.08.4(b) (ii)	
show retaining device connected to bilge pump handle(s)	3.23.4	
rig the storm jib (or if none, the heavy weather jib) with jib sheets ready for use	4.26.4(a), (e)	
rig the trysail with sheets ready for use	4.26.4	
can trysail be set without removing mainsail from luff groove or mainsail cars from track?	4.26.4(b)	
install equipment for steering without the rudder - has it been tried?	4.15.1(b)	
rig radar reflector at least 4.0m above the water as it would be used	4.10	
prepare to demonstrate nav lights both main and reserve	3.27	
fix shut cockpit lockers as if for heavy weather	3.02.1	
can crew stay clipped on along and across deck?	4.04.2(b) (ii)	
are lifelines taut?	3.14.2	
show jackstays rigged for use	4.04	
static safety lines at work stations? how many?	4.04.2(b) & 5.02.5(b)	

MAN OVERBOARD

date and place of last MoB drill?	6.04.1	
how many of this crew has done MoB drill on this boat?	6.04.1	

PYROTECHNICS (FLARES)

remove each flare from container and have laid out for inspection.	4.23	
red hand flares -how many? All SOLAS?	4.23	
red parachute flares -how many? All SOLAS?	4.23	
white hand flares -how many?	4.23	
orange smoke flares -how many? All SOLAS?	4.23	
can crew members describe “”blind”” how these flares operate?	4.23	

INSPECTOR'S REPORT TO RACE COMMITTEE

I inspected the above yacht on (date): ______________________

Location: ______________________

Comments: ______________________

____

____

____

____

____

____

____

____

____

____

____

____

Signed ______________________

Printed name ______________________

APPENDIX D

For information only
Quickstop and Lifesling

MAN OVERBOARD – QUICK STOP AND THE LIFE SLING (OR SEATTLE SLING)

When a crew member goes over the side recovery time is of the essence. In an effort to come up with a recovery system that is simple and lightning quick, the US Yacht Racing Union Safety at Sea Committee, the US Naval Academy Sailing Squadron, the Cruising Club of America Technical Committee and the Sailing Foundation of Seattle, Washington, joined forces to conduct extensive research and sea trials. The result of their collaboration is the "Quick-Stop" method of man-overboard recovery.

The hallmark of this method is the immediate reduction of boat speed by turning to windward and then manoeuvring slowly, remaining near the victim. In most cases, this is better than reaching off, then gybing or tacking and returning on a reciprocal course.

QUICK-STOP

1. Shout "man overboard" and detail a crew member to spot and point to **the victim's position** in the water. The spotter should not take his eyes off the victim (see Figure 1).

2. Provide immediate flotation. Throw buoyant objects such as cockpit cushions, life rings and so on. These objects may not only come to the aid of the victim, but will "litter the water" where he went overboard and help your spotter to keep him in view. Deployment of the pole and flag (dan buoy) requires too much time. The pole is saved to "put on top" of the victim in case the initial manoeuvre is unsuccessful.

3. Bring boat head-to-wind and beyond (see Figure 1).

4. Allow headsail to back and further slow the boat.

5. Keep turning with headsail backed until wind is abaft the beam.

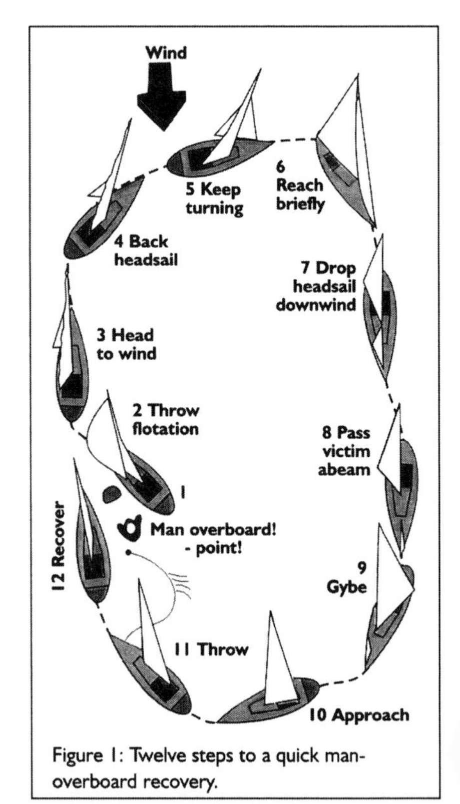

Figure 1: Twelve steps to a quick man-overboard recovery.

6. Head on beam-to-broad reach course for two or three lengths then go nearly dead downwind.

7. Drop the headsail while keeping the mainsail centred (or nearly so). The jib sheets are not slacked, even during the dousing manoeuvre, to keep them inside the lifelines.

8. Hold the downward course until victim is abaft the beam.

9. Gybe.

10. Approach the victim on a course of **approximately** 45 degrees to 60 degrees off the wind.

11. Establish contact with the victim with heaving line or other device. The Naval Academy uses a "throwing sock" containing 75 feet of light floating line and a bag that can be thrown into the wind because the line is kept inside the bag and trails out as it sails to the victim.

12. Effect recovery over the windward side.

Quickstop Under Spinnaker

The same procedure is used to accommodate a spinnaker.
Follow the preceding instructions. As the boat comes head-to-wind and the pole is eased to the head stay, the spinnaker halyard is lowered and the sail is gathered on the fore deck. The turn is continued through the tack and the approach phase commences.

Quickstop in Yawls & Ketches

Experiment with your mizzen sail. During sea trials, it was found best to drop the mizzen as soon as possible during the early phases of Quick-Stop.

Quickstop Using Engine

Use of the engine is not essential, although it's advisable to have it running in neutral, during Quick-Stop in case it is needed in the final approach. Check first for trailing lines!

SHORTHANDED CREWS

When there are only two people sailing together and a man-overboard accident occurs, the remaining crew member may have difficulty in handling the recovery alone. If the victim has sustained injuries, getting him back aboard may be almost impossible. The Quick-Stop method is simple to effect by a singlehander, with only one alteration to the procedure: the addition of the "Lifesling", a floating horsecollar device that doubles as a hoisting sling. The Lifesling is attached to the boat by a length of floating line three or four times the boat's length.
When a crew member falls overboard the scenario should proceed as follows:

1. A cushion or other flotation is thrown while the boat is brought IMMEDIATELY head-to-wind, slowed and stopped.

Reproduced with the kind permission of US Sailing.

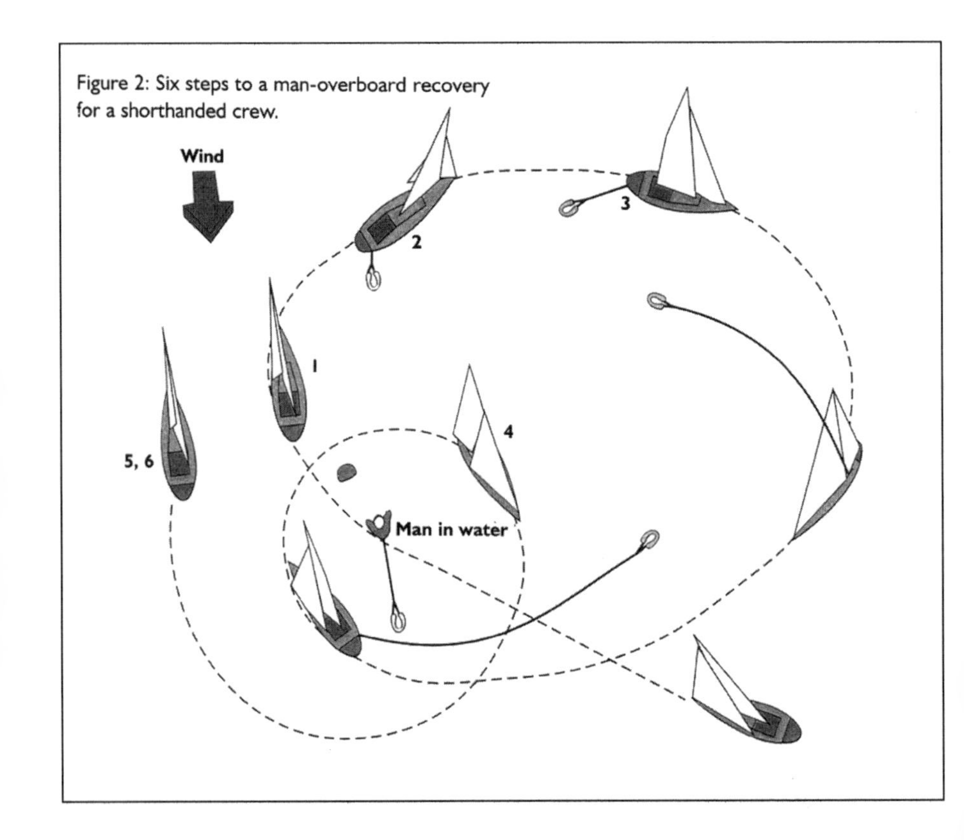

Figure 2: Six steps to a man-overboard recovery for a shorthanded crew.

2. The Lifesling is deployed by opening the bag on the stern pulpit and dropping the sling into the water. It will trail astern and draw out the line.

Reproduced with the kind permission of US Sailing

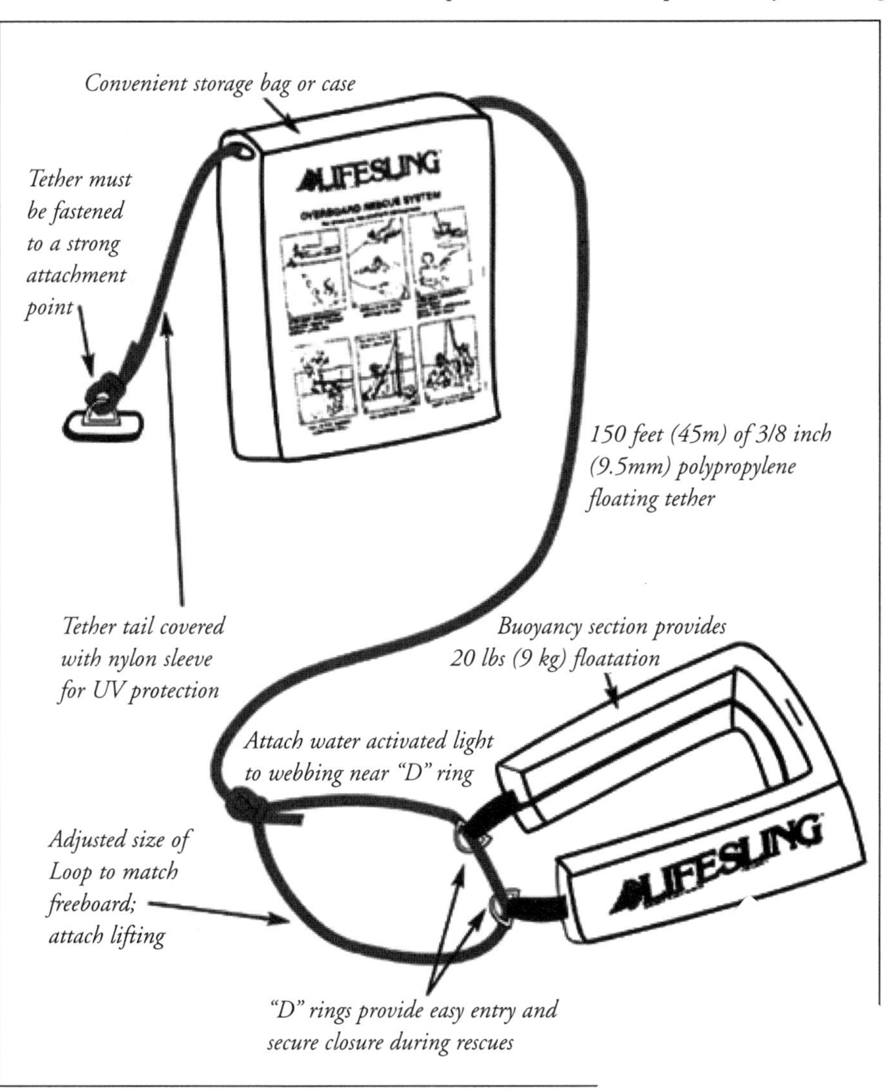

3. Once deployed, the boat is sailed in a wide circle around trailing. The jib is allowed to back from head-to-wind, in

4. Contact is established with the victim by the line and sling being drawn inward by the boat's circling motion. The victim places the sling over his head and under his arms.
5. Upon contact, the boat is put head-to-wind again, the headsail is dropped to the deck and the main is doused.
6. As the boat drifts slowly backward, the crew begins pulling the sling and the victim to the boat. If necessary, a cockpit winch can be used to assist in this phase, which should continue until the victim is alongside and pulled up tightly until he is suspended in the sling (so that he will not drop out). But see following page for advice on a horizontal lift, which is preferable when there's a choice.

PARBUCKLE DEVICE

This is an alternative to the hoisting rig. A patent version is known as the Tri-buckle. Another version is rectangular, like a climbing net. The net, or triangle of strong porous material, is clipped to the toe rail, the triangle top or net extremity clipped to a halyard extension. The casualty is manoevred or dragged alongside into the triangle or net then rolled onto the deck by hoisting the halyard.
Hypothermic aftershock may be minimised by this method which keeps the casualty essentially horizontal.

THE HOISTING RIG

Note: Since the hoisting rig was developed, more evidence has emphasised the value in keeping a victim horizontal particularly after long or hypothermic immersion. A parbuckle or horizontal lift is highly desirable (see below).

1. With the floating tether line, haul the victim alongside, preferably on the windward side, from amidships to the quarter, wherever there are available cleats and winches.
2. Pull up on the tether line (with winch assistance, if necessary) to get the victim's head and shoulders out of the water and cleat it. The victim is now safe.
3. Attach a three-or four-part tackle to the main halyard, haul it up to a predetermined point, about 10 feet above the deck or high enough so that the victim can be hoisted up and over the lifelines. Cleat off the halyard.
4. Attach the lower end of the tackle to the (previously sized) loop in the tether line that passes through the D-rings of the sling.
5. Reeve the running end of the tackle through a sheet block or snatch block on deck and put it on a cockpit winch. Hoist the victim aboard by winching it on the running end of the tackle.

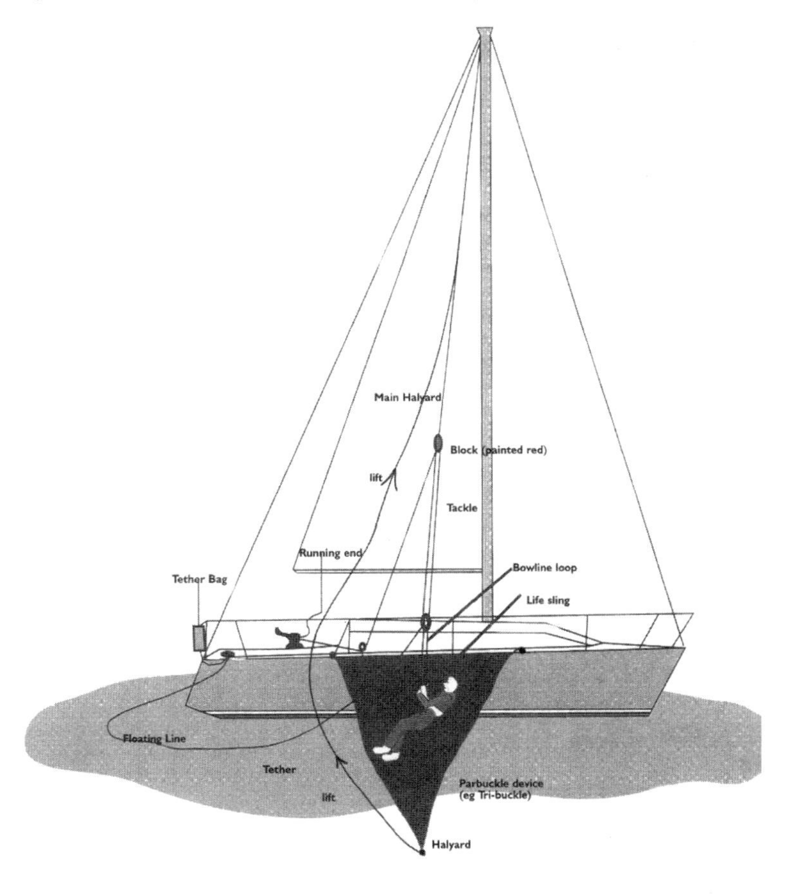

APPENDIX E
Hypothermia

WHAT IS IT?
A condition in which exposure to cold air and/or water lowers body core temperature. Death can result from too low a brain and heart temperature.

WHY BE CONCERNED?
Hypothermia, even mild cases, decreases crew efficiency and increases risk of costly accidents. ***Proper planning against hypothermia can give a winning competitive edge.***

PREVENTION
- Wear warm clothing and a lifejacket/harness. Have proper foul-weather kit for all crew. Dry suits are excellent. Insulate all areas of the body, especially the high heat-loss areas: head, neck, armpits, sides of chest and groin. Keep warm and dry, but avoid sweating; wear layered clothes.
- Rotate watch frequently.
- Get plenty of rest, prevent fatigue.
- Eat and drink normally, *no alcohol.*
- Prevent dehydration; watch urine colour (drink more if colour becomes more intense).
- Avoid seasickness.
- Take into account special medical problems of crew members.
- Regularly train crew in Man Overboard recovery.
- Have two or more crew trained in CPR (Cardio-pulmonary Resuscitation).

SURVIVAL IN COLD WATER (under 75°F, 25°C)
- **If boat is in trouble**, put on dry or survival suits if carried. Radio for help; give position, number of crew, injuries, boat description. Make visual distress signals. Stay below if possible. Remain aboard until sinking is inevitable.
- **If going overboard**, launch life raft and EPIRB (Emergency Position Indicating Radio Beacon). Take grab bag, visual distress signals and waterproof hand-held VHF. Get into raft, stay out of water as water conducts heat out of the body 20 times faster than air. Remain near boat if practicable.
- **If in the water**, crew should stay together near the boat. This makes everyone easier to find, helps morale. Enter life raft, keep dry suit or survival suit on if worn.
- **If not wearing dry suit or survival suit**, make sure you wear a lifejacket, keep clothes and shoes on for some insulation and flotation. Keep hat on to protect head. Get all or as much of body out of water as soon as possible – into raft or swamped boat or onto flotsam. Avoid swimming or treading water, which increases heat loss. Minimise exposed body surface. A splashguard accessory on the lifejacket greatly improves resistance to swallowing seawater and also accommodates involuntary "gasping" when plunged into cold water.

WARNING

- First aid for severe and critical hypothermia is to add heat to stabilise temperature only. Rapid re-warming, such as a hot shower or bath, may be fatal; it will, at least, cause complications. Allow body to re-warm itself slowly.
- Body core temperature lags behind skin temperature during re-warming. Keep victim protected for extended period after apparent full recovery or medical help arrives. *Many hours are required for full return to normal temperature even though victim says he has recovered.*
- Always assume hypothermia is present in all man overboard situations in which victim has been exposed for more than 10–15 minutes
- Victims may also be suffering from near drowning, thus needing oxygen. Observe for vomiting.
- In a helicopter rescue, protect victim – including the head – from rotor blast wind chill

HYPOTHERMIA FIRST AID

ALL CASES

- Keep victim horizontal
- Move victim to dry, shelter and warmth
- Allow to urinate from horizontal position
- Handle gently
- Remove wet clothes – cut off if necessary
- Apply mild heat (comfortable to your skin) to head, neck, chest and groin – use hot water bottles, warm moist towels
- Cover with blankets or sleeping bag; insulate from cold – including head and neck
- Report to Doctor by radio

HYPOTHERMIA FIRST AID

MILD CASES

- Primary task is to prevent further heat loss and allow body to re-warm itself
- Give warm, sweet drinks – no alcohol – no caffeine
- Apply mild heat source to stabilise temperature and/or
- Re-heat to point of perspiring
- Keep victim warm and horizontal for several hours

MODERATE CASES

- Same as above
- Offer sips of warm liquid only if victim is fully conscious and able to swallow without difficulty – no alcohol – no caffeine
- Have victim checked by doctor

SEVERE CASES

- Obtain medical advice as soon as possible using your radio
- Assist victim, but avoid jarring him – rough handling may cause cardiac arrest or ventricular fibrillation of heart
- No food or drink
- Observe for vomiting and be prepared to clear airway
- *Ignore pleas of "Leave me alone, I'm OK" victim is in serious trouble –* keep continuous watch over victim
- Lay victim down in bunk, wedge in place, elevate feet, keep immobile; no exercise
- Apply external mild heat to head, neck, chest and groin – keep temperature from dropping, but avoid too rapid a temperature rise

CRITICAL CASES

- *Always assume the patient is revivable – hypothermic victims may look dead –* don't give up – pulse very difficult to feel, breathing may have stopped
- Handle with extreme care
- Tilt the head back to open the airway – look, listen and feel for breathing and pulse for *one to two full minutes*
- If there is any breathing or pulse, no matter how faint or slow, do not give CPR, but keep a close watch on vital sign changes
- Stabilise temperature with available heat sources, such as naked chest to back warming by other crew member (leave legs alone)
- If no breathing or pulse for one or two minutes, begin CPR immediately. *Do not give up until victim is thoroughly warm – alive or dead.*
- *Medical help imperative – hospitalisation needed*

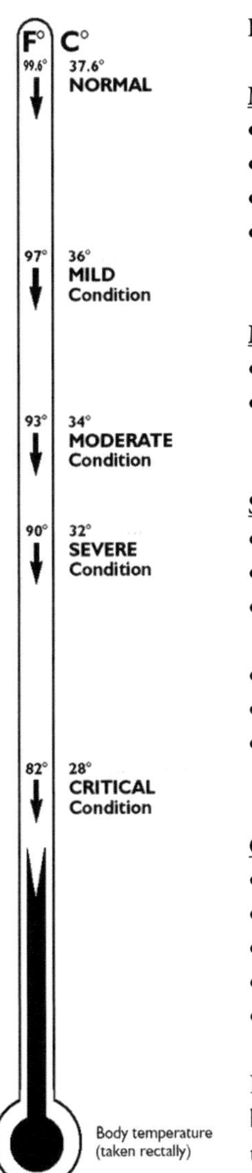

RANGES OF HYPOTHERMIA SYMPTOMS

MILD CONDITIONS (97-93°F, 36-34°C)

- Shivering, cold hands and feet
- Still alert and able to help self
- Numbness in limbs, loss of dexterity, clumsiness
- Pain from cold

MODERATE CONDITIONS (93-90°F, 34-32°C)

- Same as above
- Confusion, loss of time estimation and reasoning power

SEVERE CONDITIONS (90-82°F, 32-28°C)

- Shivering decreases or stops
- Further loss of reasoning and recall, confusion, abnormal behaviour.
- Victim appears drunk; very clumsy, slurs speech, denies problem and may resist help
- Unable to help themselves
- Victim semiconscious to unconscious
- Muscular rigidity increasing

CRITICAL CONDITIONS (82°F, 28°C and below)

- Unconscious, may look dead
- Little or no apparent breathing
- Pulse slow and weak, or no pulse found
- Skin cold, may be bluish-grey colour
- Very rigid

Note: Most physical symptoms vary with each individual and may be unreliable indicators of core body temperature. Only a low temperature rectal thermometer gives reliable core temperature (the mouth cools too rapidly). In general, as body temperature fails, symptoms will increase.

Reproduced by kind permission of
US Sailing, 15 Maritime Drive, PO Box 1260, Portsmouth, RI 02871
and Richard Clifford.

APPENDIX F

Drogues and Sea Anchors

TERMINOLOGY

The term "***drogue***" generally means a device dragged from the stern of a vessel which allows the vessel to continue to make steerage way through the water but at reduced speed. The term "***sea anchor***" generally means a device streamed from the bows of a vessel which practically halts the vessel in the water.

LIFERAFTS

Every liferaft has a sea anchor supplied as part of its equipment. A sea anchor is critical to the safe use of a liferaft and dramatically reduces the chance of liferaft capsize. Its secondary function is to limit drift. A spare sea anchor may be carried in a grab bag. Sea anchors in liferafts should comply with ISO 17339 and the opportunity should be taken at service intervals to ensure this.

There are 5 basic design requirements for an ISO 17339 compliant life raft sea anchor:

(1) It should be a cone with minimum mouth diameter of 400mm for up to 10 person raft, 500mm for 11 to 25 persons, and 800mm for lifeboats over 9m. Other shapes may be used so long as it develops drag equivalent to a cone of this diameter. The minimum drag requirements at 3kt tow speed are 35kg for up to 10-person rafts, 54.5kg for 11-25 person rafts, and 140kg for life boats over 9m.

(2) The material must be porous and rot proof allowing water penetration of 100-120 l/s/m^2. Note this requirement is a bit unusual since a typical material for small sea anchors is plastic coated polyester, which is not porous.

(3) It must have a braided construction towline at least 30m long and at least 8mm diameter with a breaking strength (including knots and attachments) at least 750kg for rafts up to 10-person and 1000kg for rafts greater than 10 persons. Any knot will reduce the breaking strength by approximately 50%, so to have a 750kg system strength would require 1500kg (3300lbs) line, which is generally the breaking strength of 12mm polypropylene line or 8mm polyester line.

(4) The sea anchor shroud lines must be designed to prevent the sea anchor from tumbling through itself. The shrouds and attachments should exceed 90kg in strength for up to 10 person rafts, 140kg for 11-25 person rafts and 360kg for lifeboats over 9m.

(5) The sea anchor must be stable when towed at up to 6 kts.

(6) The sea anchor mouth must be reinforced by a corrosion resistant ring (usually stainless wire) that will open immediately on deployment and remain open.

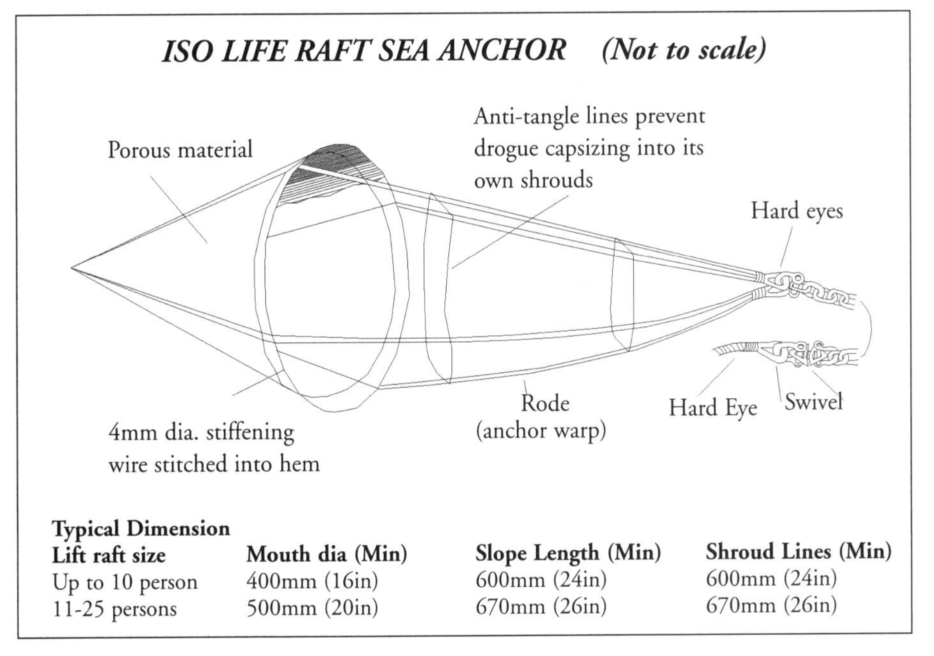

Typical Dimension

Lift raft size	Mouth dia (Min)	Slope Length (Min)	Shroud Lines (Min)
Up to 10 person	400mm (16in)	600mm (24in)	600mm (24in)
11-25 persons	500mm (20in)	670mm (26in)	670mm (26in)

DROGUES ON YACHTS

A number of research programs have been conducted including one for the RORC by the Southampton University Wolfson Unit. In tests drogue deployment repeatedly prevented typical yacht forms from being slewed sideways and rolled in heavy breaking seas.

Deployment of a drogue over the stern means that heavy water will break over that part of the yacht, so all openings must be properly secured shut.

A "series-drogue" (many small cones secured to a long rode) invented by Donald Jordan has the ability to continue to provide drag even if part of the device is "surfing" under a wave crest. It should be noted that the series drogue requires a strong attachment point (see system loads in the table below) with a chafe free lead aft to the water.

Recommended series drogue specifications

Vessel displacement	*System load*	*# cones*	*Rode length*
10,000lbs	***8,000lbs***	***100***	***246ft***
20,000lbs	***14,000lbs***	***116***	***277ft***
30,000lbs	***20,000lbs***	***132***	***303ft***
40,000lbs	***25,000lbs***	***147***	***332ft***
50,000lbs	***30,000lbs***	***164***	***361ft***

SEA ANCHORS ON YACHTS

The most common form of sea anchor for yachts is the "parachute" anchor developed from aviation parachutes. Specialist manufacturers have accumulated much data to demonstrate the effectiveness of the device which can enable a vessel to take seas bows-on, reduce drift to the order of one knot, and resist capsize. ***The rode and attachment point for the sea anchor should be strong enough to hold the full displacement of the vessel (on racing boats, often a bridle to the primary winches). The most common failure mode for sea anchors is the rode/bridle chafing thru. Thus the rode must be extremely well protected from chafe all the way from the attachment point out over the bow.***

Recommended sea anchor specifications

Vessel displacement	*Sea anchor diameter*	*Rode diameter**
10,000lbs	*6ft*	***1/2 inch***
20,000lbs	*9ft*	***5/8 inch***
30,000lbs	*12ft*	***5/8 inch***
40,000lbs	*16ft*	***5/8 inch***
50,000lbs	*21ft*	***3/4 inch***

* ***Recommended rode length is 10 tim***e LOA

APPENDIX G
TRAINING
Model Training Course Offshore Personal Survival

With acknowledgements to IMO (International Maritime Organisation), AYF (Australian Yachting Federation) and RYA (Royal Yachting Association) whose publications have been consulted in the preparation of Appendix G.

INTRODUCTION

1 **Purpose of the model course**. To help provide training under ISAF Offshore Special Regulation Section 6. The model course is not the only means of providing such training. Other courses meeting the needs of Section 6 may apply to the appropriate MNA for ISAF Approval (see Introduction paragraph 7).

2 **Use of the model course**. The chief instructor should review the experience and knowledge of the trainees before the course starts and revise details of the course plan accordingly. Trainees, who should have practical offshore sailing experience, should be encouraged to prepare for the course by familiarising themselves with the topics in Special Regulations 6.02 and 6.03. See also the reading list in A 4.2. Particular skills when suitably documented, may be accepted to excuse a trainee from that part of the course.

3 **Presentation.** The presentation may have to be repeated in various ways until the instructor is satisfied that the trainees have attained a good understanding of each topic.

4 **Evaluation.** The final activities on each day are examinations, which should be used together with instructors' continuous assessments to provide a overall evaluation. The pass mark is to be taken as 60% in each of the marked units.

5 **Implementation.** Detailed requirements are given below. Thorough preparation is the key to successful implementation of the course.

6 **Structure of the model course.**
Part A describes the framework for the course, with aims and objectives and notes on suggested teaching facilities and equipment.
Part B provides an outline of lectures, and practical sessions. A suggested timetable is included but it is more important that trainees achieve proficiency in the required skills than that a strict timetable is followed.
Part C sets out the detailed syllabus.

7 ISAF Approved Training Courses and Trainee Certification.

7.1 The status of "ISAF Approved" together with authority to use the ISAF logo may only be awarded to a training course by an ISAF MNA (Member National Authority) who must be satisfied that the course delivers training as required by Special Regulation 6.01. A grant of approved status carries with it a duty on the MNA to ensure that the course provider continues to deliver appropriate training over the course of time. An annual review may be appropriate for this purpose. The MNA must remove approved status if and when it judges this necessary.

7.2 It is not necessary for a training course to follow Appendix G Model Training Course in order to receive approval as in 7.1 above. The overriding requirement is that the course must deliver the training required by Special Regulation 6.01.

7.2 An MNA which lacks experience in offshore training or for other reasons needs advice should contact the ISAF Secretariat – Offshore and Technical Department. The OTAP is appointed by and reports to the ISAF Offshore Special Regulations sub-committee.

7.3 A sailor holding an in-date "pass" certificate (each has a validity of 5 years) from an ISAF Approved Offshore Personal Survival Course shall be accepted by a race organiser as having complied with the requirements of ISAF Offshore Special Regulation 6.01.

7.4 "Pass" certificates issued at an ISAF Approved course shall carry the statement "ISAF Approved Offshore Personal Survival Course" and may carry the ISAF logo.

7.5 Unless otherwise stated in the Notice of Race, it is not mandatory that a training course for compliance with SR 6.01 is "ISAF Approved" however this status is encouraged wherever possible.

Part A Framework

A1 **Class Size** The maximum recommended class size is 20. When smaller work groups are established, this will allow for about four in each group. A suggested minimum number for the class would be ten. Otherwise it is difficult to promote discussion in smaller work groups.

A2 **Instructors** should have:
- wide experience of offshore sailing including sailing in severe weather
- a thorough knowledge of the course material
- a thorough knowledge of the requirements of the ISAF Offshore Special Regulations
- a good understanding of teaching methods

A3 **Facilities and equipment**

A 3.1 A suitable classroom is required with desks or tables and chairs. It should be possible to move the furniture around so that a variety of room arrangements can be used. Ideally, extra rooms will be available for when the class is split into groups, since each group should have a separate space in which to work.

A 3.2 The main room should be provided with the following equipment:
- a whiteboard or blackboard
- a flip chart
- writing materials for trainees
- an overhead projector (OHP) for transparencies
- a computer projector (with additional sound channel if not integral)
- a video tape player compatible with the computer projector
- a PC or laptop with CD-ROM drive, all compatible with the computer projector
- a reflective screen designed for use with the computer projector
- adequate electric sockets located so that the equipment can be positioned safely.

A 3.3 Group rooms should be provided with a table and chairs and some form of board and writing materials.

A 3.4 A video camera may be useful and should be compatible with the computer projector or alternatively must produce video tapes compatible with the video tape player.

A 3.5 A warm-water swimming pool with all appropriate safety equipment, personnel and facilities making it suitable for demonstration and training with lifejackets and liferafts. A wave-generator may provide added realism.

A 3.6 An outdoor location with appropriate safety equipment, personnel and facilities making it suitable for demonstration and training with pyrotechnics and fire extinguishers.

A4 Recommended Reference and Display Material

This section will be updated as information is submitted from MNA's. Course providers are encouraged to refer to materials relevant to their own areas of operation.

A 4.1 For the Instructors

Printed Material
- ISAF Offshore Special Regulations complete with separately-printed Appendices A2 (Liferafts) and G (the present document)
- ISAF RRS (The Racing Rules of Sailing)
- International Regulations for the Prevention of Collision at Sea
- Admiralty Summary of Notices to Mariners (NP 247)
- IAMSAR (International Aeronautical and Maritime Search and Rescue) manual, or manual for small craft (in preparation)
- ALRS (Admiralty List of Radio Signals) Volume 5 GMDSS (NP 285)
- SOLAS (Safety of Life At Sea Convention) Consolidated Edition
- International Life-Saving Appliance (LSA) Code
- Appropriate ISAF MNA Training Booklet or if none, at least one of
- RYA Practical Course Notes on Sea Survival
- AYF equivalent
- US Sailing Equivalent

Video Tapes

A Highway of Low Pressure

CD-ROMs

COSPAS-SARSAT

A 4.2 For the Trainees

A 4.2.1 Possession of:

- ISAF Offshore Special Regulations
- ISAF RRS (The Racing Rules of Sailing)
- International Regulations for the Prevention of Collision at Sea
- Admiralty Summary of Notices to Mariners (NP 247)
- IAMSAR (International Aeronautical and Maritime Search and Rescue) manual, or manual for small craft (in preparation).
- First Aid at Sea (Justins and Berry, published Adlard Coles) or equivalent
- Appropriate ISAF Member National Authority Training Booklet or if none, at least one of
    - RYA Practical Course Notes on Sea Survival
    - AYF equivalent
    - US Sailing Equivalent

A 4.2.2 Knowledge of:

- ALRS (Admiralty List of Radio Signals) Volume 5 GMDSS (NP 285)
- SOLAS (Safety of Life At Sea Convention) Consolidated Edition
- International Life-Saving Appliance (LSA) Code
- International Medical Guide for Ships (WHO, World Health

A 4.2.3 Recommended further study:

- The Offshore Special Regulations Handbook by Alan Green (Adlard Coles)
- The Grab Bag Book (F & M Howorth, Adlard Coles)
- Instant Weather Forecasting (A Watts, Adlard Coles)
- Heavy Weather Sailing (A Coles & P Bruce, Adlard Coles)
- Essentials of Sea Survival (F Golden and M Tipton, Human Kinetics)

Part C Detailed Syllabus

paragraph numbers refer to session numbers in Part B

Session 1 Introduction

1.0 The instructor gives an overview of the course and administrative arrangements, and explains the assessment and exam procedures. If the course has ISAF Approval (see introduction paragraph 7) the certificate will be so endorsed. The instructor should also deliver a final course timetable.

1.1 The importance of training both in formal sessions and also as part of the routine in running a sailing yacht.

1.2 The importance of a "safety ethos"
1.3 The crew brief including safety equipment, stowage details, emergency procedures, responsibilities and how to send a Mayday call and use EPIRB and flares in case the skipper and key crew members are incapacitated. Show stowage chart required in Special Regulations: crew experience and fitness must be adequate
1.4 Responsibility of person in charge for safe conduct of vessel and oversight and direction of crew actions. Responsibility of crew members for their own safety and in the discharge of their duties, to contribute to the safety of the vessel and the rest of the crew.

Session 2 Care and maintenance of safety and other equipment
2.1 Routine to check, service, clean, dry, fit and adjust to wearer, and correctly store safety equipment. Give examples eg safety harness, inflatable lifejackets, liferafts etc.
2.2 Checks to continue under way including eg rigging (pins in place and undistorted, wires not fractured, running rigging not unduly chafed, shackles seized when appropriate), seacocks, stern gland, toilet plumbing, etc.
2.3 Availability of reserve navigation lights and general spares.
2.4 Marking of floating equipment with vessel name.
2.5 Check and overhaul dan buoy, jon buoy, MoB modules, lifeslings etc.
2.6 Understand that dormant water or dirt in a fuel tank may be kicked up and taken into the engine in very rough weather - ensure that engine oil and fuel filler caps etc are kept clean and secure.

Session 3 Storm sails
3.1 Storm and heavy-weather sails including those on board the trainee's boat.
3.2 How are they set?
3.3 Where are they stowed?
3.4 importance of practicing from time to time even in light weather.
3.5 Understand the changed pressures on the rig when using reduced sail in very heavy weather.
3.6 Dangers of heavy water breaking over the boat and carrying away poorly-stowed sails and sails set too low down.
3.7 Danger of heavy metal shackles in storm sails
3.8 Importance of bright colour in storm sails.
3.9 Value (in some boats) of lashing down the main boom in heavy weather and setting a trysail without the boom.

Session 4 Damage Control and Repair
4.1 Plan to minimise damage in forthcoming heavy weather
4.2 Remedial action including use of spare materials and tools to cope with:-
 .1 loss of rudder/steering
 .2 loss of mast
 .3 flooding due to (a) collision damage forward, (b) amidships, (c) aft, (d) seacock failure
 .4 stranding

.5 severe weather damage eg (a) hatch ripped off, (b) coachroof split
.6 loss of keel and/or capsize
.7 collision with another vessel, a submerged object (eg container), sea life, etc.

Session 5 Heavy Weather – crew routines, boat handling, drogues

5.1 Detailed examination of risks, solutions and contingency plans including crew routines for:-

.1 general working in exposed positions – hooking on before leaving hatchway, remaining hooked on at all times (dual hooking), telling someone when going forward, when lifejackets and harnesses shall be worn, value of personal EPIRBs (PLBs) especially with on-board D/F
.2 preparation for rough weather – secure stowage for moving items.
.3 ensure jackstays rigged
.4 rough weather operations
.5 severe weather strategies
.6 galley operations lee strops, preparing hot food in thermos containers in advance of heavy weather
.7 importance of high visibility of yacht in heavy seaway: display of orange surface, use of white light or strobe light on deck or in rig (also of use on a dull day) consider flying radar reflector if robust type.

5.2 boat handling in a seaway noting in particular helming techniques and effect of conditions on boat and crew taking into account:-

.1 strength of wind
.2 duration of high wind
.3 length of fetch
.4 wave pattern
.5 definition of wave height and length including assessment methods
.6 wave refraction
.7 multiple wave patterns
.8 waves in tidal/current conditions
.9 predicting dangerous wave conditions
.10 angle of boat to a seaway and to individual waves
.11 early sail changes, sail change procedures, knowing the boat and its characteristics and tendencies
.12 heaving-to
.13 assessing options eg to stand off or cross a barred entrance

5.3 Effect of a drogue on a boat in severe weather

Session 6 Man overboard prevention and recovery

6.1 Prevention

.1 lifelines to be maintained in accordance with Special Regulations
.2 harness to be clipped on at night and in rough weather (see C5.1.1)
.3 drawback of plain harness hooks

.4 harness crotch straps prevent "slip-out"
.5 use the sea toilet in bad weather not the stern
.6 encourage the use of shorter safety line and in particular lines with mid-line clips as being most adaptable (highlighting issues with being towed in the water at speed while in a harness and how a shorter line (less than 1m) both aids recovery and reduces potential risk particularly on high performance boats)

6.2 Recovery
.1 well-drilled routine (see Special Regulations Appendix D)
.2 "Mayday" on radio is valid if necessary
.3 quickly accessible hoisting rig
.4 value of horizontal lift and retention of horizontal position
.5 procedure and team ready to re-clothe, re-warm and check recovered person for injury, advising shore if necessary
.6 use of whistle, SOLAS-type lifejacket light, strobe light.

6.3 Search Patterns
.1 Explain the most common standard search patterns for finding a lost MOB (Expanding Square Search, Creeping Line, Parallel Search and Sector Search)
.2 Navigation consideration (establishing a datum and then what affects the position of the MOB relative to the boat and the ground)
.3 Importance of search lights, the use of PLB and high visibility clothing

Session 7 Giving Assistance to other craft

7.1 Legal and rules requirements
.1 SOLAS obligations apply to all ships on all voyages**
.2 Racing Rules of Sailing**
.3 moral imperative
.4 communications obligations**
.5 log-keeping obligations**

***see supplement one (below)*

7.2 manoeuvring close to a vessel sinking
.1 keep other vessel and shore informed
.2 be prepared to recover personnel from the water or a liferaft
.3 tactics if other vessel is on fire

7.3 understand that another yacht may be the only source of help.

7.4 towing and being towed

Session 8 Hypothermia

8.1 Actively counter its development by wearing proper protective clothing

8.2 Know the symptoms- shivering, irritability, lethargy, stumbling, slurred speech, loss of memory, victim feels cold, looks pale, breathing slow, pulse weak, leading to collapse and unconsciousness.

8.3 treatment - see First Aid at Sea by Justins and Berry or other textbook

8.4 do not – give alcohol, rub the skin to warm, or give up resuscitation.

8.5 value of immersion suits, thermal protective aids (TPA's)

Session 9 SAR organisation and methods

9.1 with regard to the SAR authorities in the areas sailed, know:

- .2 their landline number to advise them of passage planning if appropriate
- .3 how to call them in emergency
- .4 what facilities they have (and don't have)
- .5 if helicopters are in use, know the sea-rescue system (hi-line, basket pick-up, winchman bridle, etc.) and whether a pick-up from a deck, in the water, or in a liferaft is preferred
- .6 know what radio frequency to expect to use for direct contact
- .7 know what fixed-wing aircraft may be deployed
- .8 understand fixed-wing search patterns, signal flares
- .9 have a knowledge of global SAR organisation
- .10 how to cope with rescue attempts from passing ships
- .11 knowledge of new IAMSAR for small craft

Session 10 Weather Forecasting

10.1 sources of weather forecasts

10.2 terms and definitions and their exact meaning

10.3 Beaufort wind scale compared with mph (statute miles per hour) and speed in knots (nautical miles per hour), and sea state scale. Know that wind gusts may exceed forecast speeds by 40% or more and wave height may exceed forecast height by 87% or more

10.4 logging own weather observations of cloud, wind, sea, barometer, sea temperature (sometimes critical) and air temperature, etc.: making own deductions

10.5 be prepared for local abnormalities

Session 11 Liferafts and Lifejackets (theory)

11.1 Liferafts (theory)

11.1.2 knowledge of liferaft standards: SOLAS, ISAF Appendix A Part II and ORC and ISO 9650 Part 1 Type 1 Group A plus OSR requirements.

11.1.3 stowage, care and servicing of liferafts

11.1.4 liferaft emergency packs

11.1.5 grab bag contents and application

11.1.6 two key elements in combating liferaft capsize – drogue, ballast water pockets

11.1.7 the capsize mechanism and the re-righting procedure

11.1.8 when and how to launch a liferaft

11.1.9 protecting a liferaft in the minimum time it is alongside after launch

11.1.10 boarding a liferaft if possible dry: use of dry suits if possible

11.1.11 boarding a liferaft from the water: importance of boarding ramp and grab lines

11.1.12 crew organisation both before boarding and within liferaft:: signalling for help, watchkeeping, damage repair, medical, water, food, keeping up morale, psychology of survival.

11.1.13 knowledge of physiological shock of cold water and hypothermia (see session 8) and its effect on human performance in tasks like liferaft operation and survival.
11.1.14 use of SART (optional in grab bag).

Session 11.2 Lifejackets (theory)
11.2.1 Understand the terminology in your part of the world: know the difference between a 150N lifejacket (or equivalent title) capable of turning over an unconscious person in the water to the face-up position within 30 seconds, and a lesser device which may only aid buoyancy.
11.2.2 Understand the accessories required in Special Regulations: whistle, marine-grade retro-reflective material, yacht's or wearer's name
11.2.3 Understand the accessories and attributes recommended in Special Regulations: light in accordance with the SOLAS LSA code, compliance with EN376 (ISO 12402) or near equivalent, crotch strap, splash guard
11.2.3 Know the relative merits and methods of use of all-inflatable buoyancy and part-fixed, part-inflatable, automatic inflation, gas inflation on demand, mouth-only inflation.
11.2.3 Know the importance of a good fit, lifejacket organised for quick donning, compatibility with harness.

Session 12 Exam (1)
This exam is one of two. Time for answering questions -about 15 minutes, with 5 minutes for marking after swapping the papers amongst the class. Questions should be set to be answered quickly, eg multiple-choice, with at least two questions needing some narrative or listing. Overall assessment for the course will be a combination of the two exams plus the tutors' assessments during class and practical work. (See introduction paragraph 4)

Session 13 Liferafts and Lifejackets (practical)
.1 a pool with a wave-making facility will add realism
.2 trainees to don shirt and trousers plus oilskins and to try swimming first without, then with 150N lifejackets. Majority of exercises with all trainees wearing 150N lifejackets.
.3 inflate a liferaft and transfer a full complement into the raft (a) from the poolside (b) from the water (show difference between boarding with ramp and without): paddle the liferaft for a distance.
.4 capsize a liferaft and have each trainee right the raft whilst swimming
.5 trainees to haul into a raft one survivor who plays helpless
.6 In fully-loaded raft trainees to check out all equipment, including that in grab bag, deploying or using everything including food and water.
.7 trainee to attempt heliograph signalling (using spotlight in roof) from liferaft (more difficult if in wave-making pool).
.8 trainees to operate WT VHF hand-held and WT hand-held GPS talking to instructor as if a rescue vessel.
.9 trainees to try lifejackets both with and without crotch straps in place.
.10 each trainee to experience use of the splashguard in wave conditions.
.11 group to investigate ability of lifejacket to self-right.

.12 forming circle in water to aid visibility/morale – HELP/Huddle techniques
.13 towing an unconscious person
.14 assistance using throwing line to recover nearby survivor
.15 the opportunity of using the pool may be taken to demonstrate MOB modules, Lifeslings, lifebuoys etc.
.16 if a darkened pool is available, demonstrate retro-reflective tape.
.17 trainees who depend on spectacles may consider having an indestructible pair as part of their personal survival kit.

Sessions 14/15 Fire precautions and fire fighting (theory and practical)

.1 fire theory
.2 most common causes of fire in small craft
.3 prevention
.4 equipment – fire extinguishers, fire blankets, services, tested, maintained, fit for purpose. Advantages/ disadvantages of various types of extinguisher.
.5 practical operation of fire extinguishers (actual fire is not required in this training course)

Sessions 16/17 Communications equipment (VHF, GMDSS, satcomms) (theory and practical)

.1 VHF main installations and hand-helds.
.2 Special Regulations requirements for VHF 25W output, masthead antenna, emergency antenna.
.3 SSB (knowledge of email and other services via some shore stations, daily cruising yacht schedules, etc.).
.4 Satcoms: A, B, C, D and M. Non-INMARSAT types (eg Iridium).
.5 Terrestrial cellphones. Limitations.
.6 GMDSS, DSC, AIS.
.7 Aviation VHF and its use in SAR.
.8 Obligation to log communications connected with distress working**

***see Supplement below*

Sessions 18/19 Pyrotechnics and EPIRBs (theory and practical)

.1 pyrotechnics required in Special Regulations: hand flares, parachute flares, smoke signals. Usage, precautions, range of visibility, duration, behaviour in high winds, altitude of parachute flares and avoiding conflict with aircraft, different operating mechanisms.
.2 stowage of pyrotechnics including some for ready use.
.3 use of white flares
.4 understand the operation of the 406 MHz EPIRB and its ancillary 121.5 beacon; the phasing out of 121.5 MHz as a distress alert system but its use in local area homing by SAR units and yachts with special-purpose D/F receivers on board in conjunction with PLB's.
.5 understand the operation of ARGOS-type beacons.
.6 understand the integration of distress beacons in the GMDSS framework.

.7 Draw attention to Inmarsat Safety Services' web link: www.inmarsat.com/safety which contains a wealth of information about maritime safety and security – including reception of maritime safety information via Inmarsat C or mini-C. It is useful for more than GMDSS alone.

Session 20 Exam (2)
This exam is one of two. Time for answering questions -about 15 minutes, with 5 minutes for marking after swapping the papers amongst the class. Questions should be set to be answered quickly, eg multiple-choice, with at least two questions needing some narrative or listing. Overall assessment for the course will be a combination of the two exams plus the tutors' assessments during class and practical work. (See Introduction paragraph 4 for marking details).

Supplement One
1 The Racing Rules of Sailing state:-
1 SAFETY
1.1 Helping Those in Danger
"A boat or competitor shall give all possible help to any person or vessel in danger"

2 SOLAS Convention Chapter V
Regulation 33 (replaces old Regulation 10) states:-
"The master of a ship at sea which is in a position to be able to provide assistance, on receiving a signal from any source that persons are in distress at sea, is bound to proceed with all speed to their assistance, if possible informing them or the SAR service that the ship is doing so. If the ship receiving the distress alert is unable or, in the special circumstances of the case, considers it unreasonable or unnecessary to proceed to their assistance, the master must enter in the log-book the reason for failing to proceed to the assistance of the persons in distress and, taking into account the recommendations of the Organization++, inform the appropriate SAR service accordingly.
++Refer to the immediate action to be taken by each ship on receipt of a distress message in the IAMSAR Manual, as it may be amended."

Reference to the original text and its context is strongly recommended.

3 Annual Summary of Admiralty Notices to Mariners NP 247
Section 4 Paragraph 1 states:-
"The radio watch on the international distress frequencies, which certain classes of ships are required to keep when as sea, is one of the most important factors in the arrangements for the rescue of people in distress at sea, and every ship should make its contribution to safety by guarding one or more of these distress frequencies for as long as is practicable whether or not required to do so by regulation."

Part B Outline Timetable *(2 pages)*

ISAF Offshore Special Regulations Appendix G Model Training Course Part B Day 1

Session	SR	Topic	theory*	practical	start	stop
1		Introduction	00:30		11:00	11:30
	6.02.0	**Training topics for theoretical sessions**				
2	6.02.1	care and maintenance of safety equipment	00:15		11:30	11:45
3	6.02 2	storm sails	00:20		11:45	12:05
4	6.02.3	damage control and repair	00:20		12:05	12:25
5	6.02.4	"heavy weather – crew routines, boat handling, drogues"	00:25		12:25	13:00
		break			13:00	14:00
6	6.02.5	man overboard prevention and recovery	00:30		14:00	14:30
7	6.02.6	giving assistance to other craft	00:15		14:30	14:45
8	6.02.7	hypothermia	00:20		14:45	15:05
		break	00:15		15:05	15:20
9	6.02.8	SAR organisation and methods	00:30		15:20	15:40
10	6.02.9	weather forecasting.	00:30		15:40	16:10
	6.03.0	**Training topics to include practical, hand-on sessions**				
11	6.03.1	liferafts and lifejackets (theory)	00:30		16:10	16:40
12		exam	00:20		16:40	17:00
		Day 1 total tuition including breaks		06:00		
		Day 1 net tuition		04:45		
		Day 1 net breaks		01:15		

*includes breaks

ISAF Offshore Special Regulations Appendix G Model Training Course Part B Day 2

Session	SR	Topic	theory*		practical	start	stop
13		liferafts and lifejackets (practical)			02:00	09:00	11:00
		break	00:15			11:00	11:15
14	6.03.2	fire precautions and fire fighting (theory)	00:15			11:15	11:30
15	6.03.2	fire precautions and fire fighting (practical)	00:30			11:30	12:00
16	6.03 3	communications equipment	00:20			12;00	12:20
		"(VHF, GMDSS, satcomms. etc- theory)"					
17	6.03.3	communications equipment	00:25			12:20	12:45
		"(VHF, GMDSS, satcomms. etc- practice)"					
		break	00:45			12:45	13:30
18	6.03.4	pyrotechnics and EPIRBs (theory)	00:20			13:30	13:50
19	6.03.4	pyrotechnics and EPIRBs (practical)			00:30	13:50	14:20
20		exam	00:20			14:20	14:40
		Day 2 total tuition including breaks	02:05		03:25		
		Day 2 net tuition		01:05			
		Day 2 net breaks		01:00			
		net total tuition including breaks	08:05		03:25		
		net tuition		05:50			
		net breaks		02:15			

Part D - Guidelines for an Offshore Personal Survival Refresher Course

For sailors whose certificates have expired, a refresher training course of about 8 hours training may be arranged. It should contain these sessions:

Session 1 (1 hr)	Update on recent changes in Offshore Special Regulations, national relevant documents or any other changes of importance
Session 2 (1 hr)	Update on new safety equipment
Session 3 (1 hr)	Update on recent lessons learned from fatal accidents and incidents in offshore races
Session 4 (1 hr)	Update on national/regional changes in Maritime Search and Rescue organisations, resources, locations etc as well as in relevant meteorological services
Session 5 (2 hrs)	In water training with life vests, liferafts, lifeslings etc
Session 6 (1½ hrs)	Medical and/or fire-fighting training as appropriate regarding national regulations.
Session 7 (½ hr)	Written exam

Detailed contents are to be developed by the appropriate Member National Authority. After the course has been passed with accepted written exam, a new certificate for another five year period may be issued.

APPENDIX H
ISAF Code for the Organisation of Oceanic Races

An Oceanic Race is defined as any Offshore race over 800 miles.

1. Organisers of oceanic races should consult with the **SAR (Search and Rescue) authorities** through whose areas a race is proposed to pass. Topics to be considered should among others be;
   Mutual responsibilities
   Resources
   Satellite communications coverage
   Position reporting systems
   Safety equipment on board
   Lessons learned from recent events
   Exchange of communication addresses, phone numbers etc

2. A **Risk Analysis** should be made, covering topics like;
   Meteorological conditions (icebergs, major currents, fogbanks, eddies etc)
   Commercial traffic, separation zones etc
   Stability requirements
   SAR assets and coverage
   Piracy and other security matters etc

3. **Environmental aspects** as wild life protective zones should be considered.

4. A **Notice to Mariners** about the race should be produced, usually in cooperation with the organizers national authorities.

5. An **Organization Chart** shall be established with key appointments like the Race Director (when applicable), Chairman of the Race Committee, Principal Race Officer, Safety Officers, Medical Officer, media personnel etc.

6. The Race Organizer should from the participating boats require;
   Crew lists with names, nationalities, contact details, PLB data and telephone numbers to next of kin
   For all boats all data that is registered for radio and data communications like call signs, Maritime Mobile Service Identity(MMSI), EPIRBs etc
   Boat details and descriptions (including electronic pictures)
   Owners/Helmsman declaration regarding liability

7. A Race Control Centre should be organized with Duty Officer 24/7. The watch roster should include relevant means to reinforce the working capacity. It may be appropriate to

arrange a training course for the duty officers before the race, including potential incident scenarios. A visit for skippers and navigators to the Race Control Centre may be arranged before the start of major long races, if possible also to appropriate Maritime Rescue Co-Ordination Centres (MRCC).

At the Race Control Centre a Log Book should be maintained. A format for daily situation reports (sitreps) should be developed. A Voice recorder should be available to record radio communications and crisis management.

8. A **Safety Information Package** about the race, boat descriptions and details (including electronic pictures), safety equipment, radio communication and medical resources, key personnel at the Race Control etc should be distributed to participating boats as well as the appropriate MRCC's.
9. A **Crisis Management Group** should be organized with the Chairman of the Race Committee, the Safety officer, Medical officer and others as relevant. The team should include media and legal representatives from the organizing body.
10. A **Crisis Support Group** with psychologists, medical and clerical personnel should be available for major incidents, both for immediate support to crews and dependants as well as for crew debriefings at later stages. This may be arranged by the Race Committee or the authorities controlling the area.
11. There may occur incidents that are significant, but still not that serious that MRCC and SAR units will get engaged. For such incidents the Race Organizer should consider to maintain a network of contacts and resources across the racing area to be able to support with towing, transport of equipment etc.
12. The organizer shall produce a **Safety Contingency Plan**, including typical series of actions at accidents as derived from the Risk Analysis. One topic to be covered is when and how to contact dependants, sponsors etc at various stages of lost contact, requests for assistance or emergency calls.
13. All yachts shall be equipped to standards which at least comply with the relevant level of Special Regulations as adopted by ISAF. Additional requirements may be prescribed, like additional radio and medical equipment.
14. In accordance with Special Regulations, an adequate number of crew members on each yacht shall have **Survival Training**. Apart from the basic requirements for ISAF Personal Survival Course as stipulated in Spec Regs Annex G, the Race organizer can also prescribe;
    What level of sailing together in the actual boat that may be required
    Which practical training sequences that shall be required to by the crew to be performed, like MOB drills, helicopter evacuations etc.
15. A **Safety Check** should be performed before the start, it should include;
    - Safety equipment
    - Appropriate certificates for radio and satellite communication equipment
    - Check of individual and collective training
    - Endurance capacity and redundancy of capabilities characteristic for oceanic races like water provision, medical training etc

    The full responsibility for safety however always remains with the Person in Charge.

16. A **Positioning Reporting system** should be available, linked to the official race webpage.

17. **Meteorological services** may be allowed to be downloaded from public meteorolog ical centres or may be centrally provided from the Race Organizer to reduce satcom costs.

18. Races shall be conducted in compliance with the ISAF Racing Rules of Sailing and the COLREGS, whenever it is appropriate for these rules and regulations to be applied. Special attention should be given to traffic separation zones and to give way to commercial traffic.

19. A race organizer when appropriate should, in addition to supplying the relevant SAR authorities of the event, also supply;
- a T**elemedical Service Assistance Service (TMAS)** or inform a TMAS that the organizers have available on demand the following;
- for each boat:
a list of medicines and medical equipment
details of any TMAS or private medical service arranged by the boat
for each crew member:
name and contact details of physician who certified the crew members fit for entry (when applicable)
name and contact details of the crew members home physician
methods for gaining quick access to medical records if necessary
details of first aid and medical training received

20. The **Notice of Race** may include ;
Insurance requirements
Which individual and collective training that is required
What meteorological data and forecasts that will be allowed
Other matters as appropriate

21. The **Sailing Instructions** may include instructions;
To continuously monitor VHF Channel 16
To have the AIS active at all times or to activate the AIS in reduced visibility and passages with extensive commercial traffic
For any other safety matters as appropriate

22 A **Lessons Learned meeting** about safety issues should be arranged after the race.

APPENDIX J
CATEGORY 5 SPECIAL REGULATIONS
for inshore races

Category 5 Special Regulations are intended for use in short races, close to shore in relatively warm and protected waters where adequate shelter and/or effective rescue is available all along the course, held in daylight only.

With the exception of recommended item 3.14 pulpits etc. for which see the main body of Special Regulations, all the items relevant to Category 5 are shown in Appendix J.

Category 5 - Part A Basic

The following regulations shall be observed:-

Regulation	Item
1.02	**Responsibility of Person in Charge** The safety of a yacht and her crew is the sole and inescapable responsibility of the person in charge who must do his best to ensure that the yacht is fully found, thoroughly seaworthy and manned by an experienced crew who have undergone appropriate training and are physically fit to face bad weather. He must be satisfied as to the soundness of hull, spars, rigging, sails and all gear. He must ensure that all safety equipment is properly maintained and stowed and that the crew know where it is kept and how it is to be used. He shall also nominate a person to take over the responsibilities of the Person in Charge in the event of his incapacitation.
2.03.1	**suitability of equipment** All equipment required by Special Regulations shall:- a) function properly b) be regularly checked, cleaned and serviced c) when not in use be stowed in conditions in which deterioration is minimised d) be readily accessible e) be of a type, size and capacity suitable and adequate for the intended use and size of the yacht.
3.08	**hatches & companionways** 3.08.1 No hatch forward of the maximum beam station shall open inwards excepting ports having an area of less than 0.071m2 (110 sq in).
3.08.2	A hatch fitted forward of the maximum beam station, located on the side of the coachroof, opening into the interior of the boat ,and of area greater than 0.071m2 shall comply with ISO12216 design category A and and be clearly labelled and used in accordance with the following instruction: "NOT TO BE OPENED AT SEA" Attention is drawn to SR 3.02.1

Regulation	Item
3.08.3	A hatch shall be: a) permanently attached b) capable of being firmly shut immediately, and remaining firmly shut in a 180 degree capsize (inversion) c) and on monohulls so arranged as to be above the water when the hull is heeled 90 degrees. Hatches over lockers that open to the interior of the vessel shall be included in this requirement. A yacht may have a maximum of four (two on each side of centerline) hatches that do not conform to this requirement, provided that the opening of each is less than 0.071 sq m (110 sq in). Effective for boats of a series begun after January 1, 2009, a written statement signed by the designer or other person who performed the downflooding analysis shall be carried on board. For purposes of this rule the vessel's displacement condition for the analysis shall be the Light Craft Condition LCC (in conformity with 6.3 of the EN ISO 8666 standard and 3.5.1 of the EN ISO12217-2 standard). (Monohulls Only)
3.08.4	A companionway hatch shall: (a) be fitted with a strong securing arrangement which shall be operable from the exterior and interior including when the yacht is inverted (b) have any blocking devices: i capable of being retained in position with the hatch open or shut ii whether or not in position in the hatchway, secured to the yacht (e.g. by lanyard) for the duration of the race, to prevent their being lost overboard iii permit exit in the event of inversion
3.08.5	On monohulls if the companionway extends below the local sheerline and the boat has a cockpit opening aft to the sea the boat shall comply with one of the following: a) the companionway sill shall not extend below the local sheerline. Or b) be in full compliance with all aspects of ISO 11812 to design category A
3.08.6	On monohulls with a cockpit closed aft to the sea where the companionway hatch extends below the local sheerline, the companionway shall be capable of being blocked off up to the level of the local sheerline, provided that the companionway hatch shall continue to give access to the interior with the blocking devices (e.g. washboards) in place
3.09	**cockpits**
3.09.1	cockpits shall be structurally strong , self-draining quickly by gravity at all angles of heel and permanently incorporated as an integral part of the hull.
3.09.2	cockpits must be essentially watertight, that is all openings to the hull must be capable of being strongly and rigidly secured
3.09.3	a bilge pump outlet pipe or pipes shall not be connected to a cockpit drain
3.09.4	A cockpit sole shall be at least 2% LWL above LWL (or in IMS yachts first launched before 1/03, at least 2% L above LWL)

Regulation	Item
3.09.5	a bow, lateral, central or stern well shall be considered a cockpit for the purposes of 3.09
3.09.6	In cockpits opening aft to the sea structural openings aft shall be not less in area than 50% maximum cockpit depth x maximum cockpit width
3.09.7	Cockpit volume i) age or series date before 4/92:- the total volume of all cockpits below lowest coamings shall not exceed 9% (LWL x maximum beam x freeboard abreast the cockpit). ii) age or series date 4/92 and after:- as in (i) above except that "lowest coamings" shall not include any aft of the FA station and no extension of a cockpit aft of the working deck shall be included in calculation of cockpit volume iii) IMS-rated boats may use instead instead of LWL, maximum beam, freeboard abreast the cockpit; the IMS terms L, B and FA.
	Cockpit drains Cockpit drain cross section area (after allowance for screens if fitted) shall be:- i) in yachts with earliest of age or series date before 1/72 or in any yacht under 8.5m (28ft) LOA - at least that of 2 x 25mm (one inch) unobstructed openings or equivalent ii) in yachts with earliest of age or series date 1/72 and later - at least that of 4 x 20mm (3/4 inch) unobstructed openings or equivalent
	US SAILING prescribes that cockpit drains shall be accessible for cleaning.
4.01.1	**sail numbers** Yachts which are not in an ISAF International Class or Recognized Class shall comply with RRS 77 and RRS Appendix G as closely as possible, except that sail numbers allotted by a State authority are acceptable
Category 5 - Part B **Portable Equipment** The following shall be provided:-	
3.23.5 (e)	one manual bilge pump
3.23.5 (f)	one bucket of stout construction with at least 9 litres (2 UK gallons, 2.4 US gallons) capacity plus a lanyard
3.24.1 (b)	one compass (a hand-held is acceptable)
4.05.1	one fire extinguisher required if electrical system, engine or stove on board
4.06.1	one anchor
4.17	yacht's name on buoyant equipment
4.22.1 (a)	a lifebuoy with a drogue, or a lifesling without a drogue. Marine grade retro-reflective tape shall be fitted.

Regulation	Item
4.24	a heaving line shall be provided of length 15m-25m (50ft-75ft) readily accessible to the cockpit or helm
	US SAILING prescribes that the heaving line be of ¼ inch (6mm)minimum diameter, floating, UV-inhibited and readily accessible to the cockpit.
5.01.1	each crew member shall have a lifejacket as follows: (a) equipped with a whistle (b) fitted with marine grade retro-reflective tape (d) if inflatable, regularly checked for air retention (e) clearly marked with yacht's or wearer's name
	US SAILING prescribes for Category 5 lifejackets as above or US Coast Guard approved Type III Personal Floatation Devices.
	US SAILING prescribes that all personnel on deck shall wear properly fitted personal floatation while starting and finishing. At other times during the race, floatation shall be worn on deck except when the Captain of the boat directs that it may be set aside.

Category 5 - Part C
Recommendations

3.14	*pulpits, stanchions, lifelines*
	-see main text of Special Regulations 3.14 etc.
4.01.2	*sail numbers for display when sails are down*
4.07.1 (a)	*a flashlight*
4.08.2	*a first aid kit*
4.11.1	*a waterproof chart*
4.13	*an echo sounder or lead line*
4.16	*tools and spare parts*
4.24	*a "throwing sock" type of heaving line - see Appendix D*
4.26.9	*mainsail reefing to reduce the luff by at least 60%, or a storm trysail as in 4.26.6.*
5.01.2	*lifejacket equipment or attribute:* *(a) a lifejacket light in accordance with SOLAS LSA code 2.2.3 (white, >0.75 candelas, > 8 hours)* *(b) at least 150N buoyancy, arranged to securely suspend an unconscious man face upwards at approximately 45 degrees to the water surface, in accordance with EN396 (ISO 12402) or near equivalent* *(c) a crotch strap or thigh straps* *(d) a splashguard: see EN394.* *(e) if inflatable, supplied with a compressed gas inflation system*

APPENDIX K
Moveable and Variable Ballast

Notwithstanding the maximum length limit of 24m in the standard, this Appendix invokes International Standard ISO 12217-2, Small craft – Stability and buoyancy assessment and categorization – Part 2: Sailing boats of hull length greater than or equal to 6m. The functions KFR (Knockdown Recovery Factor) and FIR (Inversion Recovery Factor) are defined in ISO 12217-2, except as modified by this Appendix.

This Appendix applies to Monohull Yachts only. Unless specifically stated, a requirement applies to Special Regulations Categories 0, 1, 2, 3 and 4. This Appendix does not apply to boats racing under Category 5.

1 Stability

1.1 Boat Condition

In the calculation of stability data:

(a) Deck and other enclosed volume above the sheerline and cockpit volume shall be taken into account.

(b) Mass shall be taken as Minimum Operating Mass as defined by ISO 12217-2, paragraph 3.5.3.

1.2 General Standards

In the assessment of ISO category for yachts fitted with moveable and/or variable ballast, ISO 12217-2, paragraph 6.1.4 b) shall not apply. Boats shall comply with paragraphs 6.2.3, 6.3.1 and 6.4. Calculations shall be for the ballast condition that results in the most adverse result when considering each individual stability requirement. ISO 12217-2 Annex C, paragraph C.3.3, first sentence, the word 'may' is replaced with 'shall'. ISO 12217-2 Annex C, paragraph C.3.4 shall not be used in the calculation of righting lever.

1.3 Knockdown Recovery

Boats with moveable/variable ballast shall comply with the following minimum values of Knockdown Recovery Factor (FKR) calculated in accordance with ISO 12217-2 paragraph 6.4.4 with the modification that the reference to ISO 8666 paragraph 5.5.2 changed to incorporate actual mainsail area and centre of effort. The lesser of FKR90 and FKR-90 shall be used:

SR Category	0	1, 2	3	4
FKR	1.0	0.9	0.8	0.7

Boats with age date prior to 11/04 may seek dispensation from this section 1.3 by application to ISAF.

1.4 Capsize Recovery

For boats racing under Special Regulations Category 0, Regulation 3.04.1 is modified to read:

3.04.1 Either with, or without, reasonable intervention from the crew, a yacht shall be capable of self-righting from an inverted position. Self righting shall be achievable whether or not the rig is intact. Boats with moveable/variable ballast shall comply with this requirement in flat water using manual power only and shall demonstrate that any equipment to be used in re-righting the boat is ready for use at all times and will function and is useable by the crew with the boat inverted. Re-righting the boat shall not require flooding any part of the boat.

Boats with moveable/variable ballast shall comply with the following minimum values of Inversion Recovery Factor (FIR) calculated in accordance with ISO 12217-2:

SR Category	0
FIR	0.9

Boats with age date prior to 11/04 may seek dispensation from this section 1.4 by application to ISAF.

APPENDIX L
CATEGORY 6 SPECIAL REGULATIONS
for inshore races

That Category 6 is defined as:-

Category 6 Special Regulations are intended for use in races where:-

- participating boats may not be self-sufficient
- the races are short in duration and close to a single manned shore base, in relatively warm and protected waters, in daylight and good visibility
- participating boats can be observed by race organisers at all times
- safety/rescue boats are available all along the course sufficient to enable any competitor to be returned to the shore base in a timely manner
- safety/rescue boats are of a suitable designed and properly equipped and are manned by adequately trained and competent personnel including, for each race, at least one skilled in first aid

That the Requirements for Category 6 are:-

Unless otherwise prescribed in Notice of Race and/or Sailing Instructions, where class rules include items of safety such rules shall override the corresponding part of these Regulation.

All equipment required by Special Regulations Category 6 shall:-

- function properly
- be regularly checked, cleaned and serviced
- when not in use be stowed in conditions in which deterioration is minimised
- be readily accessible
- be of a type, size and capacity suitable and adequate for the intended use and size of the boat.

All boats sailing in Category 6 shall be fitted with:-

- A strong point for the attachment of a tow and/or anchor line.

All boats sailing in category 6 shall carry:-

- A personal flotation device (PFD) for each person aboard to ISO 12402-5 -Level 50 or equivalent
  US SAILING prescribes for Category 6 lifejackets as above or US Coast Guard Type III Personal Floatation Devices.
- A knife
- If the hull is not self-draining or is able to carry more than 150 litres of free water, a bucket or bailer of not less than 1 litre capacity
- If a trapeze harness is carried it shall be to ISO DIS 10862
- A paddle or means of propelling the boat when not under sail

APPENDIX M
HULL CONSTRUCTION STANDARDS (SCANTLINGS)
for Monohulls pre-2010 and Multihulls

		Category
M.1	A monohull with Age or Series Date before the 1 January 2010 shall comply with OSR 3.03.1, 3.03.2 and 3.03.3 or with this appendix. A multihull shall comply with this appendix.	MoMu0,1,2

Table 2			MoMu0,1,2
LOA	earliest of age or series date	race category	MoMu0,1,2
all	January 1986 and after	MoMu0,1	
12m (39.4 feet) and over	January 1987 and after	MoMu2	
under 12m (39.4 feet)	January 1988 and after	MoMu2	

M.2	A yacht defined in the table above shall have been designed built, maintained, modified and repaired in accordance with the requirements of either:	MoMu0,1,2
	a) the EC Recreational Craft Directive for Category A (having obtained the CE mark), or	MoMu0,1,2
	b) the ABS Guide for Building and Classing Offshore Yachts in which case the yacht shall have on board either a certificate of plan approval issued by ABS, or written statements signed by the designer and builder which confirm that they have respectively designed and built the yacht in accordance with the ABS Guide,	MoMu0,1,2
	c) ISO 12215 Category A, with written statements signed by the designer and builder which confirm that they have respectively designed and built the yacht in accordance with the ISO standard,	MoMu0,1,2
	d) except that a race organizer or class rules may accept when that described in (a), (b), or (c) above is not available, the signed statement by a naval architect or other person familiar with the standards listed above that the yacht fulfills the requirements of (a), (b), or (c).	MoMu0,1,2
M.3	Any significant repairs or modifications to the hull, deck, coachroof, keel or appendages, on a yacht defined in table 2 shall be certified by one of the methods above and an appropriate written statement or statements shall be on board.	MoMu0,1,2

APPENDIX N
MEDICAL TRAINING
Model Training Course for an "OSR Compliant First Aid Course"

Part 1 – Introduction

1. **General**
   Below is the framework for an MNA to establish a minimum First Aid training course suitable for offshore racing.

2. **Target**
   The target of this course is to provide the Person in Charge of an offshore racing yacht with a crew member that is capable of taking care of common injuries and illnesses on board, as well as to take charge of the immediate medical actions at a major incident on board. Furthermore to advise the Person in Charge when a request for outside assistance is needed, as well as to advise when to retire from the race and proceed to nearest harbour.

3. **Use of the model course.**
   Instructors should have a knowledge of the unique situation of offshore sailing in terms of delivering medical care. It is suggested that instructors be suitably trained and ideally a medical doctor, paramedics or nurse.

   For an MNA wanting to establish a course without the specialist knowledge to correctly train and administer instructors it is suggested that they approach a suitable training partner. Training partners could be STCW 95 training centres or land based first aid training providers who have personnel with suitable sailing experience but crucially an understanding of the liability issues. Should an MNA require advise please contact the ISAF Secretariat – Technical Department.

4 **Evaluation**. The final activities of the day should be an examination, which should be used together with instructors' continuous assessments to provide an overall evaluation. The pass mark is to be taken as 70% in each of the marked/evaluated units.

5 **Implementation** Detailed requirements are given below. Thorough preparation is the key to successful implementation of the course.

6 **Literature**
The following books further study and are not endorsed by ISAF but merely are books suitable for background reading:
Medical Emergency Afloat
First Aid at Sea (Douglas Justin and Colin Berry, Adlard Coles Nautical, London) ISBN ISBN 9781408105993
First Aid Afloat (Dr Robert Haworth) ISBN 9780906754887
Skipper's Medical Emergency Handbook (Author Dr Spike Briggs, Dr Campbell Mackenzie) ISBN 9780713689372
Doctor on Board: A Guide To Dealing With Medical Emergencies (Author Jurgen Hauert) ISBN 9781408112724
MCA Ship Captain Medic book is now available free at HYPERLINK "http://www.mcga.gov.uk/c4mca/mcga07-home/workingatsea/mcga-medicalcertandadvice/mcga-dqs_st_shs_ships_capt_medical_guide.htm" http://www.mcga.gov.uk/c4mca/mcga07-home/workingatsea/mcga-medicalcertandadvice/mcga-dqs_st_shs_ships_capt_medical_guide.htm

International Medical Guide for Ships, World Health Organisation, Geneva
General First Aid
First Aid Manual 9th Edition (Author St John's Ambulance Brigade) ISBN 9781405335379
Non English Publications
Pan Pan Medico A Bordo (HYPERLINK "http://www.panpan.it/" http://www.panpan.it/)
Le Guide de la medecine a distance, by Docteur J Y Chauve, published by Distance Assistance BP33 F-La Baule, cedex, France. An English translation is being planned.

Part 2 - Syllabus
The course is planned for 8 hours and includes following sessions;

Session 1 Introduction
1.0 Marine medical environment and characteristics
1.1 Literature

Session 2 First aid kits for the Special Regulations races categories
2.0 Cat 4 contents (recommendations)
2.1 Cat 2-3 contents (recommendations)
2.2 Cat 1-0 (if relevant)

Session 3 Tele medical communications
3.0 Support options (Medical advice services through official bodies)
3.1 Radio/Mobile phone options for support
3.2 Licences/certificates for VHF/HF radio communications

Session 4 First Aid – The basics
4.0 Basic anatomy/physiology
4.1 L-ABCDE (Scene safety, Airway and cervical spine control, Breathing, Circulation and bleeding, Disability, Expose and protect from the environment)
4.2 Stopping of serious external bleeding

Session 5 Offshore accidents and actions onboard
5.0 Typical accidents onboard (wounds, cuts, sprained wrist etc)
5.1 General illnesses, fatigue etc
5.2 Actions and treatment
5.3 Helicopter evacuation
5.4 Transfer of casualty to rescue vessel

Session 6 Special offshore medical conditions
6.0 Seasickness
6.1 Hypothermia (Person recovered from sea)
6.2 Dehydration
6.3 Brain concussion
6.4 Keeping the blood sugar level up (what to eat and drink)

Session 7 Cardiac and respiratory arrest
7.0 Cardiopulmonary resuscitation (CPR)
7.1 Artificial respiration
7.2 Use of Defibrillator

Session 8 Systematic Accident management
8.0 Damage and causality evaluation
8.1 Decisions and actions – when to call for outside assistance, when to retire and proceed to nearest harbour
8.2 Observation and treatment of patients

Session 9 Psychology Treatment
9.0 Human reactions in distress
9.1 Treatment of psychological breakdowns
9.2 Crisis group management
9.3 Debriefing procedures

Session 10 Practical training
10.0 CPR
10.1 Patient observations and treatment
10.2 Radio medical training
10.3 Decision making – When to call for assistance, when to retire?

Session 11 Examination
11.0 A questionnaire of 25 questions, requirement >70 % correct

INDEX
Alphabetical Index 2008-2009

'his index is intended to be a quick guide to the Regulations. It is not exhaustive. See also the iagrammatic guide and list of contents.

ISAF Special Regulations Governing Offshore Racing Index

Notes

Polar Diagrams
(Performance Package)

Most sailors are familiar with the Polar Diagram used by serious racers to help them achieve the best performance their yacht can provide. However, this information is not useful solely to racers. Every sailor who wants to get somewhere faster, whether for fun or safety, can use the information in the Performance Package for practical application or personal edification.

The Performance Package is a 2.4MB Excel spreadsheet containing:

- True wind polar diagrams for wind speeds from 6 to 24 knots, showing both spinnaker and genoa curves, illustrating sail crossovers
- True wind polar diagram showing the best performance curve at all wind speeds
- Detailed polar tables at one degree increments of true wind angle
- Summary VPP output in tabular form at each wind speed, at 5 degree increments, suitable for printing, laminating and displaying onboard
- Tables for use in popular onboard tactical programs that include Deckman, Expedition, Ockam, Maxsea, Nobletec
- Documentation that provides invaluable advice on the practical use of polars.

The polar diagrams and their tables can be used as a constant standard measure against actual performance so that even when no other yachts are in sight the skipper can determine whether the boat is sailing up to potential. Many races are lost when sailing at a distance from competitors or in darkness, because the flow of wake, the angle of heel, and the feel of the helm are not always reliable indicators of optimum performance.